Enfield Libraries

(3)

R

Ridge Avenue Library
Ridge Avenue
London N21 2RH
Tel: 020 8379 1714
Fax: 020 8364 1352

10/03

24.

R7

GW00400425

Please remember that this item will attract overdue charges if not returned by the latest date stamped above. You may renew it in person, by telephone or by post quoting the bar code number and your library card number.

www.enfield.gov.uk

759

RZ

ENFIELD
Council

LS131

30126 01752965 9

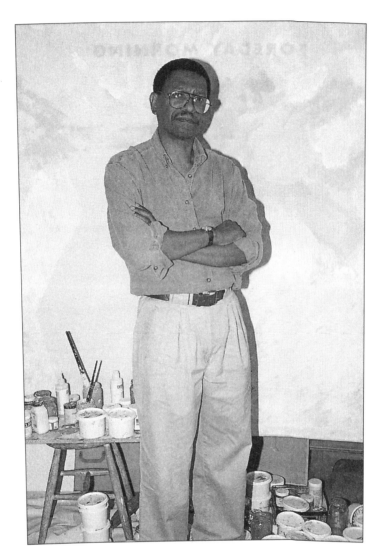

The author in his studio

FOREDAY MORNING

Paul Dash

——

BlackAmber Books

Published in 2002 by
BlackAmber Books
PO Box 10812
London SW7 4ZG

1 3 5 7 9 10 8 6 4 2

Copyright © Paul Dash 2002

All rights reserved

The moral right of the author has been asserted.

No part of this publication may be reproduced, stored in
a retrieval system or transmitted, in any form or by any means,
electrical, mechanical, photocopying, recording or otherwise,
without prior permission of the publisher.

A full CIP for this book is available from the British Library.

ISBN 1-901969-11-8

Typeset in 10/12 point Sabon
by Guy Typographics Limited
Printed in Finland by WS Bookwell

London Borough
of Enfield
Public Libraries

017529659

759.2 DAS

RL 10 03

For Jean, Luke, Nicholas and Rebecca,
who had to survive my moods and selfish ways
during the writing of this book.

Also for Karen, George, Gerald, Levi, John,
my father,
the abiding memory of my mother,
and new settlers everywhere.

Contents

———

List of Illustrations   8

Acknowledgements   9

Foreword   11

Introduction   15

Part I: Barbados   17

Part II: Britain   111

Illustrations

———

Figures

	The author in his studio	frontispiece
1	Passport photo of the author, aged 10	17
2	A typical one-room chattel house	19
3	A windmill pumping water for agriculture	21
4	My parents on their wedding day	26
5	Fairfields Cross Roads, where I lived as a child	77
6	The author at an Award-winning ceremony in 2002	111
7	George in his REME uniform	121
8	Magdalen College, one of my favourite places	144
9	My mother outside our new house in Annersley Road	153
10	My father posing with the Austin Cambridge	155
11	Emerging into adulthood: myself, aged about 15, at Fern Hill Road	178
12	Gerald, every inch a boxer, photographed with my Box Brownie camera	185
13	The Carib Six; I'm at the extreme right, playing the piano	194

———

Plates

1 *Dancing in the Streets*, *c*. 1961–2, oil on hardboard
2 *The Conversation*, 1963–4, oil on hardboard
3 *Dance at Reading*, 1964, oil on hardboard
4 *Mat*, 1976, paper collage with gouache
5 *Mas*, 1976, paper collage and watercolour
6 *Dam*, 2001, paper collage
7 *Ibou*, completed 2002, reworked paper collage with gouache
8 *Great American Pin-Up*, work in progress, paper collage

Acknowledgements

——

This book would not have been written without the help and support of several friends. Firstly, I must thank Kathy Yearwood for inviting me to speak at the Barbados High Commission in 1997. Secondly my thanks to my publisher who was present at the High Commission and invited me to write these memoirs. Much thanks must go to Helen Simpson, my editor, who knocked the book into shape – without her help and advice, it would simply not have been publishable. My appreciation, too, goes to Ann Lloyd for her insight and her keen eye at the later stages of the manuscript. A huge thank you must also go to Chris Searle, a dear and reliable friend who, at short notice, kindly agreed to write the Foreword. Thanks to Professor David Halpin who, as Professor for Research in the Education Department at Goldsmiths, suggested that I applied for study leave to research the book in Barbados. My thanks to George, Jo and Louise who kindly put me up for a month in Barbados while I worked there, and to all those relations and friends whose names have been mentioned in these pages. Finally, many thanks to Jean, my wife, for being the reliable safety-net in my life that allows me to take risks, and to Luke, Nicholas and Rebecca for their respect and love.

Foreword

———

Paul Dash's *Foreday Morning* is a story of two countries, of two realities of childhood: and both are expressed through a narrative of uncommon insight and striking pictorial clarity.

Childhood is, of course, an integral and constant theme of Caribbean writing. No other part of the world has expressed the tensions, paradoxes and awakenings of girlhood and boyhood with such moving and complex truth as this necklace of islands. From Merle Hodge's Trinidadian chronicle in *Crick Crack Monkey* to Patrick Chamoiseau's *School Days* of Martinique, from Joan Riley's harrowing novel of a Jamaican girlhood in a British inner city, *The Unbelonging*, to novels of adolescence and learning from great writers of Barbados, like George Lamming's *In the Castle of My Skin* and Austin Clarke's *Growing Up Stupid under the Union Jack*, the tradition of the literature of childhood has developed to a potent Caribbean tradition. Dash's story belongs to the flesh and blood of that achievement, and, like Selvon, Riley, Linton Kwesi Johnson and contemporary novelists like Caryl Phillips and Alex Wheatle, he adds a 'metropolitan' dimension to it.

Dash is a skilled and powerful visual artist, and this soon becomes apparent, too, in his use of language. As he describes his Barbados boyhood in communities like Fairfield and Station Hill, there is a certain crystalline, or perhaps more accurately coralline, quality of light to his writing of these 'mesmerising childhood moments' and their Caribbean setting. His words reflect that 'clarity of the light and the brilliant effervescence' around him, whether it is the images he offers of a terrified burning mongoose hurtling across a canefield, a group of boys collecting melting tarmac from the edge of a local road to improvise a homemade cricket ball, a sudden shocking sighting of the tiny body of his dead baby brother 'enmeshed in a network of blue veins', or the patience of a mother showing her own unique skill in making frothy, cooled tea by pouring the fresh brew the two feet between two cups without spilling a drop. These are preciously vital and memorable moments of a startling narrative expressed with a pellucid, tropical clarity of light and language which renders Dash's story Caribbean to its core.

But in 1957 the eleven-year-old Dash arrived in England to join his parents, who had migrated two years before. In this new country, the environment immediately 'dark and cool', he went to live with them in Oxford. Not the gleaming city of spires and elite teachers and learners, but Motown Oxford, the city of car workers and industrial greyness. His migration was to become a part of the British working class, and his education in a local secondary modern school in the Oxford industrial suburb of Cowley was to reflect that. Suddenly he feels less visible, less of an individual Caribbean person as a part of 'the whole working class of a neglected city sub-stratum' as he stares, with a stranger's eyes, through the great gates of the colleges at 'the steeples and fine metalwork ... an outsider looking into the world of white people with money, influence and education'.

The light changes, too – as does the character of his writing. It becomes more sombre, sometimes almost tenebrous, more reflective of the racism, alienation and contrasts of this new world. The brilliance of the sun is covered, and the winters are 'bleak, cold and dark. Living under a canopy of cloud for days on end, untouched by sunlight, was a reversal of everything I had grown used to and found central to life'. Here was a world suddenly 'mixed in work, toil and greyness', and the artistic brush of Dash's words paints it within an apposite screen of shade.

What single word does Dash employ many times in his story which shows, incontrovertibly, that he is a teacher (and a most powerful one, as I know well through being his colleague)? I think it is the very teacherly word 'potential', suggesting educability, application, fulfilment and betterment. Early in his narrative, he describes the achievements of the Barbadian people with whom he shared his life and human struggle in this way. They were 'Splendid people with big voices and bold hearts enmeshed in an ecstasy of music-making, while finding a universe of potentialities within themselves and giving it expression through their art.' People without extensive material benefits make sound, carve wood, essay a cover-drive, speak of their wholeness and wealth as beings through their skills and sensibilities. Such experiences 'confirmed the value of them, the value of myself as a person, by the richness of their talents and skills'. The passage reminds me of the phrase created by another Barbadian artist, the poet Peter Blackman, who, in talking of the skills and potential brilliance of all working people, the unexalted and the essential, the men and women who hold up the world everywhere, including Barbados and Britain, spoke of them having 'excellence in the ordinary'. Dash's story manifests that same truth time and time again.

Foreday Morning is also an affirmation of the love and support of family and community, while not always an uncritical vindication of their internal relationships. Dash's portrait of his hardworking, imaginative and always powerfully loving parents, of loyal and companionable siblings and supportive relatives in a small country, is at the centre of his story and is returned to many times. It is a family strong enough to survive the drama and trauma of migration, despite being frequently assaulted by its huge and complex difficulties. And it brings me to something a thirteen-year-old St Lucian girl wrote in an East London English class in 1972, as a tribute to the courage and audacity of her own parents who made the same crossing the same year as Dash's mother and father.

Perhaps there is a unity and kinship in their remembrances. For, 'in a very strange country', she wrote, 'they had no family nor friends'. And she continued: 'For other people who emigrate to other countries they run into a lot of good luck and for other people, well, it's just working day in, day out in a country they don't really like. Once you get on the plane or boat there's no second chances. You can't change your mind, it's just too late and you think to yourself, "What have I done?" You lose all your friends and they think, "I hope she's doing the right thing, emigrating like that."'

This book embodies these authentic childhood words – and all those risks and insecurities, that life-changing daring to make an irreversible move, the bravery to face its consequences, the tenacity to achieve in the face of its challenge. All that is to be found within Dash's story, which makes it all the more remarkable as a human document. For it expresses the experience of millions who have taken the same voyage of their lives, provoking that of their children too. Here is the truth of such a journey, arrival and achievement central to the making of a new and burgeoning British people whose provenances are everywhere but whose home and future are here.

Chris Searle
London, September 2002

Introduction

———

After giving a talk at the Barbados High Commission in London in 1997, I was approached by BlackAmber and invited to write a book on my childhood in Barbados and Oxford. I was flattered – as indeed I still am – to be asked, and not a little excited at the prospect. Since then the reality of meeting deadlines on top of a demanding job at Goldsmiths College, alongside other commitments, has at times made me wonder if I wasn't a little ambitious and unrealistic in accepting the invitation.

More especially, writing a book in which the quality of prose is particularly telling proved extremely daunting and occasionally even frightening. Arriving at a style that suited me, a method of recording views and experiences which keeps the reader engaged, while being true to my memories, has been one of the most difficult challenges I have ever faced in my professional career.

I am grateful to a number of writers, both living and dead, whose examples provided me with models of what could be achieved. Edward Said's *Out of Place*, with its layered complexity that folds many diverse moments into a multidimensional form; Berlioz's *Memoirs* (translated by David Cairns) with his articulate comment on a life of exciting discovery and creative significance in his extraordinary book of memoirs; the beautifully lilting prose of Richard Wright's *Black Boy*; and the delicate poetry of Laurie Lee's masterpiece *Cider with Rosie*: all these played a significant part in showing me the possibilities inherent to the genre. Having tried different approaches, it was the recollection of Nelson Mandela's *Long Walk to Freedom* that gave me an insight into the type of work I should write. This book is the outcome.

PART I

—

BARBADOS

Fig. 1 Passport photo of the author, aged 10

I WAS BORN IN BARBADOS ON 25 JUNE 1946, in Fairfield Cross Roads, Bridgetown, where my parents had lived for some years. Daddy did various jobs, from cooper to bus inspector. Mama had children from an early age, but worked for a limited period. I had two elder brothers, George, born on 8 July 1933, and Gerald, born on 11 June 1943.

Fairfield is a densely populated but surprisingly lush district. My first memories of the area are framed by images of mahogany, bougainvillea, pine, sugarcane, palm and a mishmash of fruit trees, coconut and giant casuarinas. Beneath them we played marbles, argued, exchanged gossip and did unspeakable things to insects and small creatures.

Our more affluent neighbours owned wall houses, built from the local coral stone, which stood out for their elegance and air of permanence. They were the most sought-after houses in a hierarchy of styles which placed bungalows at the apex and dilapidated single-unit chattels at the bottom. But most people in Fairfield, as in much of Barbados, lived in simple chattels, in different stages of repair. Chattels are wooden houses consisting of one or more rooms, those of just one room being shaped rather like a traditional garden shed (Fig.2). They have

Fig. 2 A typical one-room chattel house

a central door at both front and rear, each flanked by two windows for ventilation. Side windows also helped ventilation and more windows were normally inserted in the apex of the inverted V of the gable. Larger houses were a variation on this basic structure, with one or two gabled units fixed to a 'shed-roof' or lean-to extension.

Most were roofed with galvanised steel sheets, a popular, cheap building material also used for garden fencing. Galvanised steel keeps out the rain but is a poor insulator; and in stormy weather it amplifies the drumming of tropical rain to a deafening crescendo. I enjoyed the security of living beneath a deluge while basking in the dry comforts of home. In summer, the intense heat beneath galvanised sheeting can be very uncomfortable. Most people sit outdoors under large trees and take the breezes blowing in from the Atlantic, rather than stay indoors in such close, sticky conditions.

In Fairfield, the chattels were set cheek by jowl with one another in tight communities where domestic privacy was difficult to obtain. Better ones were interspersed with tiny hovels, which miraculously stood or tilted at an improbable angle on a few quarried stone blocks. Sprouting from stout posts was a network of electric wires, which linked many of the houses. It formed an aerial graveyard for kites at Easter and a deathtrap for foolhardy children the year round, a stubborn legacy of empire which, like open storm gutters, remains a feature of the region. The danger was not so much of kites crashing into the wires as of children's temptation to climb a pole to free a snared, precious kite. My father tells me of a boy who was trapped in this way and electrocuted, his charred body taking some hours to remove. Gerald loved kite-flying and soon picked up the nickname 'Kites'.

Many homes were painted to protect them against rot and add interest to the street. Vibrant colour combinations were commonplace: yellow against red, green, brown and grey. Several had decorative bargeboards and fancy architraves; woodwork as delicate as lace featured on more-up market ones.

Windmills, too, were common; they pumped water for farms on the boundaries of our district. We enjoyed their elegance and admired the power they symbolised (Fig. 3).

The natural landscape was rich in plant life: bougainvillea was abundant, its vibrant red flowers adding charm and style

Fig. 3 A windmill pumping water for agriculture

to the area. Tall elegant casuarinas or 'mile' trees swayed gently in isolated spots, their presence a constant trap for unskilled kite-flyers, whose paper playthings frequently came a cropper in the sprawling branches. Everywhere, Atlantic breezes cooled the island and ruffled the leaves of banana trees, while mature mahogany were a reminder of the abilities of craftsmen on the island. Sandwiched between chattels and growing in open fields was the omnipresent sugarcane, which offered a wide range of possibilities for play and mischief. Sitting outside the plantation economy where cane was grown for profit, these were forgotten shoots left to self-germinate. A stolen plant provided a refreshing drink for children parched in play, in a forest of elongated leaves and succulent shoots. But the fun was tempered by the presence of centipedes lurking in the cane trash and the excrement that rimmed the fields.

In Barbados, centipedes attract much same sort of the opprobrium as snakes do. A tropical centipede – 'centipee' in Bajan vernacular – is not to be equated with the puny, etiolated insect often seen lurking under garden bric-a-brac and rotting vegetation in Britain. The tropical kind is of awesome appearance and keenly aggressive instincts, often growing to about eight or nine inches in Barbados and even bigger in other tropical countries. The insect is segmented, with two pairs of legs on each of up to ten segments, and capable of giving a savage bite.

My fear of centipedes was amplified by the sight of a fully grown adult walking on a high timber in our chattel house when I was very young. It was crawling along in poor light but was clearly a centipede, though it looked deformed: there was a huge lump on its body. When I took a closer look, I found that the centipede was dragging the carcass of a mouse, which it had found or killed. A whole mouse! No wonder centipedes hold the place they do in Barbadian folklore.

Centipedes breed in damp, unmolested spots. As much of Barbados's fine arable land is given over to sugarcane production, the dense, damp vegetation and extensive cover are an ideal environment for them. We children played a great deal in canefields when we could get away with it – there isn't a finer place for tag or hide-and-seek – but we were always on the lookout for centipedes. My blood used to run cold at the sight of one nestled between cane stalk and leaf. I always put as much space as possible between myself and it.

Our home was in a side street a stone's throw from the crossroads that gave the district its name. From our front window we got clear views of the highway, where the daily traffic carved deep furrows into the tarmac. 'Wild boys' careered on homemade scooters*, while other youngsters pulled toy trucks and buses made from recycled timber, tin and pieces of salvaged metal. Donkey carts regularly trundled by, their owners cracking a cow-skin whip over their labouring charges, while mules and horses did similar work at a snappier

*Wild boys were youngsters from poverty-stricken homes who roamed the streets and lived off their wits. Many made splendid toys such as pull-along trucks and scooters. The popularity of hi-tech scooters today echoes a time in Barbados when scooters were a favourite form of transport for street youths.

pace. But we were largely protected from the hustle and bustle of life on the highway, and could play relatively free of worry from traffic.

There was a standpipe at the crossroads in Fairfield. It was bordered on three sides by low walls which doubled as seating for people queuing or socialising. Standpipes were the site of social gathering in most communities, the focal point of many casual encounters, and were dotted around the island within reasonable walking distance of each home. Some were quite elaborate, with surrounding parapet walls, but most were merely functional pipes with a tap, which provided clean drinking-water. Women already burdened by domestic chores fetched water in pails and buckets. A few men did their collection on donkey carts with huge tanks. This made queues form, and much bad feeling used to surface. Children old enough to carry a half-filled bucket supported the family effort by fetching water before and after school. The sight of youngsters not much bigger than the buckets with which they struggled, their bodies arching with the weight of their charges, and spilling more water than they arrived with, was common.

Many women took the family laundry to the pipe. The scrubbing and cleaning was done on a jukking-board in a tub. Jukking-boards were made from a single piece of timber, one side being roughened or ribbed. The clothes were lathered in soap and laboriously, back-breakingly worked on that surface. I remember the women scrubbing the laundry and twisting it into giant ropes to squeeze out the water. Then they made the journey home, the clean washing carried in buckets or trays balanced on a screw of cloth on their heads.

My parents had arrived in Fairfield Cross Roads via a round-about route. Daddy was born in the adjacent district of Whitehall and lived there for several years with his parents. Mama was brought up by her grandmother in Black Rock, less than a mile from Fairfield.

My father was born on 9 December 1914 and christened Hugh Ernest Nathaniel Ezekiel Dash. He was the third of three children. Samuel, the eldest, was born in 1907 and in his early teens, my father tells me, 'worked as a hawker, a potato seller'; later he became a watchman at Grazettes plantation. Ursula, their sister, was born in 1912. She died at the age of only twenty-five, after sustaining serious internal injuries from a kick to the stomach by a cow.

On leaving school at the age of fourteen Daddy started out as a cooper's assistant at the firm where his father worked, Monroe's Cooperage of Bridgetown. He earned a few cents a day making casks and puncheons. With experience this wage raised to the princely sum of three Barbados dollars a day as a qualified cooper. From this sum in later years he contributed three dollars a week to the upkeep of his father, who suffered from rheumatics, a condition which led to his retirement from the coopering trade. Three dollars, supplemented by a few cents for cigarettes, went a long way, covering the costs of groceries, drinks and other items.

Daddy was 'thrifty', to use his word, doing various part-time jobs on top of coopering. In 1934, while working as a petrol-pump attendant, he was attacked and robbed by two men. They beat him about the head and chest and escaped with a watch and $48, leaving him for dead. On regaining consciousness he found the strength to walk to the home of a local couple, Mr and Mrs Carew. They refused to help him because they were 'already in pyjamas and ready for bed'. Daddy staggered on to a nearby police station, where he was made to lie down on a bench. The station manager was called, and he and the police took my father back to the petrol station, where he described what happened, before he was driven to the hospital. For several days he lapsed in and out of consciousness, often 'talking nonsense'. His face was swollen and his side crushed by the beating. It took the ingenuity of his father to verify his identity by a birthmark. It was several weeks before Daddy could return to work, and he was left almost totally deaf in one ear.

I remember a visit to my father's workplace just before he left the trade. It must have been in 1949, round about my third birthday. Mama had prepared a hot meal, which she packed in a basket. She, Gerald and I took a bus from Louis Pickett's shop. I remember the bus's red and yellow livery, the huge wheel-arches. It was open at the sides, allowing air to flow through and keep the passengers cool. The seats were hard wooden benches arranged in rows like church pews, with standing room restricted to the footboard that ran the length of the carriage.

When we arrived at Barn's Coopering, his place of work, my father was shaping a stave with an axe. Birch chippings spun from his blade connecting with shirt and face, sometimes describing a gyroscopic arc as they fell around him. Seeing Daddy away from home, with other responsibilities and responding to some one else's instructions, was a shock: he was so different from the frightening figure who held sway at home.

But his usual authoritative manner hadn't deserted him. 'Marie,' he said, 'keep de boy from here – a piece o' dis wood gine blind he.'

The finished barrels exuded the smell of pitch and sap. Of course I could not then see the connection between them and the containers that were a vital element in the shaping of Caribbean lifestyle. But when I reflect now on the significance of my father's work and do make that connection – between preserves in the tropics and the need for storage casks, the enslavement of Africans and forced labour on plantations – the picture has many layers of meaning. The shadow of earlier times in practices in the sugar industry and my father's work, alongside less obvious signs, such as the way we used language and our culinary habits, are particularly apparent.

Mama was an attractive pale-skinned woman who took adversity in her stride. Tall and elegant, with high cheek-bones and a graceful manner, she was prized in our district for her 'high brown colour'. She even had the slightest whisper of freckles, which rose and fell across nose and cheeks to underpin her part-European ancestry. Within months of her birth on 5 April 1917 my mother, christened Marie Louise Harewood, lost her own mother, who died of an obscure illness. Soon afterwards her father migrated to the United States, and the baby was left in the care of her grandmother; she was effectively orphaned. She had several half-brothers and half-sisters, sired by a parent who fathered five children in two marriages and three in extra-marital relationships; my mother was the product of one of these latter liaisons. An eighth sibling, Elise, born to the same mother, and her husband,

Samuel, my father's brother, were to feature prominently in my life in later years.

My grandfather's children by his first marriage inherited his considerable property in Barbados. Mama and her other siblings were bequeathed nothing. She lived her childhood in poverty, and had only a minimal education. As a consequence, with the exception of Elise and to a lesser extent Violet, both illegitimate outcasts like herself, she effectively excluded her sisters and brothers from her life. She rarely spoke of them. It was only in later years that I realized the extent of her bitterness, and I discovered more about them while doing the research for this book than I learnt from her when she was alive. Her feeling of exclusion and rejection was to have an immense impact on her life at every level, including the focused way in which she devoted herself to her household. The family brought her a level of stability and kinship which she had lacked as a child. Yet Mama's silence on her ancestry is like an ache that cannot be soothed: a missing item from an important display.

My parents were married in 1939 in Bridgetown St Michael. A wedding photograph (Fig. 4) shows Mrs Biscombe's house, the modest, almost tumbledown, dwelling where their

Fig. 4 My parents on their wedding day

reception was held. My parents moved to different houses in the Black Rock and Fairfield areas before settling in Fairfield Cross Roads, renting from friends and relations for a few months. In those early years my father tried his hands at different jobs to support them. Besides coopering, he cut hair, preached, did some teaching and worked on the buses as a conductor and inspector. There were also spells of work in St Lucia and Guyana and as a seasonal worker in the USA. In a recent conversation he told me that between 1940 and 1948, he was in and out of the United States regularly, his longest period there being some fourteen months.

Mama gave birth to thirteen children, of whom just five survived to adulthood. She rarely spoke of the eight who died, with the exception of Laura, her second child, a particularly painful loss, probably because Laura survived for about nineteenth months whereas the others died very young indeed. My father tells me of another child who was lost in particularly unfortunate circumstances. One day Mama, already several weeks pregnant, came down with peritonitis. She was taken to Doctor Cummings, her GP. Despite her obvious distress the doctor, who was a white Barbadian, first treated white patients who arrived at his surgery after my mother. By the end of the day Mama still hadn't been seen, and she was told to 'Come back tomorrow'. She was subjected to the same treatment the following day and the day after that.

In the end, my father took her to his own doctor. It was a Thursday and the doctor's day off, but my father insisted that Mama be seen, saying, 'If you doan see she, she gun die because she dying.'

The doctor agreed to see her and immediately realised the seriousness of her condition. She was taken to the local hospital and underwent an emergency operation, but by then her appendix had burst and she lost the baby. It was touch and go for a while, but Mama rallied and survived; she was left with a huge scar down the centre of her abdomen. She spoke about the incident only rarely, and then only fleetingly, pre-ferring to maintain a dignified silence.

My mother's loss of yet another child left its mark on my own life. One day when I was three, while playing cowboys and Indians I burst into my parents' bedroom. I saw a tiny corpse on a bedside cupboard. The baby's body, enmeshed in a network of blue veins, was a strange ochre colour. I was transfixed by its stillness, the sticky afterbirth and the strange waxen quality of its flesh. There was an eerie silence about it, a clear sign that the baby was dead. Mama was in a mildly catatonic state, too grief-stricken to notice my presence, too distraught to weep. Daddy, too, was deeply introspective and distressed. The incident has stayed with me over the years, reminding me of the fragility of life and the finality of death.

In 1950 my father left for New York to fulfil a seasonal contract. I was nearly four and this was his fourth and last short-term working contract in the USA. I remember seeing him off at the airport, standing next to the plane, my surprise at the giant wheels that towered above me. He was gone for several months, during which time my mother ran the household single-handed.

Life continued pretty much as it always had done, but there was a more relaxed atmosphere. Fonza, Elaine Odle, the Knights family, Mr and Mrs Gittens and other neighbours and friends maintained a vigilance over our well-being which echoed the strict regime to which we were accustomed. They didn't recognise the niceties of family difference in their dealings with my brothers or me; we were part of a wider community and on the streets they acted as our guardians. Any challenge to their authority attracted a scolding or worse from our mother.

During this time we often visited our neighbours' homes, and we were accepted as members of their families. One Saturday afternoon Fonza came round and we all visited Mr and Mrs Gittens. The half-mile walk took only a few minutes, and we were soon in front of a large chattel house set back from the main road among sturdy shrubs.

Mrs Gittens greeted us with the lilting cadence of the Bajan middle classes, shaping each word with correct precision. 'How are you, Marie and Fonza? You are strangers fa true. Come in with the children and take a seat.'

The Gittenses' living-room was spotless and cool, with a polished pine floor decorated here and there with fine rugs. It was neatly furnished with well-crafted, beautifully polished mahogany furniture. A large sideboard was crowned with a pot of bougainvillea set on frilly lace decorated at the corners with yellow and red embroidered roses. A cane-bottom settee, on which my mother, brothers and I sat, took pride of place against a large expanse of wall; a similarly worked cane-bottom rocking-chair occupied our corner. I remember my fear of noisily snapping a cane strand and embarrassing my mother. The walls of the living-room held framed pictures of family and religious events: Christ crucified, the disciples at prayer, family snapshots. I felt constrained by the environment but appreciated the mauby served in a floral glass on a metal tray. Mama and Fonza chatted with Mrs Gittens. She said Mr Gittens was in his workshop at the back of the house, and Fonza suggested that my brothers and I should visit him.

The workshop was approached down a path bordered by stacked logs and lengths of timber. Mr Gittens was a light-skinned man with lazy curling hair of indistinct colouring, who sported a neatly trimmed moustache which shadowed the fine edge of his upper lip. His strong workman's hands, often stained by French polish, seemed to echo the quiet dignity of a man steeped in his craft. I was overcome by awe at the workshop, the arrangements of bandsaws, clamps, cramps, hammers and planes, the aroma of freshly cut timber and the fluffy mounds of rust-coloured sawdust. On a table was a pot of viscous glue, the consistency of liquid toffee. Furniture frames were everywhere, some second-hand in for repair, the canes broken into tangled strands; furniture still under construction hung from the ceiling, and a few dust covered-pieces were piled in shady corners. Mr Gittens's authority over wood, the way he ordered his life, his undemonstrative self-assurance, shaped the character of his workshop. As I cast my eyes around this Aladdin's cave, I developed a special respect for him and his craft.

Of equal fascination, though in a different way, was the Knights household; their property backed onto ours. Mr Knights had worked as a sailmaker for many years at the Careenage, a small inlet on whose shores, in the old days, boats were careened for repair. Occasionally he brought home a length of canvas to hand-stitch or cut to a required length. I remember the thick white duck laid out flat in his back garden, the blue guidelines chalked on its surface. Knights stitched the material with blue cord threaded through large curved needles, stooping or crouching on his haunches to do so.

But if Mr Knights's sailmaker's craft was an attraction, the lifestyle of his sons was engrossing. Vere, the second son, regularly sang operatic arias in the toilet, which was near our garden fence. He took delight in the resonant quality with which his voice was infused in the tight little outhouse: pieces from Bach, Verdi and others regularly rang out from that garden loo. Audley, the eldest brother, could often be seen strolling to the toilet with a large tome in his hand, happy to read the finest literature. Music and literature defined the Knightses' style and interests. It was a way of life rich in intellectual stimulation and refinement. The Knightses were greatly respected by all my family. We acknowledged their sophistication, even if we failed to understand the finer points of their intellectual preoccupations. In later years Vere obtained a PhD, Ronald became a GP and Audley and Vernon achieved success in other fields. While I was doing research in Barbados for this book, Ronald spoke on television in his role as a government medical officer. I couldn't help thinking that his career had been predetermined from those early days.

My experiences in the late 1940s and early 1950s laid the foundation of my sense of self. Through interaction both with children my own age and with adults, the core values and principles on which I base my life began to be formed. Much of this came about through playing with my siblings and local children. Daytime play was based largely on ball games, kite-flying, pitching and other organised sports, but evening play was often driven by the mystery of the dark hours. Then every shrub became a hiding-place for ghosts, duppies or wild beasts.

Our fear was driven by stories told around coal-pots as the evening meal simmered and adults told elaborate stories of awful happenings. These entertained in the security of large family groups, but induced near-terror when we were alone in bed or if we strayed from the family group. Every shadow, every rustle of dried leaves in the eddying breeze, every croak from an unexpected frog or scurrying flight of a startled blackbird or wood dove, fuelled our fear. Occasionally we found a frog hopping in the moonlight, or the discarded skin of a centipede, and would used it in invented tales of death and horror. But when, poking into a bush, we startled a rat or lizard, the sudden rustle and flight was like the crack of a gunshot and we ran in panic to the safety of adult company.

Most evenings local girls played hopscotch under a street lamp outside our house. I admired their skill, though to this day I cannot understand the rules. They threw a damp cloth into the chalked grid, and sought to retrieve it by using first one leg, then both, to hop on to numbered squares: one square, two squares, one square, and so on, then, the cloth retrieved, a sudden about-turn, and back again. Occasionally a land crab scuttled across the ground, its claws scraping the hot tarmac. Stones, lengths of rotting cane, roots, rotting fruit, sods of turf, would shower down on the pop-eyed mite, and it would scuttle faster and dive into a hole in a mud bank.

The varied sounds of nature, the innocent rising and falling laughter of children, the cooling Atlantic breezes: all were features of those early years. I loved the starry evenings when the stars were clear and bright against a dense navy-blue sweep of sky. When there was a full moon, my imagination was fired by the stories about the Man in the Moon. I tried to see him in every crater, but without success, so I imagined him in a white gown having supper and living a simple life in that cold, hard landscape.

Often, though, the dark of the evening led us to play much naughtier games, which made us laugh a lot but sometimes had a painful aftermath.

Another of our neighbours was an elderly lady called Mrs Gayle, a good friend of the family and a confidante of my mother, who did a little shopping for her and other neighbourly favours. She lived in a rickety old chattel house across the road from us; the street lighting was not strong enough to reach the front of her home, which was therefore enveloped in shadowy gloom at night.

My brother Gerald decided to play a practical joke on her. He had an uncommon talent. Even as a young child he could lower his voice several octaves to that of a seasoned old gentleman; it was a coarse, eerie sound, which rose from his lungs without intervention by the larynx.

One evening he took me to one side and said, 'Paul, you

know Mrs Gayle frighten o' ghost?'

'How you know dat?'

'I hear she tell Mama de udder night that she hear rattling at de door and thought it was outmen* come to steal she things.'

'Outmen ain' ghost,' I said.

'Look, man, if ya scared o' outmen ya scared a ghost.'

'Wa you tell me fa?'

'I gun play a trick pun she.'

'Wa trick you talking 'bout?'

'Follow me and find out.'

'Wa you gun do?'

'Shut ya mout and follow me na.'

We crept up the alleyway next to Mrs Gayle's house. There was a shrub by her back door, and Gerald hid behind it, his hands to his lips, barely able to contain his excitement. Then he expanded his chest and in bass tones reminiscent of the chant of a Tibetan monk belted out, 'Mrs Gayle, ah coming to get ya. Hear me, Mrs Gayle? Ah comin' fa ya now. You hear me, Mrs Gayle, I gun come in day fa ya.'

'Oh my God!' she screamed. 'Duppy outside ma door. Wa Lord, help me, Jesus, duppy outside ma house. Marie, Marie, come quick, come quick!'

Mama dashed across the road, pounded on the door and shouted, 'It's all right, Mrs Gayle, it's me, Marie. Open de door and let me in.' Eventually, Mrs Gayle did so, and Mama went in and calmed her down.

We tiptoed away to wait until the furore died down. But Mama was wise to what had happened. When we got home she was waiting for us, rocking gently in her rocking-chair while darning a pair of socks. On the floor beside her lay a stripped tamarind twig.

'Where were you two tonight?' You could tell she was mad by the deliberate articulation of every word.

'Outside, playing with some boys,' Gerald said.

I could barely take in the scene: Mama's steady, unusual calm, the tamarind twig, her refusal to look us in the eye.

'I thought I tell you not to go around interfering with people in their house?'

---

*Outmen were escaped convicts and other men on the run from the law.

Though instinct said that denial was the course for self-preservation, we couldn't lie to our mother. We kept silent.

Mama put down the sock, picked up the twig and called me to her. Inching my way towards her with the tiniest foot-steps a four-year-old could manage, I wrung my hands in anticipation of my punishment. I started whimpering.

'Wa I tell you about upsetting Mrs Gayle when she is a woman living by she self?'

'That I shouldn't upset her, Mama.'

'Right. So you starting young to do wa I say you shouldn't. I ain' gun have you growing up hard ear just like he.' With that Mama grabbed my shirt, pulled me towards her, and while dispensing two blows said, 'So take these for going over day and upsetting she.'

'As for you,' she said to Gerald, 'I gun cut ya ass for ya because you learning Paul bad ways. You is he older brother and should know better'. Mama never used vulgar language unless she was blue with rage, so it was clear she was very unhappy indeed. Realising that Gerald would be less willing to go over to her, and being enraged with him as the main source of her embarrassment, she lashed out immediately, striking him across his bare legs. He clutched his legs, trying to soothe the pain, and she took advantage of that to spin him round and unleash a volley of blows on his back and buttocks.

Our wailing reverberated in the street, penetrated each window, beat at every door. Ensconced in her creaky rocking-chair, Mrs Gayle rocked sagely, reassured that justice had been seen to be done.

After a few months' absence, my father came home. I remember his arrival at the airport, his trousers stacked at the ankle, his black brogues glittering in the harsh Barbadian light, his grey felt hat indented at the centre and worn at a rakish angle. Daddy was back, and the pattern of our lives changed again to accommodate him.

He had an air of metropolitan style, presence and confidence, which was reflected in his new clothes: broad ties of art nouveau chic, gilded tie-pins on looping chains. Double-breasted, broad-trousered suits, à la Victor Mature and Humphrey Bogart, echoed the style of Yankee city slickers. He unpacked fine leather shoes which squeaked with every thread, footwear gift-wrapped in soft paper like precious ornaments of chintz or crystal.

He brought my mother a green polka-dot dress. She looked exquisite in it. It lasted for many years, and I remember the smell of mothballs when she took it out to wear. The sleek smoothness of the material, the padded shoulders and elegance of design wreathed her in style and poise. She was confident and felt good about herself. I rarely saw her looking so confident or positive again, except perhaps fleetingly many years later at my younger brother Levi's wedding in Oxford when, as on this occasion, a new outfit bathed her in light, charm and a general feeling of well-being. For many years, polka-dot dresses were, in my assessment of the world of fashion, the measure of women's wear, the benchmark of metropolitan sophistication and style.

My brothers and I were given clothes, toys and picture-books. I spent many days flicking through the pictures, in which farmers in dungarees, without blemish or signs of wear, tended their stock. The white ranch-style fencing was always immaculate against perfectly tilled soil and manicured lawns, and whole orchards drooped with succulent fruit of rich, seductive colour. Through such exposure, an idea of America was formed, one that set that country, and indeed the white world, apart from the reality of my own life. Metal cars, trucks, buses, cowboy holsters and pistols raised our standing in a neighbourhood where such toys were dreamt of or occasionally bought as Christmas gifts. But the very preciousness of the toys inhibited play in the streets and in the dirt and dust of our back garden.

I was also given a pair of brown plus-fours. I had never seen plus-fours before and didn't know how to wear them. The proper mode was tried, but rejected because it seemed unreal: I couldn't reconcile myself to the three-quarter length of the trouser-legs, which ended just below the knees, their bagginess emphasising my spindly legs. I remember hoisting the elasticised folds up to my thighs, but that seemed equally unreal, the trousers ballooning out like puffy Elizabethan pantaloons. My legs descended from the bottom like stalks on wild mushrooms, and the hoisted trousers slid down from time to time. In frustration I asked, 'Mama, why dese pants so puff out?' She reminded me of how lucky I was and of the fact that few Barbadian boys could ever hope to wear such gear, while her face expressed her own bewilderment at their strange design. I often had to pull up the trouser legs; running was out of the question, hopping and skipping a total nightmare. Children peered in amazement at my peculiar attire but their parents shooshed them, realising that even if the wear wasn't elegant, it came from overseas and indicated our connections with a sophisticated world beyond our shores.

My father brought New York home in every pore, its beat in every pulse. In his relationship to the States he was much like a rabbit caught in a car headlights: so captivated was he by its mesmeric power that he could not move from its destructive path. He so idolised the idea of America that even where racism was clearly evident I think he found it hard to accept, couldn't begin to come to terms with the range and depth of its impact. Black and white Americans were central to the American mystique. Both had their part to play, and to attack one or the other was tantamount to dislodging the bricks on which the myth of the American Dream was founded. But I was fascinated by the way he boosted the character of Caribbean blacks who lived in the States, extolling them as toughs willing to stand up to the white man, unlike the American black man, who generally showed less fight and resistance to oppression. 'The American white man would always push round a coloured American, but he wun dare try to do de same ting to a West Indian,' he would say. Stories were told of Caribbean black men answering back and threatening fisticuffs or strikes if they weren't treated in a manner 'befitting a man', whereas the long-down-trodden American black would slink off and show a reluctance to fight back. It was almost as if Daddy could shun the reality of oppression by studying the performance of different black groups up against the white oppressor. The oppressor, on the other hand, though obliquely positioned as devil, was never directly targeted in Daddy's assaults.

Though my father brooked no serious criticism of the American way of life, the stories he told of his experiences there often illustrated the brutalities of institutional racism. He spoke of the humiliation of black segregation, in accounts of black-designated areas in bus queues, buses, cinemas and shops. On top of this there was the never-to-be-satisfied thirst for information on other aspects of American life, information which wasn't forthcoming, presumably because my father didn't venture into areas where he was not welcome.

Yet the difference was – often by implication – made obvious: the discriminatory laws and how they were regarded by 'Darkies' such as himself; and his accounts of whites' brutality to blacks. We heard of lynchings, of shootings and of executions in the electric chair. There were descriptions of indoor life, of trimming fruit trees or of working in a munitions factory. He told me of a Canadian boy whose family employed Daddy to trim their fruit trees. Their five-year-old son was not used to black people and had clearly not spoken to one before. On seeing my dad working on his parents' property he asked his mother, 'Ma, why is dat man covered in coal dust?' His mother told him to be quiet and not to say that. My father encouraged the lady to let the boy ask questions, explaining to the youngster that being brown doesn't mean you're dirty, and that 'the colour couldn't wash off even if he were to bath continuously for a week'.

Among our happier moments there were experiences that dulled the soul and left everyone feeling lost and dejected. One such moment left an indelible mark on the community in Fairfield in 1950. After returning from the United States my father worked as a conductor on the buses, later rising to the position of inspector. One of his fellow conductors, Errie Pa, had a relationship with a divorcee who had a bright fourteen-year-old-son stepson called Arlie. Errie Pa was jealous and became obsessed with Arlie's position in his lady's affections, developing a deep dislike for him. Over time Pa decided to do away with the boy, and he was seen sharpening a long cutlass.

Errie Pa, the boy and his mother lived just a metre away from another house, and between the two houses was a narrow alleyway. One day Pa jumped Arlie in that tight, confined space and struck him on the head with the cutlass, killing him outright. Someone informed the local bobby, who came after the killer. Before long other policemen arrived to complete the arrest and Pa was taken into custody.

There was of course a trial and Pa was sentenced to hang. My father visited him in prison.

Feigning insanity, Pa pretended not to remember the incident. 'Dashie, where I is?' he asked. 'Wha' I doing here?'

'You in prison, Errie,' my father said. 'You know you killed dat boy.'

'Wha' boy? Who killed wha' boy, Dashie? Wha' I doing here?'

The warden outside the cell winked at my father and showed a wry smile.

On the day of Errie Pa's execution I woke early, like the rest of the family. My parents had often spoken of what happened to convicted criminals on the day of their execution: the final meal, the conversation with a priest, the walk to the gallows. The stories filled me with dread, yet there was a macabre interest in them. At the stroke of the hour when the deed was supposed to be done, there was mild panic, then relief, a feeling of 'Well, at least it is all over now.'

But there was a dreadful feeling of loss, too. We couldn't talk to each other; nobody wanted to broach the subject. I conjured up vivid pictures of him sitting there waiting to be escorted by warders to the gallows, the rope being fitted round his neck, the panic, weeping, and the drop. I relived those images many times, playing them over in my thoughts when other executions were due in Barbados, and in later years in Britain, too. But Pa's death was the most shocking, if only because of the effect it had on everyone in the family. Although I was only four, it gave me my first inkling of the horrors of judicial execution, the sheer barbarity of the process.

Prayers were said for Pa and Arlie in my father's Methodist church. Christianity sat at the centre of our communities, the institution to which people turned at moments of stress and often of celebration, too. But churches in Barbados, as across the region, were (and still are) splintered, adhering to many different denominations. My experience of church life was similarly disjointed. Store-front churches with obscure names inspired by a quaint ritual or personal reading of the scriptures abounded: Pilgrim Holiness Church of the Holy Sepulchre, Church of Christ the King, the Blessed Episcopal Church of the Holy Father, and so on, all devoted to Christian worship but proclaiming fiercely protected, principled differences from other groups. This splintering has its roots in the history of the plantations, where missionaries from Europe competed for new converts.

Across the island there were many churches, small buildings sitting less than perpendicular on their crumbling foundations, often catering to congregations of fewer than fifty. They rocked to the sound of service every Sunday, the children starched and pressed in their Sunday best, their Sunday shoes worn only to service, funerals and weddings. Young people who played freely in puddles and trashy fields, or cleaned cow pens in threadbare clothing, donned pretty frocks and stiff suits in imitation of the adults. Mums, aunts and big sisters stepped out, pocket-book in hand, for morning's service. Many lightly powdered their faces to neutralise the effect of naturally occurring body oils, or carried a parasol for protection from the intense sunlight.

My brothers and I attended church every Sunday, sometimes two or three times in the day: Morning Service, afternoon Sunday School and Evening Service. My father's church was a popular one and was almost always full. The tightly packed little building was an uncomfortable place to be at any time of day or night. There was no air-conditioning, and some evenings, when the Atlantic breezes were light or non-existent, sweat coursed down our faces and necks and under our starched collars. How I hated the sensation of sweat under stiff, uncomfortable clothing in a tropical climate!

Preparations started the evening before, when Mama ironed her hair and 'pressed' clothing. The house was filled with the acrid scent of burnt hair, the sizzling and the puffs of blue smoke that accompanied each combing action, a feature of our weekends. Then there were the minor adjustments that had to be made on the Singer sewing-machine, as hems were lowered or waistlines trimmed. As wages were low, and the machines imported, ownership of a good sewing-machine, particularly a Singer, like ownership of a Raleigh bicycle, conferred special status on a family. My mother's machine had a dedicated timber box-base, into which it was folded after use. It helped cement our position in the community as a go-ahead and resourceful family. I enjoyed the purr of the machine, the skill with which my mother manoeuvred cloth beneath the needle-head while stitching.

Local people who owned similar machines augmented their income by making clothes and curtains. Our family ordered made-to-measure suits and dresses from local tailors and seamstresses: three-piece suits worn by my father and even by my brothers and me, and the fine cotton dresses that my mother wore. In later years many local self-taught tailors took their skills to England, where a few found employment, over a period of time, in the clothes trade.

We bathed each Sunday morning in water drawn from the standpipe. I was scrubbed in the back garden on a pile of stones, Mama throwing bowls of water over me as she lathered me with carbolic soap. Then there was the ritual of squeezing oneself into uncomfortable clothes, too thick for the climate, too stiff for the joints, too important for childish freedoms.

The walk to church was almost always uncomfortable. Our Sunday shoes pinched the toes, blistered the ankles and took layers of skin from the heels. We walked stiffly behind our parents and neighbours, the men walking together, followed by a gaggle of women, with the children at the rear. The crunch, crunch of shoe leather on gravel was so strangely satisfying that you made a beeline for gravelly surfaces to prolong it as long as possible.

Church was a strangely disjointed experience. We were required to be on our best behaviour in the room, whose heat was made worse by the worshippers' own body heat. Then there was the fanning, the constant fanning to keep cool, the flickering of prayer books and song sheets. Occasionally someone produced a manufactured fan and beat the air. I was drawn to the pretty colours and ribbed effect.

But I was mystified by the preacher quoting chapter and verse. The whole thing was more tiring than convincing: the otherworldly language, the use of 'thou' and 'thee' almost comical. I tried to believe in the miracles I was told about, but couldn't: the turning of water into wine, the feeding of a multitude from five loaves and five fishes, the parting of the Red Sea. I kept waiting to see the light but never found it, spent more time studying the worshippers than the scriptures, the way people fell to their knees, hands clasped, focused on imagined worlds. I couldn't understand their certainty in something so vague.

The closest we got to an extraordinary happening was the assent of some women to The Power, a special communion with Christ. Women – it was always women in my experience – came into The Power at evening service. It could be described as religious streaking: out of nowhere, the unexpected and bizarre. Interestingly, too, in their transports of religious fervour the worshippers never hurt themselves. Though claims could be made that they were 'in the bosom of the Lord', I think the truth is more pragmatic and self-centred.

Before slipping into The Power, a worshipper gave warning of an imminent fit by a range of signs. There was the swaying from side to side with eyes closed, accompanied by murmuring and myriad inarticulate swoons. There was also the waving of arms, again with closed eyes, grunts and various invocations to the Almighty. Sometimes the worshipper started singing a repetitive ditty which cut across the business of the service. Strong-armed worshippers stood ready in case the chosen one 'lost control', and at the moment of transport they caught the collapsing believer and gently lowered her to the floor. Furniture would be pushed aside to make way for the believer, before the fireworks began in earnest.

There would be shrieking and a tossing of arms and legs like that of a possessed whirling dervish, their hair dishevelled, clothing crumpled and tangled. A sheet would be brought to protect their dignity as clothing was disturbed and intimate areas of the body exposed. Some spoke in tongues, others foamed at the mouth, beads of sweat rolling from their brow as they gyrated in their fervour.

There was never a panic to see who was possessed; except those assisting the chosen, the congregation remained in their positions and continued singing, often reacting as if the presence of the Lord was being made manifest by the chosen one. The woman's movements had an echo in the behaviour of the congregation, many of whom held their arms aloft in expressions of deliverance, singing and sweating, their eyes closed to this world as they communed with Christ.

One of the most memorable church occasions was the harvest festival, when people took offerings to church as a celebration of plenty and as a way of sharing with the poor. The church then was a very special place to be. Bundles of sugarcane were pressed into the four corners of the building. Tucked in among rafters and pillars were fern fronds, leaves and branches, whole lengths of foliage that turned the inside of the church into a forest of green. Straw baskets and decorative buckets hung from ceiling timbers, while tables overflowed with guavas, ackees, mangoes, dunks and myriad other fruit. There were tinned foods, hams and roast meat, sweet potatoes, cassavas and yams in great mounds, soursops (huge fruit with black seeds and flesh the consistency of ice-cream) and pumpkins of giant girth. On plastic cloths, beakers of sorrel and mauby infusions sat alongside richly decorated glasses. Fabric, woven, plaited, tasselled and plain, interspersed with paper ribbons and balloons, added a further decorative note, all touched off with tubs of bougainvillea. Caribbean people like good smells, and there was no place on earth that could offer a greater variety of rich, pungent ones. With the plaintive songs of Christian worship filling the building, guitars strumming, choirs going through their paces, the church was a rich environment indeed. The food presented at harvest was later distributed among the poor of the neighbourhood; who would themselves have made an offering to the church during the festival.

Christmas

My father's choir was called on to contribute to the Christmas service. The choir sang in his Pilgrim Holiness church and at competitions around the island. Rehearsals took place regularly in our home, particularly during the run-up to a contest or an important service, or when a new hymn was being added to their repertoire. Shop assistants, field workers, schoolteachers, cane-cutters, housewives, tailors, carpenters and joiners, all skilled in the craft of making music from graphic symbols. Corpulent women in nylon dresses smelling of cheap perfume, their song books fanning the air. Sweat sitting on furrowed brows – Mrs Skeete the organ player's eyes moistened in sympathy. My father tapping his improvised lectern for quiet. Presently he would call for everyone to order, the singers tuning up like instruments in an orchestra pit: 'Mi, Mi, Mi; Doh, Doh, Doh; Doh, Re, Mi ...' Basses and tenors on one side, sopranos and altos on the other, denoting a difference of vocal texture rather than a gender separation. Then the striking of the tuning-fork. Voices in sequential order ringing out, related segments meshing in a multi-tiered descant, the disparate synthesised elements a unified whole, the participants working in harmony like workers on an assembly line.

My father's choirs filled the house with music, pulsated in the street and drew crowds. Little children standing on orange crates or large butter cans, staring in goggled-eyed at Ambizine Gail embroiled in the alto part and Mr Knight's groping determination to produce a tenor sound. Splendid people with big voices and bold hearts enmeshed in an ecstasy of music-making, while finding a universe of potentialities within themselves, and giving it expression through their art. People without material wealth make sound, carve wood, essay a cover-drive (a particular cricketing stroke), thus speaking of their wholeness and wealth as beings through their skills and sensibilities. Such experiences confirmed the value of them, the value of myself as a person, by the richness of their talents and skills. My feeling for the choir has expanded to embrace wider areas of orchestration. I am indebted to the singers of Fairfield, and more especially to my father, for my love of classical music and the controlled harmonies of Welsh choral music. Pure experience rooted in those mesmerising childhood moments as I tried to make myself unseen and unheard in my family's front room with those splendid singers.

The final preparations for Christmas were complete in most households by midnight on Christmas Eve. New cotton curtains were put up, the 'good' side facing outwards, and net curtains were hung along beams at the entrances to passage-ways and doorways, bunched and bowed with ribbons to enhance the decorative effect. Embroidered cloths, mothballed for much of the year, were taken out and placed on cupboards and small tables. Paper flowers filled pots and glasses decorated with abstract patterns, flowers, fruit, birds or other motifs. These harmonised with paper chains, lanterns and other paper-based decorations. My father bought fluted glasses from the United States, their stems streaked with emerald, the lip of each rimmed with a band of gold. They were taken out at Christmas when we entertained guests – we ourselves were not allowed to use them. He also bought a large block of ice for chilling drinks. Everyone in our neighbourhood bought ice, because few if any owned a fridge. It was kept in a cool part of the house, wrapped in burlap, what we called a crocus bag. My father chiselled ice from the block with an ice-pick, its long, pointed blade the stuff of nightmares.

We didn't have a Christmas tree, because that hadn't yet become a fixture in local Christmas celebrations. Instead, we spread marl on Christmas Eve. Armies of people, both children and adults, collected buckets of marl and spread it around their homes, in a ritual embedded in the culture of Christmas.

Barbados is a coral island, its bedrock a brilliant white coral stone. The quarrying of stone for building left a residue of fine white dust (marl) in the quarries. The whole village was transformed by the film of white dust. It created a feeling of moment, of occasion, the unique feeling of Christmas celebration. Short of the festive opening of gifts and the Christmas meal, the marl-laying was for me the most exciting Christmas experience, though it was to be many years before I realised what we were doing. Whether by sublimation or osmosis, or indeed by indirect exposure to influence through the media, popular music and cinema, Christmas couldn't be Christmas without 'snow'. In tropical Barbados, few people had experienced a northern winter, but the significance of snow in the romance of Christmas for many people in the north had been communicated to us. People in Europe and America set the style, and where they went we followed in many areas of cultural expression. This was true in the way we celebrated Christmas, as it was in the manner in which we categorised people on the basis of physiological differences such as skin colour. Bing Crosby's 'White Christmas' was one of the most popular records ever sold in Barbados.

Mama stayed up late making preparations for our Christmas feast. It was a wonderfully exciting time, dominated by the smell of cakes, freshly cooked ham, chicken and pork prepared in the spices integral to Caribbean cooking: thyme, black pepper, turmeric. Mama also dusted and polished, bringing out the sheen on the rich claret tones peculiar to mahogany furniture. Presents were placed for us in the front room.

Each Christmas morning Daddy rose early and turned up the volume on a programme of carols on our Rediffusion receiver. 'Silent Night', 'The Holly and the Ivy', 'While Shepherds

Watched', classic carols which added to the magic of the season. We had a simple breakfast before opening our presents. Mama bought us practical gifts: BVDs, the popular American manufactured underpants, vests and socks; occasionally a new shirt, pair of shoes or even a pair of trousers for school or church. Gerald and I were also given one or two simple toys, usually small, push-along donka vehicles, bows and arrows or a simple cap gun. These were very basic toys that didn't cost a great deal, but extended our range of play.

We didn't know how they arrived in our house. Like children in many other countries, we were told fanciful stories of Father Christmas inserting himself through cracks in window frames, under doors or through window jalousies to deliver them. I couldn't help thinking that, if he could do such things, maybe duppies and evil spirits could, too. For all that, Christmas was an extraordinary moment of excitement and sweet anticipation.

I remember hearing a band one Christmas 'foreday morning' as they performed door to door. Initially there was the muffled boom-boom of a bass drum. This was soon joined by the rattle of cymbals. In a moment, scraps of human sound could be heard, interspersed with rhythmic peals, before the more coherent tones of recognisable melodies. The troupes moved slowly from door to door, singing and beating out their rhythms, and were rewarded with tots of rum and slices of ham dressed with pepper sauce. I was awe-struck by the costume-clad group and the power of their music. My father didn't drink alcohol and wouldn't have approved of a member of his household doing so, either; it went against his religious principles. But I was fascinated by the ritual attached to the consumption of strong liquor: the drinks, the cute gestures, the way each sip was followed by a smacking of the lips, a grimace or even an expression of discomfort, the requests for more.

The Christmas meal was of course an important part of the festival. My mother started her preparations days earlier, often supported by my father, who enjoyed making cakes. Soft drinks were bought, and sorrel and mauby infusions prepared. All the necessary meat, spices and vegetables were bought. The ham, a vital ingredient of Bajan Christmas festivities, was kept in the larder with other perishables. We always had roast chicken instead of turkey, because Daddy didn't like turkey, finding it dry and unappetising.

Each year my father killed a bird for Christmas dinner. I could never contain my horror at the death: a bird we had fed and had come to know well being taken to the gravel bed at the bottom of the garden and slaughtered. When my father entered the hen house there was a great commotion, a flurry of feathers and general pandemonium, as if the birds had forebodings of what was about to befall one of their number. He selected a bird, grabbed it and took it down to the gravel bed. There, he pinned it under his foot and pulled the head, stretching the neck taut, then cut the neck with a sawing motion, and the blood squirted in a fine jet into the white coral stone. He held the convulsing body firmly until the thrashing ceased, then removed the head. It was a sickening spectacle. I lived in horror of having to perform such duties as a man, taking responsibility for feeding my family, choosing a bird and cutting its throat.

After the killing my mother took control, plucking the carcass and gutting it, the entrails being fed to a dog. She took out the gall-bladder, whose bitterness, we were warned, would taint the meat if broken while still in the carcass. How I hated the mucky, mushy look of it. I remember my father opening a bird's crop, revealing partially digested grain, another hateful sight, like damp droppings. I couldn't enjoy freshly killed chicken, couldn't disconnect the bird's death from the meat on my plate. Much better the anonymity of food butchered elsewhere and delivered in packs or on a plate. I thought of Jesus the fisherman, how he served five thousand people with fish and bread. In the Bible shepherds were seen as good people, but surely shepherds bred animals for slaughter? And surely fish could feel pain? There seemed no sanctuary for animals, even in heaven.

Nevertheless, as cooked by my mother, the chicken was delicious, the gravy rich and flavoursome, the meat seasoned with herbs and browned to crisp perfection. It was served with rice and a well-marinated salad of avocado, cucumber and lettuce, and was followed by a platter of fresh mango, guava and papaya. We ate well at Christmas – as indeed we did the year round.

Barbadian cuisine is partly shaped by salted preserves and tinned foods such as corned beef, pilchards and herrings. Salt cod (salt-fish to the Bajan), salt pork, salt beef, red herring, long-life milk and so on were packed and shipped to the island in barrels from other Caribbean territories, Britain, the USA and elsewhere. They extended the range of available food, adding interest and variety to our diet.

Imported food was brought to the island by ships and schooners. The Barbados harbour wasn't built until 1961, so when I was a child ships and schooners still had to anchor off the island, their cargoes being ferried ashore to the Careenage by a flotilla of small craft. Many years later I left the island via this route, sailing from the Careenage in a small ferry and boarding an Italian liner, the *Serrienta*, anchored out at sea.

Mama used to make lovely tea, which she cooled by pouring it from one cup to another, allowing the tea to fall through space for a couple of feet between the two cups. I admired the skilful way she did it: starting with the lips of the cups touching, then, as the tea flowed, drawing one cup upwards from the other in an unbroken, fluid movement, without a drop being spilt. By the time it had cooled enough to be drunk, the tea was covered with a bubbly froth, like the head on a fresh glass of beer. We loved it like that. For breakfast we sometimes had fried plantain and scrambled egg. Our breakfasts were light, with fresh eggs, bread, cheese and marmalade.

People in Fairfield didn't go hungry, but they weren't affluent, either. Food was plentiful in the fields, and most people owned their own stock: chickens, pigs, goats, black-belly sheep or even cattle. When we needed to buy meat, it was reasonably priced, but there was little cash for buying other items. My first memory of my mother's cooking is of her preparing meals in the back garden. It must have been 1949. In those days Mama cooked in a cast-iron cauldron – it was nicknamed 'hands akimbo' because of the way the handles curled at the side – over a fire built from imported coal and timber. The pure blackness of the coal fascinated me when set against the coral stone strewn about the back garden. I had never seen anything so black.

Mama cooked the most delicious stews, soups and rice dishes in that pot. We pressed bakes round the outside to nibble while the meal was cooking. Bakes are a simple bread, effectively a baked dumpling, which was an essential item in the diet of the poor. Most Barbadians ate bakes because they were cheap and easy to make, though few would have admitted to eating 'poor man's food'. If eating bakes signalled low social status, the use of calabash ware indicated destitution. Such ware was in itself a transgression of a vital code, the denial of which spelt exclusion and vilification. That code was a show of sophistication and elegance based on Euro-American familiarity and dependence on the man-made and the mass-produced.

When we moved to Britain and I learnt about African peoples and their ways of life through seeing television programmes about them, I realised that calabashes and gourds are vital kitchen equipment for many in Africa. In the Far East, people use them to glorious effect, producing exquisite tools and receptacles of beauty, strength and elegance, ideal for cooking, washing, making music and other purposes. And in the Americas many people of African ancestry use calabash ware, at times showing marvellous creativity in decorating it with delightful bas reliefs, paintings and drawings. But most Barbadians saw neither the practical and economic benefits nor the fact that calabashes are a historical link to our African past. To them the use of calabashes was a sign of failure, so much so that we children gave calabash trees a wide berth, in case anyone should think we were going to harvest the pods for use at home. When anyone was seen with a calabash it was usually in the process of being destroyed, if only symbolically – as the pods are extremely tough for even an adult to break.

The gourd's bedfellow was the tin can. Poor people salvaged throw-away cans ('tots' in the Barbadian vernacular) and used them for drinking and cooking. Simple cans were fitted with a metal off-cut as a handle, and recycled as mugs. My father was always in work and never had to resort to such desperate measures, but one met people who did, who made shoes from worn-out car tyres, who even made clothes from the burlap 'crocus bags' used to transport and store fruit and vegetables. Next to the humble brown paper bag, burlap was the cheapest, most unsophisticated material available, its use for clothing signalling desperate poverty. Such people survived on a diet of breadfruit, salt-fish and bakes, plus fruit and vegetables grown on a strip of land or cadged from neighbours and friends. Breadfruit trees grew everywhere, and for the most part still do. The sheer abundance of the savoury fruit made it a common meal for poor people, because it was cheap and did not need elaborate preparation. Today in the finest Barbadian restaurants and bars, breadfruit, once the staple diet of the poor, is a valued ingredient in cooking, a marker of the Bajan way of life. On visiting the island with my family in 1998, I couldn't suppress a whimsical smile when I thought of how the poor had fought to preserve their dignity in a land where appearance and style matter. It was extraordinary to see black and white Bajans and tourists tucking into breadfruit and salt-fish with relish.

Not the least remarkable thing about the breadfruit is the way it reached the West Indies. After the mutiny aboard the *Bounty* in 1789, the mutineers cast Captain Bligh and the crew members who supported him adrift in an open boat without charts – but with the breadfruit seedlings collected in Tahiti. In an astonishing feat of seamanship, Bligh got boat, men and seedlings to Timor, nearly four thousand miles away. The mutiny on the *Bounty* not only provided the material for a great movie but supplied an important ingredient of a way of life which sustained many and has given enormous pleasure and satisfaction to generations in the Caribbean.

Cooking in the garden in an iron pot, like scrubbing clothes on a jukking-board was a communion with the past, not a welcome one, maybe, but a lived part of that reality just the same. Within a few years things began to change rapidly as the trappings of the modern era kicked in. In 1952 my parents bought a four-burner kerosene cooker with a detachable oven. As the fuel didn't generate smoke and was relatively clean, a kitchen was built. For the first time my mother could cook indoors, bake coconut bread, conkies and other cakes and roast meat in her own oven. Until then, most of our meat was fried and our cakes baked, for a nominal fee, in the ovens of the local baker.

Throughout the year food was bought fresh in small quantities to satisfy each day's needs. Meals weren't left overnight for reheating, this being regarded as the worst culinary practice – there was the fear of ptomaine ('tomay' in the vernacular) – because food went bad quickly in the tropical heat. Perishables were usually cooked and eaten on the day they were bought. Fish-sellers appeared in the evenings, carrying on their heads trays of flying-fish, red snapper, sprats and other fish. On special occasions my mother did her food shopping at Eagle Hall or another market. I remember going with her to a market where there was a wide selection of fish, some with scales and some without, crabs, sea-cats (octopus) and sea-eggs, dolphin, barracuda and swordfish. But what interested me most was a huge shark hanging by its tail in front of a stall. It must have been eight feet long and the prize catch in the whole market. Stories of how it was caught were told and retold: the struggles at the side of the boat, the hours of sweating, the near-fatal accident when a man slipped and almost fell into the sea. My mind went back to a story my father had told of a shark which on being gutted was found to contain pieces of machinery, an old shoe, several cans of palm-tree butter, and other tinned food. The savagery of sharks was constantly discussed with wide-eyed fascination and was, to our mind, justification for their slaughter.

Fresh fish was central to the Bajan diet. We enjoyed all types from the smallest to the largest, the spiky to the squirmy, the goggle-eyed to the near-featureless, but flying-fish was the most popular. I remember the excitement generated on the first evening of the fishing-season at the sound of the plaintive cry of 'Fish, fish, six for five cent', or some such figure, and the mad dash with a few jingling coins to buy some. That night puffs of steam and smoke could be seen everywhere, and the mouth-watering smell of fried fish immersed everyone in bonhomie and satisfaction at the catch. Peering through the fence, one saw neighbours scaling and gutting or frying fish against a backdrop of anxious, bug-eyed children willing the cooking to be over so they could tuck in.

We helped Mama prepare ours. Sitting in the garden on a low wooden stool, scaling and gutting by the light of an oil-lamp, the thin, filmy scales sticking to my body and clothing, I pulled at the bloodied intestines and marvelled at the smell of the sea that wafted up from them. The washed fish were seasoned and turned into a pouch-like shape by inserting the tail through the mouth, before being floured and fried. Some were kept back for soup, others steamed or baked. The roes, a great delicacy in Barbados, were put aside to be fried in oil or butter and eaten with crackers. We made the best of a wonderful resource.

Sea-eggs are edible sea-urchins. Large and pinky-white, they once thrived on the coral reefs of the island, where it is relatively easy for a moderately skilled diver to harvest them. But easy access made them vulnerable to over-fishing, and they are now a protected species. When I lived in Barbados they were another favourite delicacy. We removed the salmon-pink flesh with a spoon and fried it in oil or butter over a gentle fire for a minute or two. When ready they had an orangey scrambled-egg consistency. The flavour remains unique in my gastronomic experience.

Some Saturday nights we bought black pudding and a pan of souse. Of all dishes, with the exception of sea-egg and possibly salt-fish and cou-cou, black pudding and souse define the Bajan culinary taste. Black pudding is made from sweet potato, pig's blood, herbs and other ingredients. Souse is a spicy pork dish, usually served cold, and consists largely of pig trotters, other pork trimmings, spices and onion. The smell of black pudding sizzling in a hawker's pan is like none other. Waiting in line with other hungry customers for pudding and souse, pennies in one hand, enamel bowl in the other, was a moment of tingling excitement and mouth-watering anticipation. The bats that essayed their darting, angular flights in the night sky, the scuttling land-crabs darting to a borough on a sticky embankment, and the nearby children who played tag on the fringes of enshrouded canefields, were common to those evenings. Returning home with my precious bearings, waiting in sweet anticipation while my mother divided the pudding and distributed it, was pure heaven. Cou-cou, popular with some Barbadians, is made from corn-meal and is often served with red-herring or other toppings.

We bought meat from shops, but occasionally a neighbour slaughtered a pig, black-belly sheep or goat, providing fresh meat and welcome income for their household. Similarly, we bought milk from hawkers who sold it freshly drawn each morning from a tethered cow. It was sold by the gill, half-pint or pint.

Preserved food such as salt beef, corned beef, salt pork, salted pigs' tails and salt-fish was often left in our larder for considerable periods before being cooked and eaten. This didn't matter with salted cod or herrings, but home-prepared salt beef and salt pork sometimes acquired a peculiarly rancid taste which I came to enjoy. Most food was kept in the larder, a cupboard fitted with fine mesh wire front for ventilation. It was meant to be mouse-proof but mice often got in, leaving a scattering of droppings behind them. Traps were set and many killed. I remember the flattened bodies and the startled look on their tiny faces. Like most people, Barbadians abhor rats, regarding them with the same revulsion as snakes. An occasional rat took a chance to raid our larder. Tough and elusive, they were difficult to catch, but their presence sent everyone into a panic.

Around midday, especially in June, July and August, the heat became so intense that I often dropped off to sleep. The hot sun induced a sound lassitude, cast a spell of silence on the landscape. We didn't have Spanish-style siestas, but people and nature withdrew to darkened spaces and reduced their pace to a crawl or even a full stop. Occasionally a cockerel could be heard squawking as if bewailing the heat, comb flopping to one side, beak open as if it were panting for air. Few ventured out at midday. I wondered at the shimmering heat-waves often generating mirages in the streets, the sight of mirror images and unreal water which made the rooftops shimmer.

There were few people anywhere, few sounds to connect with, and even the birds seemed to melt into the darkness of the trees and undergrowth. Workers stood off work for a couple of hours; carpenters building houses in adjoining streets slowed to an occasional burst of activity before falling silent altogether. What pleasure to walk in a shady lane and hear the whistle of a breeze whipping through bamboo groves, making their elongated leaves jingle like door chimes, the riot of leaves bursting with sound on mango, and tamarind trees; bananas and palms bouncing in the current of air. People moved with a special sloth, an unfussy rhythm which conserved energy. Even the speech of many became slower, more of a drawl than a clear enunciation of words.

Nobody went out in the sun unless they had to. To this day the sight of white people sunbathing in terrible heat fills me with a sort of horror of discomfort.

Women used parasols made of gossamer-thin, colourful fabrics which held back the sun's rays without shutting them out completely. Slow-moving women in the heat of midday, working their hips to the rhythm of time, parasol held aloft, working their way down an alleyway, up a side road. The beating sun, stillness all around.

Craftsmen and hawkers plied their trade from a front room, in the shade of a tamarind tree, a back yard, under a street lamp or in some other advantageous spot. You could buy pudding and souse, coconut bread in which chunky lumps of coconut were embedded, a perfectly tailored suit or a multi-tiered wedding cake. A neighbour in Dash Road, an adjoining street, sold snowballs from his cart, standing under a cluster of coconut trees for shade, his ice-block wrapped in a hessian bag. From the giant cube he shaved thin slivers with a machine which looked very much like a carpenter's plane. At the centre of this tool was a chamber which collected the shaved ice. When dropped into a customer's cup, the frozen mass would be flavoured with a squirt of cherry syrup, pineapple or other sweeteners. In the long, hot, steaming days of summer, few treats were more welcome to us or more fully appreciated.

To escape the heat, Mama and Daddy sometimes took us to the seaside. The walk took us from the poorer district through a more affluent one, the character of the houses changing from wooden practicality to shimmering white-painted stone authority. Houses with splendid verandas and decorative stone worked balustrades, homes with perfect tiled driveways and picket bush fencing. No palings here, or even galvanised sheeting for fencing. Here the comfortable black or white bourgeoisie reclined in confident elegance in shaded nooks on well-crafted mahogany furniture to read *The Advocate*, *Bim* or some foreign journal. Men with reading-glasses pushed right down the bridge of their noses, cocking a snook at my lowly status in their middle-class confidence. Many on rocking-chairs gently rocking. Sometimes an older person, overcome by sleep, folded into a cane-backed rocker, a crumpled paper on their lap.

My heart missed a beat on one trip, when a white boy pretended to shoot me with a rifle, from the nozzle of which a cork popped when he pulled the trigger. I really thought my time had come. The experience has stayed with me over the years because of my coming eye to eye with a white boy not much older than myself in this uneven and threatening way. The fact that he was ensconced in his parents' home, from where he looked down on me as I walked with my parents, and his possession of a toy rifle such as I had never seen before, was instructive.

Holding my mother's hand as we made our way to the sea, I marvelled at the illusions created by the heat. A panting dog, its tongue hanging from one side of its jaw, moving slowly, and frighteningly, in our direction from a few hundred paces away, its body mirrored in a broken reflection in the air. The tops of giant casuarinas singing and bending in the wind as the breeze blew in from the east, coming off the hills and striking the treetops. Then, as we neared our objective, the intensity of sea smells, the richness of sea-weed. Occasionally a fisherman with his catch on his shoulder or carried in one hand. Three or four octopuses hooked from the mouth, their arms bouncing with the tread of their bare-foot owner. Another successful fisherman with snapper on a pole, twine fastened through their gills and looped through their bloodied mouths. I gawked at the multicoloured shimmer of their scales. A woman with a load of sea-eggs making her way rapidly to market with a large catch on a tray on her head, the tray sitting on a flat pad for better balance. Many youngsters passed us with buckets of sea water, much of it splashing and spilling, and in the buckets crabs trying to escape or huddling with fear in a mass, their pink-brown colour betraying their suitability for cooking and the short journey to a terrible end.

The ocean, on Sunday morning visits, offered gleaming prizes, which crawled or squirmed their precarious existence in brackish water in the cupped hulls of fishermen's rowing-boats. I loved peering into them and seeing the unwanted catch left behind: tiny flat fish of emerald and gold, some-times with a band of white, peculiar crabs with rough spiky shells that cleverly imitated rock and chips of stone, tiny silver fish that flitted about in their marine prison on seeing my head appear above the rim of the boat. The flotsam and jetsam that girdled the sea in beached offerings were nervously explored for the treasures lurking there. The smell of the sea trapped in the shell of a conch, or the sticky, drooping arms of a sea-cat, always captivated me and whispered of distant lands and hidden stories beneath the waves. The sea was special; you respected its power, its dangers and its sheer iridescent beauty.

We owned a wind-up gramophone on which my father played fragile 78rpm records of Billy Eckstein, Sarah Vaughan, Nat King Cole, Bing Crosby and other popular American musicians. He also had a large collection of church music and carols bought locally and in the USA. The weight of the arm and the fragility of the discs meant that the slightest error could result in a damaged or even broken record. My brothers and I were never allowed to operate the gramophone, and Mama didn't care to, either. She steered clear of modern technology and allowed my father a free run of it. The sound quality may have been poor – tinny and lacking in resonance – but we were grateful for the music. I remember my mother mending clothes or doing out other household chores while humming along to 'Some Enchanted Evening', 'You Are My Sunshine', 'Beautiful Dreamer' and other favourites of the day. To me it was like magic that a machine could produce music by running a pointed nail along fine grooves on a disc.

We also had an eight-band Zenith wireless, bought by my father in the United States during one of his seasonal contracts. It was the envy of many in the street. The horizontal bands were stacked on an adjustable lid, which operated like the screen on a laptop computer. I was mesmerised by its complexity and by the way it enabled us to listen to broadcasts from countries and cities I could only dream of. Of an evening we picked up Caracas, Havana, New York, Jamaica and of course London. Broadcasts from Brazil meshed with those from New York, voices from Martinique fused with music from Mexico. In the frizzle and crackle of interference we surfed the airwaves for a signal from London and the military marches that presaged programmes from Britain. Through such contacts, pictures were formed of life in other places. These combined with my father's stories and the scraps we picked up from the press, comics, school and other sources to form often wildly distorted notions of life in other places.

We listened to fights in America involving Joe Louis, Max Schmeling, Josey Joe Walcott, Rocky Marciano and others. On fight night the atmosphere in the house was electric. For black people, sport, most notably cricket, was the only real opportunity to elevate ourselves to positions of power relative to whites. Given the macho baggage attached to fist-fighting, the performance of black boxers meant a great deal to all of us, both male and female. We crowded round the wireless, adjusting the aerial to pick up a clearer signal. These moments united the family in support of our heroes and divided the Fairfield community.

These stations and western countries were a pleasure to make contact with, but in the early 1950s the key influence on the taste of the Barbadian listening public was the BBC. Most Barbadians resonated with the British through radio broadcasts and other cultural contacts. Each evening Bajans put away their work things, made themselves comfortable in rocking-chairs and on verandas and listened as the BBC told us what was happening in the world. Radio Newsreel with its militaristic jingle attracted a near universal following. Apart from Rediffusion, which was largely a parochial station, focusing on domestic matters, we had little other access to information about the outside world. The 'foreign' stations we listened to were excellent for music and sport, but the BBC seemed to speak directly to us. The clipped accent of the English middle classes was commonplace. We pictured the world through their renditions of plays and stories transmitted from Bush House. The achievers of British and Commonwealth society, celebrated in current affairs and arts programmes, formed the backdrop to our lives. Stories of the war were told; Hitler's name was frequently mentioned but it meant nothing to me or, I suspect, to many of those around me. But a man who lived in an adjoining street named his dog Hitler. It was a bad-tempered dog and we were scared of it, so I came to associate the name Hitler with evil and danger. A local policeman who rode a motor-bike was likewise, because of his authority and power of arrest, associated in my growing mind with the Nazi leader. Much of this was driven by my untutored access to radio broadcasts on the Overseas Service of the BBC.

Television did not exist in the world of 1950s Barbados, and cinema made a limited contribution to our entertainment. The oral tradition that sits at the heart of African life-styles was central to how we shared experience and passed on histories. My father told high tales about his travels and adventures, about encounters with ghosts, confrontations with animals and even wild dogs. He often told the story of an extraordinary adventure he had had some years earlier in BG (British Guyana). I remember the first time I heard it, though the detail has been underscored by frequent retellings in different family contexts. That first occasion was a balmy summer's night, the people present were fanning themselves to keep cool, frogs croaked in the scrubland next to our home, crickets and myriad other insects chirped or flew wildly in front of the steaming pot.

My father began his story. 'Man, when I was in BG we were out in the jungle and one day man we got real tired, ya know. So this fella said to me, "Man, lets sit 'pun dat log over there and res' a while." We were tired and everybody felt like a break so we went over and sit down 'pun de ting. And you know' – laughter began rippling through his audience – 'de log started to move, we felt a little tremor, then a wiggle, and we look down and we realise we sitting 'pun a big, big boa constrictor.' Hysterical screaming, squirming of discomfort and looks of amazement ensued. The children stared dumbfounded at the storyteller. Mama screwed her face into a look of horror and disgust.

'Man,' my father continued, brushing one hand against another to indicate rapid flight, 'we gone mad.' He laughed so much that he couldn't sit up straight but keeled over, holding his tummy and throwing his head back at the sheer ludicrous situation. 'Everybody took off in every direction – I couldn't see no man jack for smoke.' Tears rolled down his cheeks and he coughed, remembering and recreating the sheer joy of the event. In the meantime Mama, who loved a good yarn as much as anyone, looked as if she was caught in a boa constrictor's coils, squirming and twitching as she imagined the event.

Daddy elaborated on the yarn with stories about boa constrictors swallowing animals whole after suffocating them. He told us that the snake, having swallowed an animal, didn't move from that spot until it had digested its meal. He described how the snake's shape changed when it swallowed something big: the head and forepart the usual shape, then a lump in the middle, and then the hind part and tapering tail. I sat behind my mother, my arms thrown round her waist for protection, unable to quell visions of myself being killed that way. To this day I have an inordinate fear and dislike of snakes; there can't be any doubt that my father's story-telling was a key contributor to that.

Another evening my father spoke of rats which climb coconut trees, chew their way through the shell of a coconut to the jelly, gorge themselves, and then, unable to climb back down the tree trunk, use the coconut as a 'parachute', leaping from the shell just before it hits the ground. There were also yarns about dangerous outmen who terrified whole districts of the island. My imagination went wild with thoughts of cutthroats lurking in our garden or behind a bush to grab me and chop me up. Every shadow, every creak in the house, every rustle in the bushes, was a potential threat. I clung to my mother for dear life, feeling more vulnerable and helpless than I had ever done. It is just as well we had chamber-pots or 'topsies' under the bed, because my fear of the outdoors after dark was so profound that nothing would have got me to use the loo without adult protection.

My father's ghost stories, though, were an altogether different matter. The sheer otherworldliness of 'ghosts' was such that protection was of no account – even adults were fair game for poltergeists. One warm summer evening the family was gathered in the gentle glow of a kerosene lamp in our front room. Daddy sat in a rocking-chair gently rocking back and forth, the floorboards creaking as he did so. The street lamp threw a cone of light to the pavement below, but around it there was inky blackness. An occasional neighbour shouted a greeting as they walked by, but there was little movement outdoors, little traffic, either motor-driven or animal-drawn. The stillness and quiet of the evening seemed to induce my father to speak of his experiences with ghosts, and he told the story of a ghost in Trinidad which became active at night, harming people by blowing scentless fumes through keyholes.

His favourite ghost story was particularly frightening because it was based on his own experience in an area near our district, and he swore by all the stars that it was true. This is how it went. One evening after work my father, then a young man, was tired and wanted to get home as quickly as possible, so he took a short cut across the Grazette estate canefields, which he knew well. It was a moonlit night and the cane was young, only about a metre high, so he could see a long way. As he walked he saw a strange shape in the cane ahead of him. He knew there shouldn't be anything there – there were no trees or shrubs in the area, and no small shed had been built there. In any case, the shape was strangely human.

Daddy could feel panic rising. His immediate instinct was to run the other way, but his father had always warned him not to run if confronted by a threatening person or animal, because that would 'put you at a disadvantage and could spell disaster'. With that in mind he held his course. As he approached, the apparition rose jerkily from a crouch to stand upright, then started to move towards him. But its movement was more of a glide than the undulating stride pattern a person would normally make. My father found the strength to continue walking as the creature moved towards him. Before long he and it were close to each other. As their paths crossed, it gave off an awful smell, unlike anything he had smelt before, and it made an inarticulate and guttural sound, a kind of 'hum' which came from deep within it. When it was past him, my father seized the opportunity to bolt with all the speed he could muster, arriving home in utter exhaustion and terror.

Stories like that kept me well away from the tiniest outcrop or domestic clump of sugarcane at night. The vast majority of adults, too, were wary of the fields after dark, the tales of ghosts and outmen lurking in such places too credible to ignore. Much of that fear, I am sure, was given credence by a primordial belief in the supernatural and a spirit world rooted in African mythology, and retained in the memories of people throughout the diaspora.

Not all my father's stories were about the supernatural. He

spoke of one awful experience when the dentist, unable to extract a firmly fixed tooth, resorted to putting his knee in the patient's chest to get greater leverage. Most worrying of all was a statement, supposedly made by Joe Louis, that he was 'scared of no man but a dentist'. That one phrase probably did more damage to the dental health of young Barbadians, certainly those exposed to my father's story-telling in Fairfield, than all the sweets they ate.

My mother, too, contributed stories. Hers were usually about people in the neighbourhood, peculiar incidents or occurrences or practical jokes that showed up eccentricities or weaknesses in individuals. A famous one was of a man nicknamed Judge Monkey.

Judge Monkey and his brother, Amos, quarrelled a lot. One day they had a nasty row which resulted in a tussle on the ground. Amos held Judge Monkey in a fierce arm-lock and demanded that he say the Lord's Prayer without making an error before he would release him. Poor Judge Monkey did as he was told, reciting the Lord's Prayer with clear and precise articulation: 'Our Father Who art in Heaven hallowed be Dy name' and so on and so on. Neighbours gathered and witnessed Judge Monkey's humiliation as he went through the verse, grovelling on the floor, his face pushed into the dust.

Judge Monkey wasn't one to tolerate an insult, even from his brother. The hurt and humiliation of the scene grew and festered within him. A few days later he acquired several sticks of dynamite and a fuse from a nearby quarry and took them home. At an appropriate moment he charged the dynamite, lit the fuse and jumped Amos, wrestling him to the ground, the dynamite jammed between them. Judge Monkey reminded his helpless brother of their recent fight, and said, 'You remember the Lord's Prayer? Well you better say it now, because today our ass will be in "Dy Kingdom come".' Happily the 'charged' moment was defused by the quick thinking of their nephew, who managed to pull the fuse out of the dynamite before it could detonate.

Stories like these were, with Daddy's wireless and gramophone, our main source of family entertainment. We didn't have television, but there was always someone with a yarn to share. The difficulty was that we couldn't always separate fact from fiction and some of the things that we were told in those days have shaped us as people, quite often not to our best advantage.

In general, people in Fairfield Cross Roads were very healthy. No one went hungry, let alone starved. Everyone was fussy about cleanliness, particularly personal hygiene. But in the tropical climate bacteria and viruses flourished, and medicine was expensive, so some people died unnecessarily from treatable illnesses such as tuberculosis and pneumonia. TB was regarded with much the same fear as cancer is today. As I said earlier, my mother survived a level of maltreatment which could easily have killed her, and she lost eight children in her lifetime.

A friend of mine called Hewey died when I was four. The service and the burial were emotionally charged moments. I recall the mourners singing 'There's a friend for little children' as the small white coffin slid into the ground. I remember, too, the outpouring of emotion, the brightness of the day, the black clothing. The savage reality of death struck me forcibly as something uniquely aweful and mysterious in the whole complexity of human life.

My mother was over-zealous in her efforts to protect us from infection, particularly pneumonia. The trauma of losing so many babies had made her mindful of the dangers to which we were exposed. Her medical remedies were severe. When I became ill, even with a common cold or a fever, she lathered my chest and back with strong-smelling ointments, put me into a thick woollen vest, administered a hefty dose of castor oil and sent me to bed. The castor oil gave me violent diarrhoea for a day or so; the woollen vests were unbearably uncomfortable, itchy and hot. I spent years in fear of catching colds and flu because of my mother's remedies and their horrible discomfort. Even now I greatly dislike steamy, clammy bathrooms and showers; sun blocs require great mental resolve before I can apply them; woollen garments are rarely worn next to my skin and never on my chest or back.

Yet now I can well understand her concern. Doctors were expensive, and Barbados's lack of a national health service led to the high infant mortality in my own family and others. Mama's unwillingness to allow us to venture unsupervised beyond the boundaries of our home, for fear of falling into a well, being hit by a bus or some other calamity, was a clear sign of her insecurity. When we went to the seaside we were rarely allowed in the sea beyond the shallowest edge, even though my father was a strong swimmer and could have protected us. Macabre images of drowned people, published in grizzly detail in *The Advocate* certainly didn't help. To this day Gerald and George are non-swimmers. I eventually taught myself to swim in 1974 while holidaying on the island at a popular local hotel. The picture many have of a tropical idyll in which people spend much of their time on a beach, drinking coconut water or sipping rum and Coke while taking frequent dips in the ocean, couldn't be further from the truth.

To reduce the risk of disease the streets of Fairfield were periodically fumigated. Men with large cans strapped to their backs sprayed the sidewalks, the foundations of the houses, inside the storm gutters and around latrines. A latrine is effectively a shed inside which a seat is located above a deep pit. Soils were periodically collected from these pits and emptied in some distant place by men on trucks. Their work was the most loathsome anywhere. When they were around we disappeared, preferring not to see the awful contents or be near the dreadful smells that came from the pits. Not surprisingly, rats, mice and cockroaches proliferated in the village and were a serious threat to health.

There were other dangers, too. Playing outdoors, often barefoot and handling knives, cutlasses, sickles and other sharp blades meant that we often acquired cuts and bruises, some of which could be quite serious. My mother's medicine cabinet contained iodine, plaster, bandages, various lints, ointments and peroxide, this last being used to clean and disinfect wounds. Gerald, an adventurous and semi-wild lad, was always hurting himself. When he was eight, he cut himself on the thigh with a sharp knife while whittling a piece of box-wood for a kite frame. It was a deep wound and should have been stitched. My mother cleaned it with peroxide and applied clean sticking plaster. The peroxide bubbled in the wound when first applied, and my heart went out to Gerald as he screamed and writhed in pain.

Other dangers came from our wider lifestyle. I remember seeing faeces in canefields, and bushes writhing with tapeworms. Canefields were a natural outdoor lavatory, offering privacy and, in the trash that proliferated everywhere, a natural toilet paper. People in their desperation defecated in the fields, covering the mess with a layer of trash. Stepping on this mess while playing filled one with horror and a feeling of being thoroughly unclean.

School

In September 1951, at the age of five, I went to school for the first time. I was kitted out with knee-length khaki socks with colourful tabs at the side, and prepared in the pristine and formal manner common to Barbadians to this day. I remember the small, whitewashed wooden building, the headmaster waiting at the top of a flight of steps to welcome the new students. My father escorted me up the steps, told me to be a good boy and went outside the school gate. I remember how I felt standing there, unprotected and hopelessly alone, looking up at the headmaster. Deeply frightened by this figure and the power and authority I knew he wielded, and feeling disconnected from the swirling flood of children around me, I took to my heels and ran back to my father as fast as I could. Seeing my distress, he took me home.

It remains one of my most cherished memories of him in those early days. His usual manner was blunt and dictatorial: you challenged him at your peril. I had openly defied him, yet, far from ordering me back into the classroom under threat of a hiding, he was warm, sensitive and understanding.

Later that day Mama spoke about the incident. She gently coaxed and encouraged me without offering the slightest hint of reprimand. She asked, 'You want to learn so you cun read tings and become a big shot like de people in de big houses?' I said I wanted to do arithmetic and learn about history. 'But,' I said, 'I doan want dem to beat me.'

My picture of school had been heavily influenced by stories told by my father and other adults, and even by children, of teachers who delighted in caning or strapping their students. It seemed a very harsh place, where a child could expect a hiding for any misdemeanour or incorrect answer to a question. George's stories of teachers 'peeling the skin of de ass' of this or that boy filled me with fear and deep foreboding. School seemed a good idea in many ways, and I certainly wanted to learn, but I was terrified of being beaten.

'Nobody gun beat you, or dey will have Boss and me to deal with,' Mama said. She understood my fear and reassured me that if I worked nobody would lay a hand on me. Only hard-ears children and dunces got beaten, she insisted, and I was neither a hard-ears nor a dunce.

Two weeks later the experiment was tried again at a larger school; I think it was Saint Barnabas primary. My father waited nearby until I had settled. There was no repeat of the earlier incident. I took to the teachers and started my formal education.

Schooling in Barbados was, even for children as young as myself, formal and very strict, operating on the principle of 'filling the pot' as opposed to that of 'lighting a fire'. Teacher had the answer to most things, and it was for us dutifully to take from them what knowledge we were capable of imbibing. Classes were enormous, children seated in serried ranks while information was transmitted to them. Discipline was total. Sometimes the class worked in the school grounds in the shade of a fruit tree. That was most enjoyable because of the cooling breezes: school classrooms were often uncomfortably hot.

Age wasn't necessarily a determining factor when children were placed in classes; the classes were a movable feast. Ability was the main factor, so you might at any time find yourself working alongside children much older or younger than yourself. The curriculum was very narrow, but what we did was based on the principles of British grammar-school education, even though we were at primary level, and the teaching methods were therefore geared to the more academically able. Parents expected this of schools, and the teachers delivered.

We learnt the scriptures. Coming from backgrounds where the Christian faith was at the centre of our lives, this was easy for most of us, but even here the readings were done by rote, the children repeating verse and texts mechanically: 'Honour thy father and thy mother that their days may be long in the land which the Lord thy god giveth thee.' And 'Thou shalt not covet thy neighbour's house nor his oxen nor his ass nor anything that is his.' I don't remember a single teacher from that time; there is just a blurred image of someone standing at a blackboard on which large letters had been written and the class learning. Yet somehow I learnt to read, and learnt my tables, too.

In those early years, we didn't have exercise books but wrote with a sharp point on quarried slates. Your slate was effectively an open page on which you worked out solutions to problems set by your teacher. At the end of each session, or when you had completed a task, the work was erased. There was no way of documenting what had been learnt, apart from demonstrations in the classroom. We therefore had to develop a good memory. Those who had difficulty concentrating, or couldn't remember facts and figures, found school-work less than enjoyable.

Though partially protected by thin pieces of moulding round the edges, slates were easily damaged or broken. Students dropped them while playing or simply while walking to and from school, because the large slates were difficult for small hands to hold securely along with satchels and other belongings. Many were broken at home in the small, cramped chattels. Such breakages almost always met with a beating and the withdrawal of privileges. Coupled with the high expectations of parents and the rigours of academic learning, incidents like this were a reminder that schools were tense and difficult environments for many children. You learnt to focus on the business of learning with all the energy you could muster, and you also learnt to take care of your equipment. Barbados being a poor colonial country, people found it difficult to meet the minimal cost of state education; some even found it hard to raise the money to replace a broken slate. Children were taught to appreciate the difficulties that were caused when things got lost or broken.

There were no school meals. Some children took sandwiches, but the vast majority, including me, had their food brought by their mother or a relation. Mama's cooking was a welcome treat: both nurturing and reassuring, it was like home from home, something to look forward to in a very stressful environment. She brought peas and rice, cou-cou, homemade soup and other savoury things. I particularly enjoyed her corn-bread pone and coconut bread, washed down with a cool glass of sorrel or mauby.

My first experience of formal learning had occurred when I was four. My father decided to teach me to read. I was made to sit between his legs on a low bench. He read a line from a book and I repeated it word by identified word. Inevitably I made mistakes – mispronounced something, for instance – and each time my father gave me a hard, stinging slap on my bare leg. The lesson rapidly degenerated into an exercise in fear, tear-stifling and blow anticipation. The more I cried or made mistakes, the angrier he became. I tried with less and less success to follow the text. I remember the feeling of help-lessness, my mother hovering in the background wanting to intervene decisively but doing so only tentatively, for fear of sending my father ballistic with rage.

'Boss, give him time to pick it up,' she said.

'Marie, he will do as I say. I doan need any advice from you.' Slap. 'Hurry up. Repeat what I said.' My father's shouts were hostile, aggressive, without love or mercy. They terrified me.

I still find it hard to understand what could have induced a father to treat his child like that; what made him step outside the affection stimulated by his children's innocence and fragile dependency, to adopt such an aggressive attitude. But I can now see that his actions were greatly influenced by the culture of which he was a part, one in which where children were flogged. A significant part of this influence was a very narrow and literal interpretation of the Bible's words: 'Spare the rod and spoil the child.'

Barbadians like most Caribbean people have a deep belief in the Christian faith: they are more God-fearing and regular worshippers than the descendants of the European mission-aries who converted them. Much of their belief is taken raw from the metaphorical language used in the Bible: where symbols are used, people often interpret them as truth which must be followed without deviation from the Word. 'Spare the rod and spoil the child' has therefore been interpreted to mean that you must beat your children if they are naughty or lazy or disobedient, because otherwise they will grow up to be bad people; after all, it says so in the scriptures. This attitude, combined with the sheer ignorance of many parents, meant that many children were brought up in a climate of fear.

Sport

Cricket was our passion. Just about every boy in Fairfield, so long as he could hold a bat and had the coordination to wield it, played cricket. We made bats from lengths of half-rotten timber, off-cuts discarded by carpenters, or even from the spines of palm-fronds, which, cut to shape, looked very much like an early English cricket bat. Stumps were anything of appropriate size, from an oil can to a length of timber or a scrap of corrugated-iron paling. We often played with worn-out tennis balls, the fur long departed and just the black rubber base remaining. Occasionally a boy brought in a knitted ball made from a length of string stitched round the hard core of a pebble which had been padded with cloth and paper. People supplying balls always got first bat, and if they were skilled or lucky could stay in a long time.

There were many skilful players of all ages. Some executed the most delicious shots, square cutting to perfection, playing cracking cover drives with immaculate timing or essaying correct defensive strokes. The passion for cricket spilt into everything, dominated every moment, was the lifeblood of the community. We played it in the streets, in every unused field, on beaches and in back gardens. No matter the size of the space, we created a game to meet its dimensions. We played with soft balls for the most part, as we of course had no pads or other protective gear. Composite balls – 'rubber-lined compas', as we called them – were occasionally purloined for a more up-market game. They were hard and quite bouncy so they could do a lot of damage; most players took this into account when bowling.

One game we played was called marble cricket, which was designed for small areas. The pitch was about half the normal length, the stumps and bats similarly reduced in size. The bowlers and batsmen knelt on one knee, while the fielders stood normally and the wicket keeper crouched. Boundaries were twos and fours, as opposed to fours and sixes. The ball was made of tarmac collected at around midday, when the sun was at its hottest and the road surfaces began to melt. Great chunks would be taken the side of a road or from an area damaged by trucks and other traffic. At home the tar was carefully heated over a flame, beaten into a sphere the size of, say, a golf ball and cooled in water.

Other forms of cricket included tip and run, played where there were more children than were needed for two full teams. The player had to run whenever he made contact with the ball, no matter how far the ball travelled or how faint the touch. Inevitably, there were lots of run-outs, and a rapid turnover of batsmen.

No matter what type of cricket was played, there were always spectators. Many spoke their minds from the boundary, making an endless string of comments on the game as if it was being played at professional not street level. 'Paul, wha' ya doing na, man? Move your foot and hit de ball, man, and stop fanning outside de off-stump.'

When you tried a sweet cover-drive or positioned yourself correctly for a pull-shot, the comments were equally forceful, supported by bursts of applause. 'Shot, man, shot! Wunna see da? He hit da ball like he hate it, man – da is what I call a shot. Da cover-drive went through de covers like a ball a fire.'

Sometimes a supporter couldn't resist running onto the pitch to do some impromptu coaching. 'Look, man, when the ball bouncing just short of a length get on the back foot and angle the bat down, or sway out of the way an' let it pass ya so.' Laker, an older boy and friend of my brother George, was always issuing instructions: 'Kites, a bouncer ain' a problem, man.' Laker threw back his right arm and stared Gerald in the eye, his face focused on some inner arena of action. 'Rock back, and when you going forward straight bat'. He went through the motion of a perfect defensive shot, gesturing with his hands, without the need for a bat. There was a flurry of fingers and wrist movements, a wonderful illustration of Caribbean theatre based on the spectacle of cricket.

Few things in sport are more satisfying than performing well before a knowledgeable crowd of neighbours and village people at a cricket match in the Caribbean. I happily found myself in that position a couple of times. One will stay with me for along time. It was a simple knockabout match between two sets of boys from the Station Hill area, where we had moved in 1953. By then I had become a batsmen of reasonable skill, with a good defence and a fair range of strokes. The match was hotly contested because many residents had gathered to watch. Conscious of the growing interest, both teams began to compete with greater resolve. Boys who usually ran up without making a significant effort, batsmen who showed a distinct lack of determination when facing fast bowling, and fielders who chased far-flung boundary shots as if their feet were fixed in concrete, excelled themselves.

I went in to bat early and soon settled into a groove, playing good defensive shots and standing up to everything the bigger boys sent down at me. We were playing with a knitted ball, which was bouncy and really hurt when it hit an unprotected shin, chest or arm. The sight of this skinny little lad standing up to bouncers and short-pitch deliveries caught people's interest. I was seeing the ball like a proverbial breadfruit. I remember Gerald's exhortations from the boundary: 'Paul Pea Dice' [one of his many nicknames for me], 'keep ya bat straight and doan forget to move ya feet, and keep ya eye on de ball.'

Then a large boy from the other side took his turn to bowl. Mindful of the scrutiny he himself was coming under, he charged in with even greater fierceness, unleashing a vicious bouncer which reared up towards my throat. Quick as a flash I got inside the delivery, rolled my wrist over and swept the ball away to the boundary like a rocket. I don't know where the skill came from; I guess it had been there for a while but needed the right moment to show. The crowd roared their approval.

Gerald was hysterical with joy. 'Jesus, ya see da boy?' Shot, Paul Pea!' followed by a cautionary 'Watch de ball, Paul, watch de ball.'

Expletives were bandied about by a couple of drunks, as people tried to find words to express their pleasure in my effort. I felt two feet taller. My batting grew in that moment in leaps and bounds, and I knew I had turned another corner in my development as a player. More importantly, I enjoyed being the subject of such adulation.

Gerald is three years older than I am, and he was proud of his little brother. My cricketing success was also his, and he was both protective and supportive. Time like that cemented the bond between us, as similar incidents in other contexts cemented my relationship with all my brothers. They were priceless moments, which indicated my individuality and potential ability to win the respect of others. They were character-forming. They showed me, too, that poverty or modest circumstances need not be a barrier to fullness of soul.

I felt valued and respected. It mattered not at all that I was playing not at Kensington Oval, or even for a school team, but on a scruffy strip of wasteland between chattel houses on a poor Caribbean island in the 1950s, alongside other children and in front of an audience of family and friends. Young though I was, I sensed my achievement's importance for me, for Gerald and for everyone one else in the family. They were proud that Paul Pea Dice showed courage under fire and good technique with the bat. It was an experience which inspired my confidence as a player for many years. I felt free in a way rarely equalled in my childhood. I had been given a glimpse of the wealth of potential within me. These reflections remind me today of the self-affirming moments that occur for all people who interact positively in the community of which they are a part, moments which may not always be articulated but are fundamental to our sense of identity.

We owned an almanac which included portrait photographs of the West Indies cricket team: Ramadhin, Valentine, Weekes, Walcott, Worrell, Atkinson. They were our idols. I still remember the stripes on their pullovers, the cut of their hair. When a test match was played people gathered round radio sets to follow the commentary, building a mental picture as the game unfurled. Big grins would break out at the fall of an England wicket or at the description of a well-crafted West Indies boundary: a Worrell late cut, a Walcott cover drive. When we lost a player the atmosphere was very different, gloom and despondency descending in a heavy pall.

There was a gladiatorial edge to cricket, akin to bull-fighting: the bowler the bull, the batsman the matador, the cricket field a site of conflict. Spectators enjoyed fine batsmanship but at the same time bayed for blood: they liked to see people hit, enjoyed the spectacle of the kill. Even at street level, when a bowler turned to run in the moment was charged with excitement. Cricket was not only a contest between bowler and batsman, bat and ball, but also a duel between good and evil. Players invested the ball with an animated presence, speaking of it as if it were a demon, something which had to be tamed. In a similar vein, the bat took on life, the spectators uttering 'No' on its behalf as a firm defensive shot blocked a threatening delivery. Each delivery became a trial, a test of ability, determination and sheer grit. Through cricket we gained enormous self-respect. It put us in the front line alongside those with real power and authority, besides offering a wealth of impromptu entertainment.

The memory of cricket in Barbados in those early years will stay with me always: the whiz of a delivery as it sped through, the heat and sweat as you concentrated on the next delivery, the smell of rubber on compositional balls, the attendant comments from the boundary as you essayed a perfectly timed shot, all part of a delicious pleasure.

Second only to cricket in Bajan popularity is dominoes. It is a national obsession. People play outdoors under trees, in bars, while watching cricket in a park, at the seaside, in fact wherever and whenever a group of four can cosily meet in a space and improvise a surface to play on: a scrap of timber, a sheet of stiff card or any reasonably flat and rigid material of suitable size. George is a skilled player, and in the early 1950s he played for Tudor Bridge Domino Club, based at Louis Pickett's shop. I rarely got to see him play – my father's restrictive religious beliefs did not allow our setting foot in a rum shop peopled by 'drunkards, sinners, smoking and swearing ruffians' – but we were very aware of his reputation.

On the few occasions I saw him in action, playing with friends under a tree or at a friendly local venue, I was bewitched by his ability to 'read' a game, to deduce early on from the pattern precisely what 'cards' each person held. This insight enabled him to set traps which ensnared his opponents. When a trap was sprung and the guileless opposition inveigled into a disastrous course of action, there would be an outburst of card-slamming by George as he blocked avenues of play for his opponents and opened the way for himself and his partner to win. In the prolonged analysis that inevitably followed, he would explain how his opponent had been outsmarted. George's ability to tell what people had in their hands was to my mind a magical skill. I could not work out how he did it, bearing in mind the effort that each player made to keep their cards quite literally close to their chest and away from the prying eye of opponents.

Post-game analyses are an essential feature of dominoes in the Caribbean. Whenever it is played there is argument, sometimes leading to violent altercations: wife pitted against husband, friend against friend, brother against sister. More often than not, players argue over the wisdom of playing a particular card or over the timing of a play, justifying their action and insisting that a different card would have led to a win. Four voices giving different accounts of play to anyone and everyone who cares to listen, all seeking understanding and recognition of their line of argument. Then as now, dominoes was a reliever of tension, a perfect means of defusing the anxieties of life's travails.

'Man, why didn't you play de tray? You could see I only had double deuce.'

'You should 'a notice by my double blank dat I was in trouble – I couldn't play no tray there. And wha' 'bout he, man? If I play tray, he could kill my sixes.'

'Ya see de way I put dat one 'pun he? It was a real bait, man, a decoy, and he walked right into de trap. First of all de tray, then de blank.'

'I was hoping you would play tray blank. If you had done dat sooner, de whole thing would 'a been over fass.'

Then the appeal to the audience: 'Wunna see da? Boy, I popped some licks in 'e ass there, an' 'e now know who is boss.'

I always liked the tension when a pair or, in a game of cutthroat, an individual was about to be beaten 6:0. On such occasions the tension was almost palpable. Every eye in the garden, house or play space focused on the table, each card was read and analysed with feverish excitement. And at the moment of a successful 6:0 drubbing, the cards would be slammed down with board-splitting force, the successful player often showing great contempt for his inferior opponents: 'I tell ya doan [*slam!*] fool 'round wid me [*slam!*] cause I gun [*slam!*] bus ya backside.' With the realisation of victory, there would be an explosion of hollering and celebration from the spectators, and a shaking of hands by the successful team players as the cards were violently shuffled for the next set.

More entertainingly, super-cool players showed a total lack of celebration or joy in their feat, as if, even against respected opponents, it was an everyday occurrence. Such players limited their emotional displays to a cool, dispassionate stare, indicative of their brilliance, at their opponent or anyone willing to catch their eye. There was no sign of glee at a job well done, but a serious cool, reminiscent of a man contemplating a savage fistfight.

Another very popular sport was kite-flying. At Easter, the traditional season for kite-flying, the skies were a dappled spread of reds and oranges, pinks and blues, the switchy tails flickering in the Atlantic breezes as the kites caught the wind. Most of the locally made one followed particular patterns such as 'star', 'propeller' or 'trouser'. Many kite-makers used the berry from the clamma cherry tree, or clammy cherry, for sticking the tissue to the light boxwood frame. This was better than flour paste, which could be messy and attracted rodents at night. Many kites did, in fact get eaten, the rustling and chomping of mice and rats feasting on the paste was a dispiriting end to a laboriously constructed and carefully crafted flier. Most were Bermudan tissue-paper and boxwood kites with paper 'bulls', which vibrated, buzzing at different pitches depending on the size of the bull. More elaborate were Singing Angels, octagonal kites with a bull attached to each of the eight sections; a good Singing Angel could make a tremendous din. Then there were bent-stick and box kites. Poorer children, who couldn't afford professionally made kites, flew simple ones made of wrapping paper and trash spines (the spines of sugarcane leaves). Wealthier white kids often flew imported box kites, which I loathed because they were boring and unimpressive and stifled fun by their lack of flexibility.

Some children used inferior string for their kites. Many days were spent spotting kites that had broken free and soared higher and higher until they disappeared from sight, in some cases even flying out to sea. I was fascinated by those moments, the kite tumbling or floating as it vanished. Lower-flying kites were trailed by hopeful local children, though they risked being challenged by a distraught owner or, worse, chased by a dog. There was something wonderfully calming about a kite under control and flying at great height. I was entranced by the whole process and enthralled by the simple beauty of the kites.

Throughout such seasonal changes you felt compelled to conform to the prevailing toy. During Easter, even where people owned good cricket equipment, we simply didn't play cricket. Kites dominated our imaginations completely until Easter Monday, when there was a big finale; and at the end of the day the whole festival of flying ended as abruptly as it started.

Compared to cricket, dominoes and kite-flying, football wasn't taken seriously. There were occasions when we chased a ball, punting it from pillar to post, but we played without any real art or understanding of the skills of football. But children can be cruel, and in the Caribbean people went to great lengths to secure a good belly-laugh, even at the expense of others, in the innocence of sport. One day someone got it into his head to play a practical joke on a boy in our district. A football match was arranged, and an old felt hat was taken apart and stitched into a football shape. But the practical joker had his own wicked agenda. There was bad blood between himself and another local lad who, he decided, needed to be taught a lesson, so he stitched a large stone into the 'ball' and padded it with cloth.

Later that day two sides were formed for the match. When everything had been set up, the enemy promptly volunteered, as expected, to kick the game off. After a pretence at objecting, he was allowed to do so. Someone had placed the ball on a marked spot, making the whole thing look authentic. Aware that dawdling would probably result in someone beating him to it, he didn't bother to adjust the position of the ball but kicked it so hard he seemed determine to punt it into the Caribbean Sea. There was a dull thud, followed by a cry of pain, and the ball travelled just a few feet. I remember the shock on his face as he realised what happened. It was that dreadful moment between doing something awful to yourself and the pain registering. Then there was a loud scream and he began to shake. I remember a trickle of blood as a he collapsed in shock. Life on the streets could be cruel at times.

Sam Marshall's Farm

One evening while my parents were entertaining guests Gerald organised a raid for coconuts on Sam Marshall's farm. The farm was just down the road from our home – the perimeter gully was less than 100 metres away – but for me, who rarely ventured from home without permission, this was a frightening venture indeed.

The farm was said to be a forbidding place, and scary stories surrounded the family, their lifestyle and the measures they had taken to ensure the security of their property. Sam Marshall, so the stories went, was a fearsome character, with big dogs which could tear a man apart. Some people said he owned a gun and wasn't averse to using it on thieves who dared trespass on his land. We lived in fear of him and yet I could hardly remember ever seeing him, let alone his ferocious dogs or his mysterious rifle. Despite the rumours, and the myths that grew up around Sam Marshall, young children ventured on to his land to steal coconuts. It was the sort of dare you couldn't resist, certainly not if you were to have any street cred or be able to hold your head high in the community.

The evening of our raid was dark, with no moonlight to speak of, so we would be able to travel for some distance without being seen. There were eight of us. Most were about Gerald's age, around eight to ten, but to me they were giants. We gathered beneath a tamarind tree to plan our action, a motley crew of scared yet strangely exhilarated children. Our self-appointed general decided that we would go in hugging the ground in the near-total darkness, enter the field by the access road, pick up a couple of coconuts each, then dash for home as fast as we could. We would have to be careful because of Sam Marshall's dogs, and of course he had a gun and, being a big shot, wouldn't think twice about using it.

We set off. On the way Gerald whispered, 'Paul, keep close to me and do exackly wha' I say. No matter wha' happen, do wha' I say and doan let me out a ya sight.' I knew Gerald as well as anyone, and I could tell by the urgency in his voice that this was serious. It was going to be a moment of challenge, and I mustn't let him down in the eyes of his friends.

We slipped down the gully and into the field. Immediately we started to step on coconut husks, shrivelled old things which were clearly past their best. We had to venture further in. Within a short while we found good coconuts and started to gather them.

Then someone close by whispered, 'Sush, you hear that?'

'Wa?' asked someone else.

'Listen,' came the first voice.

By now my heart was pounding like the pistons in a steam engine. I was scared, but it was a delicious fear, because I didn't know what was likely to happen.

There was the sound of a twig snapping, and in a split second all hell broke loose, everybody running blindly in all directions. Gerald grabbed my hand and shouted, 'Run, Paul, run!' I was hysterical with fear but ran till the soles of my feet felt as if they were on fire. I could feel the teeth of Sam Marshall's Alsatian sinking into my buttocks, chewing my ankle, tossing me to the ground and grabbing my throat. I tried to scream but the sound wouldn't come out. Delicious fear gripped me by the throat and released hot urine down the inside of my short pants. Gerald, running ahead, shouted, 'Paul, follow me!' I was gasping for tears but couldn't find them. By now we couldn't care less about skulking in the dark, we merely ran in the middle of the road and fled home as fast as we could.

Gerald and I burst into the garden at top speed. I ran behind my mother, feet bloodied from grit and thorns, and not a little soiled with dog muck. Of course, Mama instantly realised from our faces that something was up. The truth came out and we were scolded, made to wash, and sent straight to bed with the threat of a good slapping if we weren't careful.

That incident was typical of what children in my village regularly got up to. Much of the fear was imaginary – and all the sweeter for that. But the feeling of community, the fact that we could explore and make discoveries in a reasonably safe environment, and the feeling of being part of something bigger than oneself, made that part of my life rich and very special.

The loss of a sibling left its mark on all of us, but Levi's birth in 1952 was a moment of wonder and celebration for the family. He, like most children at that time, was born at home. Mama was attended by Mrs Garner, who acted as midwife to women in the district. I remember the mystery of the whole thing, being shut out from my parent's bedroom, the requests for basins of warm water, the adjuration from adults to go out and play. Then, after what seemed an interminable time, the cry of a fine new voice, which came in short spurts.

Soon we were told that we had a new baby brother, and were introduced to him. Mrs Garner had clothed him in a nappy, or diaper as they are called in the Caribbean, which seemed much too big for his little body, though in fact he was a big baby. A broad band of white cotton material was also bound around his midriff, keeping the nub of his umbilical chord in place. We were told of its remnants being buried, and the importance for his future prospects of doing it right. In my awe and excitement at being with and related to this new person, I tried to stroke his soft black hair but was warned of the dangers of touching the 'soft spot' at the top of his head. I craned my neck to get a look at it and witnessed the rhythm of his heartbeat pulsing there. I loved the newness of him, the smell of talcum already applied and that ineffable freshness of baby skin. But already in my childish way I couldn't resist thinking of future games in which he would play his full part; a brotherhood of Dashes against the world.

Fairfield was a short street, though when I was a small child it seemed the length of the world (Fig. 5). The crossroad, though just 50 metres from our home, seemed a long way away. Children from the district met to play on the path outside our house and in the narrow street. We played cricket and pitched marbles. Children who had homemade trucks and buses would 'drive' by, to my chagrin. I always wanted a truck made from scrap but never got one. They were blue-riband toys which gave the games created an authenticity far removed from other forms of play. Trucks and buses were working toys, which had the feeling of the

Fig. 5 Fairfields Cross Roads, where I lived as a child

real vehicles we saw on the highways collecting cane and picking up passengers. Many showed clever refinements of style determined by their makers' ingenuity, imagination and skills. There were steering-wheels and huge curling wheel-arches, moveable bonnets which swung up and down like gull-wings, and grilled radiators. The trucks pulled lengths of cane like real Bedfords.

I was given tiny metal trucks, matchbox motorcycles and buses, bought for a dollar by my father in a flea market or store in New York City. These bought toys hadn't the same currency as homemade ones. The earthy design and ruggedness of a locally produced truck was what I coveted. Apart from their size, I loved the way the trucks rocked and the axles swivelled as they struggled over stubborn grass, pebbles and clumps of soil, like real heavily laden trucks negotiating the gouged furrows in a canefield. I was enraptured by way mud gathered in the wheel-arches as the vehicles were pulled down pot-holed lanes and along the borders of ploughed fields. I imagined an engine straining for power, as it tried to haul its burden of cane out from gully to highway.

Homemade buses brought equal pleasure, though adapted to the transport of people rather than cane. Miniature passengers, crafted from scrap cloth and cork and other recycled materials, were seated in rows, their bell ropes looping above the conductor's footboard. Some buses were painted Transport Board red for added authenticity and mystique, the bright red and corn-yellow of the drapery signalling an experience of public transport which we understood.

Trucks and buses were high-denomination currency, but homemade scooters were best of all. They came between toys and road-worthy vehicles, much as roller-blades, roller-skates and even bicycles are today. Scooters enabled children to travel at breakneck speed around our neighbourhood and have lots of fun into the bargain. In Fairfield I wasn't old enough to ride a scooter but I loved the idea of them, the sound of the ball-bearing wheels making their characteristic swishing as youths careered up and down the highway. Riding a scooter was to my mind like riding a stallion, requiring skill, daring and sheer recklessness. Today in the Western world, chromium metal scooters are all the rave. People pay handsome prices for them, and they are seen as chic style statements and, in some cases, a useful means of transport. Ours were mostly sturdy vehicles made to a basic local design copied by youths across the island.

My father wouldn't allow us to ride scooters because of the dangers of collision with traffic, animal-drawn or motor-powered. Apart from that, there was a stigma attached to scooter-riding because of its association with wild boys, the free spirits of the island regarded as louts and tearaways. In reality most were impoverished young people who used their wits to survive. In a family with aspirations to middle-class respectability, any association with scooters – or even with homemade trucks and buses – was frowned on, regarded as a retrograde step. So I looked in frustration at the wonderful playthings that other children had but that were barred to me.

Station Hill

In 1952 we moved to Station Hill, a district of Bridgetown two miles from Fairfield. It was the first of many moves in my childhood.

The new house was a three-bedroom chattel. It was more up-market than our old one, with two gable sections and a shed-roof extension; its windows were of fancy design with wooden jalousies, and it had an enclosed cellar. It was surrounded by fruit trees, including a large breadfruit tree which bounced and bobbed in the breeze, an avocado and a tamarind which provided copious supplies of acid fruit.

Not far away was Waterford, an area with a large open field which now houses Combermere School, one of the top grammar schools in Barbados. We sometimes played cricket there or flew kites with George and his friends.

I went to Saint Giles primary school. It was even more strict than Saint Barnabas. Each morning, immediately after the bell had been rung, the headmaster, in shirt-sleeves, waited at the end of a path that led from a gate in the surrounding wall to the front door of the school. Pupils who arrived late were given one lash on the back with a leather strap; there was no conversation between him and the students.

Corporal punishment was an ugly and regrettable aspect of life on the island. My father often told us of convicted criminals being sentenced to a flogging with the cat-o'-nine-tails, an animal-hide whip with nine strands. The offender was strapped to a bench and beaten on the back, the number of lashes being prescribed by a court of law. He spoke of victims of such beatings having maggot-infested wounds, and they were often both physically and emotionally scarred by their ordeal. The beatings and floggings had their origins in the brutality of the slave trade, at a time when overseers beat slaves mercilessly for the slightest misdemeanour. Such punishment became a distinctive feature of life in Barbados, a fixture in its psychology and culture. The cowhide, until recently a mainstay of every owner of a donkey, mule or horse-drawn cart, came out of that culture of repression.

In an arithmetic lesson we might be asked to recite a particular table in front of the class, or to answer a question such as 'What is nine times nine, Dash?' We were expected to provide immediate, word-perfect answers; failure resulted almost inevitably in a beating. We all sat in terror of being asked a question to which we didn't know the answer, and being beaten in front of the whole class. Yet this was the backbone of much of our education. In my experience there was little recourse, little sympathy or sanctuary at home. Parents in general supported corporal punishment in schools. That was how they themselves had been brought up, and they thought teachers would be failing in their duty if they did not show a similarly harsh attitude to their pupils. We were whipped by teachers and flogged at home on the slightest pretext. For many of us, being a child in Barbados at that time was a brutal experience.

Mama had always kept chickens, but with the move to Station Hill the poultry became a small business, attracting customers from the neighbourhood and beyond. I remember officers from District A police station coming to our house to buy eggs, the friendly conversations, the exchange of eggs and money. I was in awe of those men in their bristling uniforms of grey tunics, black trousers with red stripes, and white cork hats. Their bull-pizzles, often used for breaking heads in rum-shop squabbles, otherwise sheathed in a leather scabbard, hung from their broad belts. Power and authority were etched in every sinew, and visible in their easy stance.

Glendary Prison was close to the police station. Many of the wardens also bought eggs from Mama. I hid from them, fearful of the men who hanged prisoners. I thought of the chain gangs they brought to our streets to clean the gutters and pick up trash. I wondered how the prisoners passed their time when not chained together in the streets. My father told me about convicts breaking rocks. I couldn't imagine more soul-destroying work, and felt sorry for the men, who had to walk in chains to a quarry and then toil at such useless activity hour upon hour. But we were taught that sinners were not worthy of pity unless they begged for God's mercy. The pressures – the poverty and desperation – that led many of those men to commit crimes simply didn't come into the equation. What they suffered was, therefore, of their own making. Of course, a socialist dimension or a rereading of the scriptures was not possible when I was a small child.

Such thinking came over time and in different circumstances, when I had seen a bit more of the world and had time to reflect.

My mother tended her chickens with professional care. I remember her going into the coops to help a hen release a chick from its shell, breaking tiny bits away by hand without damaging skin or feathers. I witnessed their slow arrival into the world as they escaped from their oval prison: the spurts of action, the long periods of rest, the continuous chirping cry, Mama's helping hand. Eventually, there was an energetic thrusting of limbs and the protrusion of a clammy head through the hole in the shell in an ecstasy of freedom. Soon they were taken from the nest and transferred to shoe boxes. The boxes were kept beneath a mahogany crockery 'wagon' made by Mr Gittens. They fitted snugly, so that fresh air could circulate but the chicks could not tumble out and be crushed underfoot.

A few days later Mama would let the chicks out for exercise in the front room: balls of fluff in hunched gait, chirping and shitting as they investigated every nook and cranny. But there was no safe place for them. I would scoop one up and snuggle my nose into its downy feathers, feel the rhythm of its heartbeat through my hand. I was enraptured by the purity of the chicks, the little pips on their beaks, the clarity of their eyes, the softness of their down. There was often a sickly one, a quivering runt hunched in a corner or standing on unsteady, trembling legs with the mark of death upon it. Sensing the life ebbing from them filled me with dread, a strange foreboding of death and the unknown. Next morning we would find a corpse in the box.

Those moments had a strange effect upon me. I was terrified by the mystery of death and steered clear of sickly birds. But even then I knew I was being irrational: why this fear of a tiny, harmless creature which only the day before I had held and stroked without concern? Here, surely, I now believe, was a legacy of my African ancestry, the fear of death's mystery, encoded in belief systems which gave meanings to every aspect of death and dying, and attributed powers to the corpses entwined with notional 'spirit' worlds, duppies and supernatural powers. My father's belief in ghosts is another legacy of those traditions which lay outside our colonisers' control and restriction. The African in us lives in myriad ways and surfaced at such moments. Much of the fear and respect of the mystery of death embedded in African faiths has been transferred to our way of celebrating Christianity. The Lord God is spoken of with a reverence possibly lost to many Europeans. The people in The Power, the fear of dark spaces, the unshakeable belief in ghost and duppies – all of this echoes *nkisi* spirits and the voodoo rites common in West African cultures and still practised in countries such as Haiti, Cuba and Brazil.

But raising chickens had its low points. One night we were roused by pandemonium in the henhouse. There was loud squawking and a general panic from the birds.

My father got up, lit a kerosene lamp and grabbed a stout stick he kept next to his bed. 'Marie, Marie, de fowl mecking so much noise day must be a rat or mongoose in de chicken coop.'

Mama lit another lamp, and within minutes everyone was peering through the windows into the gloom. I remember the pool of light that surrounded my father as he hurried to the coop, Mama just a few paces behind. As they approached there was a flurry of feathers and an appalling cacophany as the panic-stricken birds tried to escape from their bloody cage. On entering, my father was met by appalling devastation. A mongoose had got into the coop, and there were dead chicks, feathers and smeared blood everywhere, eggs crushed underfoot in the birds' futile attempts to escape. Some had had their legs badly bitten, others had suffered serious wounds to the neck, and a few had been killed outright. Several suspended themselves upside down from the roof of the cage, others were clinging to the sides of the coop. In its killing spree the mongoose failed to escape through the opening it had created: it didn't notice or care about my father's approach. Daddy quickly opened the cage, and some birds flew out while others swirled around in an attempt to be free. In a moment the mongoose appeared from a mass of billowing feathers and panicking birds, and shot out of the coop. Daddy brought his stick down in a fury but missed, and the animal darted through a hole in the garden fence. I heard my father shout in frustration, 'Marie, ah miss de damn ting, and it gone through de bush.'

Mongooses are extraordinary animals, bigger than rats but smaller than rabbits, furtive and predatory. Introduced to the island by previous generations of travellers, they are expert at killing snakes and in the local folklore are thought to have wiped out the remnants of a snake population on the island. Over the years they have adapted to town and city life, taking food wherever they can; chicken is a particular favourite. They were a serious and hated pest, and when one was caught people did the most appalling things to it.

A few days after our hens were killed, someone in the district caught a mongoose which had been devastating his coops. The news soon got round the village. 'Paul, ya hear 'bout Mr Roach?' Gerald asked. 'He catch a mongoose and 'e gun kill it.'

Roach had put the animal in a cage, which was doused in kerosene and set alight. I remember the animal's squealing and the stench of its burning fur as it bolted round the cage in an effort to escape. Somehow it did escape, and it dashed into a nearby canefield, flames licking round its tortured body. Panic gripped the villagers as the living torch careered through their crop, leaving a trail of smoke and flames. People ran with buckets of water to douse the flames, as fire-fighters trundled their way to the blaze. At the end of the day much of an invaluable crop was lost and people wandered off despondent, the death agony of the squealing mongoose long forgotten.

At the age of eight I learnt to ride George's Raleigh bicycle. I used to tuck my skinny legs through the V of the frame and pedal hard, the crossbar in line with my shoulder. Before long I could cycle the length of the street without putting my foot down. Almost everyone I knew learnt to ride on adult bikes, using this very uncomfortable and contorted method. Few families could afford children's bikes; I cannot recall seeing a single one in a working-class black community. We became expert in bicycle technology, adept at operating the archer gears and light generators that produced power through the wheel-operated generator. Bicycles were very popular in those days. People across the island gave lifts on bikes, took their children to school and courted lovers by this means: most cyclists adapted their bikes for carrying a passenger on the crossbar. When George courted Gloria, who was to become his first wife, they often went out together on his bike, Gloria seated sidesaddle on the wooden crossbar, her cancan skirt ballooning in the breeze. They were a colourful and romantic sight.

Hurricane Janet struck in September 1955, soon after our move to Station Hill. People had been warned the previous day when, in late afternoon, sirens sounded across the island. Many boarded up their homes, protected the outhouses and penned their animals.

At first, strong winds and rain lashed the island. We stayed indoors and peered at the world through the windows, too scared to play as the winds pounded the timber walls of our home. Gradually during the evening the wind increased. My father brought in lengths of timber from the cellar and started pinning the house together from the inside, paying particular attention to the gables, which would be the first thing to go if the wind got under the roof. The house looked strangely fragile and vulnerable with the strengthening timbers zig-zagging through the centre of it. Getting from A to B necessitated scaling or crawling under the chunky wooden beams.

My father's concern was echoed by many other people in the village. I remember the fear and tension: people who were normally languid and relaxed showed unusual urgency as they boarded up windows and doors. Men climbed ladders to batten down galvanised sheets on rooftops. Fencing was strengthened, and outhouses held firm with stout timber ramparts. In people's eyes I could see their fear, a fear which brought home to me the seriousness of what we were about to experience.

The full force of the hurricane struck in the early hours of the morning. I was awakened by the roar of the wind, which whistled as it penetrated every crevice and crack in the house, and by voices and the sounds of hammering and movement. My father was frantically adjusting his reinforcements, adding the odd nail here, an extra piece of timber there. He checked the roof for signs of weakness in the carpentry, indications of a leak developing or a gap appearing, but everything held firm. He kept wandering round the house, concerned that something might give way at any moment and lead to a crisis. I of course didn't know how great the danger was, or that my father was doing more than protecting his property: he was ensuring the survival of his family.

At daylight the storm was still raging, but we had got through the worst. As the wind abated, it was possible to go out to survey the damage. There was some flooding and almost every fence in our district had been blown down. Coconut, mahogany and other trees lay across the streets and fields and the ground was strewn with coconuts. Some properties had been badly hit, some had their tin roofs completely ripped off and many were destroyed or damaged beyond repair. The devastation was difficult to take in. Gruesome stories about Hurricane Janet's power were passed around. We heard of galvanised sheets being blown huge distances, one decapitating a donkey in someone's garden. Another report said twenty-five people who had sought shelter in a country church had been killed when the roof fell in on them. We, however, had survived the ordeal.

Later that day Daddy removed the strengthening timbers from inside our house, and made good the nail-holes in the pillars and partitions, and life slowly began to return to something like normal. But across the island much work needed to be done to repair the damage to homes and businesses. My father was busier than ever, repairing or replacing tyres damaged by nails and timbers that littered many of the streets. There was a call nationwide for carpenters to help repair and make good the properties damaged in the storm.

About this time an earth tremor was felt in Barbados. In some respects it was even more frightening than the hurricane, because of the total insecurity, the realisation that not even our parents could protect us from this act of nature. There was movement everywhere: the house moved, the land moved, our parents shook. I had grown up used to the family as a rock, a secure anchorage to which I could cling when times were difficult, but the quake destroyed that security. The family, too, were fearful and helpless. It lasted no longer than a few seconds but for the first and possibly only time in my life I felt without a firm anchorage on this planet. When in water you know that, if there are difficulties, terra firma is a sanctuary offering a chance of survival. With the earth tremor the solid bedrock of life momentarily vanished, and the parents to whom I had always looked for hope stared back with fear in their eyes.

By the time as I was eight or nine, I had gained in confidence on the streets, becoming a reasonable gymnast (as well as a cricketer) able to do flips, somersaults and other tricks. Gerald positioned himself on hands and knees, and I dived over him, landing on my hands and doing a forward roll. I did somersaults from his cupped hands, twisting and turning in midair before landing perfectly on my feet. Children in the street regularly held backbend races: we bent backwards until our hands touched the ground, our bodies making an arch, and raced each other on all fours, our heads dangling between our arms. I usually won, certainly when racing children of my own age and even some much older. However, the one thing I couldn't do, something at which Gerald excelled, was the simple handstand: I couldn't keep myself vertical. This was to cost me dearly.

One day while doing a handstand on a neighbour's doorstep I lost my balance, pirouetted in mid-air and landed on my face in the road. I bled profusely from the mouth. Mama came rushing to my side and took me home cradled in her arms, my face smeared with blood, my lips rapidly swelling. I screamed hysterically. After washing my face in warm water, she squeezed me into a flannel vest and put me to bed. It was the single most traumatic, painful and unpleasant experience of my early childhood, and it greatly upset Gerald, my street guardian, and Mama, who had to deal with her traumatised and badly bruised son.

Unsupervised play outdoors exposed us to many dangers. Most children roamed the streets unsupervised, and sometimes fell from trees or got hurt in fights and wrestling competitions. Children often stepped on broken glass in canefields or on sharp thorns which penetrated deeply into their bare feet. Soon after our move to Station Hill, a girl of about five fell on an old skillet while collecting water from a standpipe, and cut great chunks out of her lips. I remember seeing the lumps of fresh tissue; it was horrifying to see the human body so defiled. Human flesh for me was something sacred, not mere meat. Animals could be killed, and their bodies dismembered and cut into portions, but the human body should remain whole for ever. The pieces of flesh that gathered dust in the street in Station Hill were a harsh awakening.

As I grew, I was given more opportunities to play outside our home. One of my favourite games was marbles, or pitching. In my highly protected state I failed to acquire the skills to win at this game, and could only admire as better players won hatfuls of marbles pitching against weaker opponents. The studied concentration as boys blasted marbles off the playing area was a special thrill, particularly for someone who couldn't play.

Pitching bears some relationship to bowling, croquet and even snooker. In Station Hill I played marbles with boys from our district. We prepared the play area on a flat, even piece of ground about eighteen feet long. Three shallow holes were dug in the ground about eight feet apart. At one end of the row of holes was a line which ran at right-angles to them. That was the starting-point for the game. Players dropped their marbles on to the line, and those who finished closest to the line went first. The aim was to pitch into each cup sequentially down the row and back again, crashing your opponent's marble out of the way with your own whenever possible.

Marbles were wonderfully exotic things, beautiful glass objects in clouds of rich colour, sometimes spotted like stars or with imprisoned seed-like forms, often dappled or striped with layers of molten glass. I was transfixed by their intricate, gem-like beauty. The pleasure I got from Gerald's collection when it was strewn across the floor for his satisfaction was akin to contemplating a field of multi-patterned butterflies or a flock of budgies on the wing. Similarly, I loved the skill and dexterity of the top players: marbles arcing through the air and crashing unerringly into others were thrilling to behold.

Many youths took delight in teasing the local 'village idiots', until the victim's patience broke and he sought retribution by chasing us and threatening violence. On the way home from school some evenings, a poor wretch would be cornered by mob of schoolchildren who, on discovering a quirk that triggered the desired response, would harry and tease the simpleton until he reached breaking-point and chased us through the streets. It was in some ways akin to bull-chasing in the streets of a Spanish village, only not nearly so dangerous. Most of these characters were older men who lacked speed and stamina, and we were fit, nimble and very quick. But the idea of a 'madman' chasing you, over-layered with the stories our parents told of the damage deranged people could do, made the experience deliciously thrilling.

There was an old man we called Bambury on the Cross who reacted with anger on being shown a crucifix or when the sign of a cross was made by hand or with a couple of implements. He would lumber after us, barefoot, his ragged clothing hanging loosely and adding to the spectacle and the feeling of danger. I was always with Gerald on such occasions; not that we instigated or became involved in riling the poor outcasts, but we enjoyed the chase. When Bambury chased us, we screamed and hid, ran down alleyways and into any safe place we could find. At those moments we lived on the edge, at least in our minds, took a special delight in the feeling of being threatened, of laying our lives on the line.

We were often caught up in street fights. Gangs of youths would hurl stones at each other in street battles after school. These fights erupted spontaneously out of nothing, but if you were in the wrong garb, on the wrong stretch of street, or in the wrong school uniform, you could be attacked and beaten blue by children from an opposing gang. Usually such fights were no more than elaborate stand-offs in which children pelted each other with rocks, the streets exploding with stones crashing around us, sending up puffs of marl like shellbursts in a battlefield. Many of us got hit, particularly younger children running too close to the line of fire or too docile to take evasive action when necessary. As a result, many West Indian adults are badly scarred on their shins, from missiles thrown in street brawls and other such encounters.

Our parents didn't take kindly to our taking part. If news got back to them of our involvement or, more seriously, if Gerald and I showed cuts and bruises from a rock fight or street brawl, we were seriously punished because of the danger we put ourselves into, and punishment in these cases meant a severe whipping. Growing up in the Caribbean was wonderful fun, but you had to have a strong constitution to survive the pummelling we all took from teachers, parents and local louts.

As a child I feared dentists with a passion which brooked no mediation. Stories of dentists who seemed to take pride in causing pain were popular. They told of extractions which had gone wrong, yarns so frightening that they made the blood curdle. My father spoke of dentists with strapping biceps and large fists, who savagely yanked stubborn teeth from resistant gums, the dentist lifting his patient clear out of the seat in the effort. One of his tales was to colour my view of dentists for many years.

'Man, I had a bad teet and it meck my face swell out like a balloon. Boy, I tel ya, my teet hurt so bad I decided I must go to de dentist.'

Mama was always at the centre of such stories, egging Daddy on while showing her discomfort with grimaces. She focused on my father, the expression on her face indicating extreme unpleasantness, possibly triggered by an offensive odour or physical injury.

She interjected, 'You shoudda heard 'ee, moaning and rolling bout 'pun the floor, grabbing 'e face and shouting, "Marie, Marie, come bring Phensic quick, dis ting killing me."'

'Anyway,' my father said, 'I got in a taxi and went to de dentist de next day 'cause I couldn't bear de pain no longer. When I got day I had to wait. I said to de woman day, "Please see me now, dis ting killing me, man." Eventually I got in de chair, all fear gone – I jus want de ting out. De dentist give me de anaesthetic, me mout went num, and he started to pull out de teet. But he couldn't get it out.'

With that there was uproarious laughter, and gestures of discomfort from some, such as myself, who were living the experience, picturing themselves in that dentist's chair.

'Wa Lord!' said my father (he often used that expression to convey extreme discomfort and shock). 'He push in dese pliers and pull, and pull. I slap 'e hand but he still pulling and nuttin ain' happening. Man, de man virtually lifted me outa ma seat.'

By now most of us had our faces buried in our hands and were expressing shock at my father's ordeal.

'I ain' gine to no dentis, not even if they pay me,' I said.

Several of the adults elaborated the story until it became totally unreal, but to our childish imaginations the dentist was one of the most frightening experiences anyone could have. This fear of dentists, and of hospitals and doctors as a whole, didn't prepare us well for life and the need for medical and dental care. For much of my childhood, both in Barbados and later in Britain, I visited the dentist rarely – and then only in a crisis.

We celebrated Guy Fawkes night with special relish. Like young people everywhere we played with sparklers, lit Catherine wheels and sent up rockets, enjoying the sound of explosions and the bursts of light in the sky. We also played with fireworks the like of which I have not seen elsewhere. They were 'bombs' the size of golf balls, which had to be thrown with considerable force against a hard surface to make them explode. Children coiled themselves into balls of energy and hurled the paper-wrapped bombs into the street against a wall. As a young child I couldn't throw hard enough, and my bombs bounced off and failed to explode. Someone always picked up my failure and launched it with zeal at a hard surface, doubling my humiliation with an explosion, not to mention the theft of my firework.

Older children played with a type of explosive which on contact with fluid gave off an explosive gas which could be ignited with a match. We collected tins, particularly Andrews Liver Salts tins with lids which were pressed in to the top surface. The bottom of the tin was pierced at the centre with a nail. We put a piece of white explosive the size of a sugar cube in the tin, spat on it, replaced the lid and shook the can hard for ten to fifteen seconds, keeping the hole in the base covered, so as to keep the resulting gases trapped inside. The can was then set on the ground and a lit match applied to the hole in the base. There would be a massive explosion, and the sound of the tin and its displaced lid crashing around as they were hurled great distances. For me they were the sounds and smells of Guy Fawkes night, a time of true excitement culled from a British political event which has been subsumed into Barbadian life.

*

When I was still very young it was determined that I should succeed academically. My parents, for whatever reason, decided I would be a professional and Gerald an athlete. Although their decision brought me many benefits, this pre-determined categorisation has always sat uncomfortably with me. For one thing, it was embarrassing, given the premium placed on academic learning in Barbados, to be so identified next to someone who was probably of similar ability but, because of physical build, personality and other circumstances, allocated a different position in the family's perception. Secondly, it put me under great pressure to succeed, which was at times difficult to withstand. Thirdly, it fixed my position in life, sketched out a role which from an early age shaped me as a person.

  Knowing my parents' ambition for me, I have always striven not to disappoint them – and indeed the whole family, who adopted their categorisation. Much that I would like to have experimented with I avoided, because people treated me differently from Gerald; it was almost as if I was a marked person. People expected me to be more circumspect and thoughtful, more intelligent in my responses to a problem, more alert to a range of possibilities in a crisis. When I fell foul of my father, he often said accusingly, 'I expected better of you.' I couldn't be free of this perception of being the inheritor of a more refined intellect. It drove me to study and acquire academic skills. I read what books there were at home, even dipping into the Bible from time to time, and did my homework religiously. When I spoke in front of my father my words were granted a special reception: he and others, who were perhaps following his example, listened to what I had to say. I felt constantly under the microscope, almost as if part of my childhood was being stolen from me. There was little room for play; I don't mean play as in toys or cricket – there was plenty of that – but play with time, with risk-taking. Risk-taking implies the possibility of getting it wrong. But, because I was supposed to be intellectually astute, I constantly had to show wisdom and special percep-tion, to 'get it right'. The fact that people respected me because I had 'brains' was at times satisfying to the ego, but the constant pressure to say the 'right thing' – that is, the thing people considered to be right – was a huge burden.

I deeply resented the fact that Gerald wasn't granted similar respect, a respect he deserved. But that would have been to burden him with all its responsibilities. He himself didn't question those constructs, being happy with the freedom to roam, socialise and taste the wider pleasures of life. I have felt compelled to achieve, and have striven to live up to my parents' expectations, but Gerald has been ignored academically: how he did or didn't do, has never seemed to matter. As a consequence, he rapidly lost confidence in his ability in this area, investing all his ambition in me. It has always weighed heavily on me knowing that he has placed himself outside a part of human life in which he was perfectly capable of performing at a high level. In the end he shut down all academic ambition and focused on being an athlete, running through a gamut of sports from long-distance cycling to boxing, fast bowling to martial arts.

In Station Hill I developed an enjoyment of reading and arithmetic, but there was little stimulus at home for academic work outside the reading of the scriptures. Nevertheless, my parents' ambition for me became a part of my life. All Barbadians wanted their children to become lawyers or teachers, doctors or judges, but there was no nurturing to allow this to happen in working-class households. It was almost as if people though wishing for success was all that was needed to achieve it, apart from the child's hard work and the teacher's skill and firmness. The culture of the home didn't support academic learning.

Our language was a Barbadian dialect at odds with the dis-cipline of standard English. Syntax was skewed and mangled relative to standard grammar, in a way that made fluency of writing or speech in the accepted mode impossible. Except in the classroom, one was constantly exposed to such linguistic use as 'Ope it in' (*open it*) and 'wunna gun' (literally 'one another going to' or *you are all going to*.) Descriptive terms, too, were outside the normal run of standard English. 'Foot' was in some contexts synonymous with 'leg', describing any part from the big toe to the crutch. An itch was called a 'bite', so something itching was 'biting' one's skin; and so on. The Barbadian dialect is so firmly built into my psyche that it constitutes much of who I am. I still find myself conjugating verbs and structuring sentences in dialect, and often, in conversation with friends, I lapse into it. When I become aware of it, the experience can be a little shocking because I appreciate the confusion it can create in my audience, if only in their perception of my ability to cope with the English language.

My Parents' Migration to Britain

People were leaving the island to start new lives elsewhere. People whom we had grown to know and respect, even love, were packing their bags and going. Friends from Fairfield and neighbours in Station Hill were selling up and starting a new life in Britain. Laker and his brother Lemuel, Blackman and Straughan, people I had known all my life, had gone or were about to leave for new and distant horizons. For a nine-year-old the implications were difficult to grasp. I was uneasy, and had a faint feeling of insecurity, but I couldn't imagine such a thing affecting my family directly. But attending farewell parties for men who were packed to go, their wives lost in thought, eyes dulled to communication, children stunned by foreboding, struck me forcibly.

I remember the slices of cake, the smell of cooked chicken and pork, the piles of rice and peas, the mauby and juicy soft drinks and, of course, the tots of Mount Gay; then, at the crucial moment, the plaintive singing of 'Now is the Hour'. Close relations wept and children wailed, grown men fought back the tears as guests, relatives and friends sang the anthem of the soon-to-leave. The experience left its mark on me. The realisation that these people really were leaving Barbados, and that in all probability I would never see them again, was too much to take in.

This ritual of farewell became a feature of Barbadian life in the mid-1950s. In the upheaval, the securities we had once had in our local community were being stripped away as people who had embodied them left the island. Throughout it all, it never occurred to me that my parents might emigrate without the rest of the family: I couldn't conceive of dislocation on that scale. Yet in December 1955 that is exactly what happened: Mama, Daddy and George sailed for Liverpool on a British liner. I went to the Careenage to wave goodbye, consumed by tears and deep forebodings. My mother was very emotional, the whole experience more like a nightmare than a dream for her as well as for those left behind.

A lot of people came to seem them off: family, members of the church and close friends. Collin, my mother's brother, Elise, her sister, and Elise's husband, Samuel, my father's brother, their children, Fonza and others. Before long they boarded the small vessel that took them out to sea. It was a moment full of fear and confusion. Never in my life had I been separated from my parents for even a day, yet now we would probably be separated for several years. As the boat pulled away I stood behind the railings, my head pressed against the metal, and waved farewell. It was a bizarre experience. Before long the boat did a left turn and disappeared from sight; I never saw the ship on which they travelled. It was the end of an era. I wasn't to know that my mother's creative life, her independence and sense of being part of a larger community, were coming to an end before my eyes. From now on, her life was to be restricted to a narrower field.

I have never discussed the issues that led to my parents making this vital decision, but I have no doubt that the decision was made by my father, the dominant figure in our home. Throughout his life he had sought new challenges and constantly uprooted himself to explore new territories. My mother had a much simpler view of life, wanted little more than the security of her family. While idolising my father and supporting many of his projects, I am certain she would have been doubtful about a decision that resulted in her separation from her three youngest children for twenty months.

Despite their assurances that we would be together as a family in a very short time, maybe less than two years, to my childish mind a year was a lifetime. The idea of joining my parents in Britain frankly meant nothing. I had no clear concept of what England was, and any fanciful notions I may have had of life in Britain evaporated in the light of my parents' departure. I just wanted things as they were when we were a united family.

Arrangements had been made for Gerald, myself and our younger brother Levi, aged twelve, nine and three respectively, to stay in Bridgetown with my mother's sister and brother-in-law, Violet and Harry Innis. Harry was a blacksmith and wheelwright. Short and fair of complexion, with wavy hair, he had many social advantages denied his wife, who was dark-skinned. From the outset they took to Levi, showering him with the affection that would have been given to their own children, had they had any, while their relationship with Gerald and me was cool and stilted. Despite that, I was immediately enthralled by Harry's workshop.

I was captivated by the horses' trappings, the reins and harnesses, straps and bits. In the yard stood a dilapidated cart with broken timbers in the flooring and a wheel leaning unsteadily at an acute angle from its axle. In the workshop, there were wheels leaning against a wall and wheel-rims hanging from the ceiling. Several harnesses hung from large spikes driven into the walls, while horseshoes of different sizes were strewn about or dangled from spikes in the wall. There was a mountain of coke, and a much-worn spade in a dark corner, and shelves of equipment, nails and tin cans used in the blacksmith's trade. The workshop was a dirty place, but none the less interesting for all that, and I was fascinated by the forge and anvil on which Harry worked each day.

The misery of being away from my parents was tempered by this environment, so different from anything I had experienced before, one which offered new perspectives on life and opportunities for exploration. I had rarely encountered horses at close quarters before, and watched open-mouthed as they were brought in and skilfully re-shod. The hard base of the hoof was trimmed with a sharp knife and long, flat nails driven in to fix the shoe in place. I couldn't understand how the hoof worked, why the horse didn't kick out at what I thought must have been a painful process. But the long nails went sweetly into the hardened tissue, painlessly pinning the perfectly shaped shoe into position. After the work was done I loved the sweet clip-clop sound as the horses left the yard, the metal shoe fitting perfectly to a hoof carved to accommodate it.

I enjoyed watching Harry at work at the forge as he heated metal to a bright orange glow, before shaping it to fit wheel-rim or hoof. I felt for him as he stood over the glowing fire in that tropical heat, sweat forming on his brow and rolling in streams down his cheeks. The way lengths of iron and the metal rims of donkey carts were shaped, his blacksmith's hammer beating the orange-white metal into shapes as effortlessly as if it were made of plasticine, was gripping. As he worked, sparks flew into his face, occasionally showering the forge with shards of glowing metal before the metal was plunged into cool water when the work was done.

Unfortunately, Harry's skill sometimes led to complacency about basic health and safety precautions. In his workshop he generally wore sandals, finding them cool and comfortable in the hot, humid environment. One day a glowing ember lodged itself between two toes of his left foot. I remember the scream. Harry had the presence of mind to splash some water on it but by then the damage had been done. The whiteness of the wound and absence of blood were shocking. The burn was deep and disabling, forcing Harry out of work for several weeks and plunging him and his wife into debt.

The stay with Harry and Violet was a short – only two or three months – and unhappy one for Gerald and me. Somehow we didn't gel. Our relationship soured, and there were longs periods of silence when communication was difficult. Things reached a point where Gerald and I became almost aggressively alienated from them. Rather than eat our Sunday meal at table, we used to bolt the rice or vegetables that were provided, wrapped the meat or chicken in a cloth and take it outside. We would climb the large tamarind tree in the garden, the meat nestled warmly in our bulging khaki trousers, and seat ourselves in the topmost branches. From our perch there, we enjoyed a splendid panoramic view of the south-west of the island down to the coast; it gave us a new perspective on Barbados. This escape suited Harry and Violet, who must have found us just as difficult as we found them; they were prepared to overlook the risk inherent in climbing a tall tree when one's hands were greasy.

From our lookout point, Gerald and I enjoyed the rich textures of a landscape which juxtaposed glimpses of red corrugated roofs against dapple-green mango and tamarind, all set against vertical trusses of cabbage palm, as mops of spiky green fronds tossed in the breeze that swept across the island from the east coast. To the spread of timber, bushes, metal and masonry, the Caribbean formed an emerald-blue backdrop, seemingly tilting to cradle the land and facilitate my view of it. We enjoyed watching tall schooners sailing in and out of Bridgetown, their sails bellying in the breeze, making the ships heel to port or starboard in a mass of swelling canvas. The rippled effect of the multiple sails, the wake of the ship ploughing her way through the sea, never failed to impress me. Schooners were the Concorde of their day, so elegant and charismatic that they took my breath away, no matter how often I saw them. The sheer refinement of humankind's ingenuity, our appreciation of form and line, coupled with the knowledge needed to harness the elements, were nowhere more finely encapsulated than in the lines of a schooner under full sail. Our stay with the Innises bequeathed me that gift, a treasure I value to this day.

Those stolen moments each Sunday afternoon, which brought relief to both sides, became a magnetic, almost hypnotic, attraction and were arguably the single most important experience we had in that household. Despite their apparent triviality – in other circumstances they would have been unworthy of note – they helped shape me as a person. They triggered deep-set values and abilities which lay dormant for years and might have atrophied with time. Had I stayed with my parents, I would not have had the experience I did in Violet and Harry's home, and I can see now that I would have been impoverished.

Despite their rejection of Gerald and me, the Innises didn't mistreat or abuse us in any way. We simply didn't get on and they didn't want us in their home. Their relationship with Levi, however, was very different. He fulfilled their desire for a family, and was someone on whom they could impress their values, aspirations and way of life. They grew to love him and he reciprocated, growing with the passage of time to regard them as his parents.

Strangely, these relationships, though apparently favouring Levi and disadvantaging Gerald and me, turned out to do quite the opposite, and still mark our lives in different ways. On coming to Britain, Levi became deeply disorientated and unhappy, regarding the Innises as parents from whom he had been torn away, and finding it difficult to re-adjust to his natural parents. That tension, especially my father's inability to comprehend Levi's trauma and disorientation, was to lead to much conflict, unhappiness and resentment. On the other hand, Gerald and I found that our experiences after our parents' departure brought us closer to nature, and it was then that my interest in colour and the physical environment was triggered.

In later years, as I studied at the Oxford and Chelsea schools of art, as my love of painting took hold of me, driven by an interest in Gauguin and Van Gogh, Cézanne, Matisse and Vuillard, it was through the play in canefields and the earthy smell of the blacksmith's forge that I understood the Impressionists and appreciated their magical rendering of light. The clarity of the Barbadian light and the brilliant effervescence of tropical colour drew clear parallels with that moment in Western art and made it real for me, part of my lived experience. Nowhere was this more apparent than in Gerald's and my move to the home of another uncle and aunt in spring 1956.

The move was the result of news filtering through to my parents that the relationship between the Innises, Gerald and me wasn't working out; Levi was to remain with the Innises. We were reluctant to leave him, but it was clear this was the best hope for an improvement in our circumstances, and we all knew he would be well looked after, because Harry and Violet doted on him.

Our new home was in Spooner's Hill, with Samuel and Elise Dash, my father's elder brother and his wife, who was my mother's elder sister. As soon as we arrived, Gerald and I felt an immediate affinity with Samuel and Elise's family: we were as one with their household.

Spooner's Hill was less than a mile from our first home in Fairfield, and not much further from Station Hill, and Samuel, Elise and other members of their family, with the exception of Wesley and Fred, the two eldest sons, had sometimes visited our home. Spooner's Hill was a semi-rural area on the edge of Bridgetown, abutting the parish of Saint George. Long Gap, the street where we now lived, consisted largely of Dash family chattels: a few houses and, between them, trees and patches of cultivated land, interspersed with open areas of weeds and shrubs. On my uncle and aunt's land, there was a derelict house owned by the family, and there was also a small chattel where my grandmother Dash lived.

Grandmother Dash was a small, taciturn and by then tooth-less old lady, who resembled my father in many ways. She had well-cushioned fingers and thumbs, which nimbly 'picked' rice of impurities when preparing it for cooking. We often visited her, roaming round the house, playing hide-and-seek in the dark cellar. Being old she must in her youth have experienced many difficulties in Barbados. She never spoke of these times but I was impressed by her deeply wrinkled face and the authority that went with her age. She connected us to the nineteenth century, when she was born, just a few years after the slave trade had ended. As such she represented a crucial link with a past about which I still knew little, and I was fascinated by the history, and indeed the promise, that she represented.

My aunt and uncle had eleven children: Wesley, Fred, Pearl, Lascelles, Velda, Ernesta, Eugene, Marlene, Yourline, Sam Sam and Darnley. Fred and and Wesley, being young men, lived away from home; the others lived with their parents. Lascelles – or Ta Ta, as we affectionately call her – and Pearl were in their middle or late teens when we moved in. The others were aged between about five and fourteen. From the outset there was real camaraderie and shared interest in our play and outlook on life. The three-bedroom chattel truly became our home.

Gerald and I shared a room with Sam Sam and Darnley. The four of us somehow slept in the same bed, one or more of us sometimes ending up in a tangle on the floor at the bed-side after a fitful night's sleep. The seven girls found space in that packed household, the three bedrooms swelling to four sleeping quarters by the conversion of part of the shed-roof to an extra sleeping area. For all the inconvenience to the family, Gerald and I were never made to feel unwelcome. I was very happy there and I feel sure that, despite already having a large family, they would have found a way to take in Levi, too, had it been necessary.

Samuel was a man of few words. He worked as a watchman on Grazettes plantation and managed a smallholding from which he eked out a living for his family. He was noted for his severity in dealing out punishment with a cowhide whip, so my introduction to the household was one of some appre-hension, if not fear. But within days this concern evaporated, as our relationship with this quiet, introspective man grew. Samuel had a simple approach to life, in which clear boundaries were set. If we respected that framework there was no problem, but if the guidelines were breached there was hell to pay.

Being meek and utterly respectful of my uncle, I never received a full whipping, though Gerald, who was more reckless, received two; he still carries a weal from one of them. In some ways these beatings, though painful, were strangely reassuring because Samuel treated all the children in his household with the same severity and warmth. Though the beatings would probably horrify people today, they were then, if not the norm, a common mode of punishment, and Samuel didn't use the whip excessively. I was quietly, if a little fearfully, fond of him.

Samuel had two dogs, one docile and sweet-natured, the other, his pride and joy, a bulldog called Bullet. Bullet was a short, squat, powerful animal with a terrible temper, who spent much of his life chained to a metal stake in the garden. He couldn't be set free because he was so violently deranged that no one but Samuel could go near him. Samuel exercised him each morning before dawn, to minimise the risk of an incident when Bullet was allowed to run free. He was chestnut brown with a white V on his chest and fine muscle tone; his handsome appearance was his only endearing quality.

Bullet knew the range of his chain. He wasn't an animal to waste energy barking and leaping at targets he was unlikely to hit. Instead he bided his time, patiently waiting for an opportunity to strike. To this end he usually lay in wait at the door of his kennel, until an unwary target came within range. His targets included chickens, piglets and people, and he attacked them with frightening speed and sheer savagery.

My cousins and I built a hutch for a few rabbits my uncle and aunt owned. The hutch was above Bullet's kennel, when he had been temporarily removed to a different area. The rabbits were fed from an opening which ran part of the way over Bullet's patch. One day someone forgot to check that the hutch door had been properly shut after the rabbits were fed. During the afternoon a couple fell out and were slaughtered by Bullet. I saw one slipping from the edge and saw the speed at which Bullet leapt to snatch it in mid-air. As a result of that and other incidents, my aunt decided Bullet must be put down. Samuel woke early one morning, took the dog into a small copse and killed it.

My aunt Elise, like my uncle, treated Gerald and me as she treated her own children. I think she had considerable affection for my mother, her sister, which communicated itself in the warmth with which she spoke of her. Like most women in Barbados at that time, Elise was a housewife who worked in the home, looking after her children. However, on top of all that she had wider responsibilities, tending the sheep, cattle and other animals that played a big part in the family economy. Again like my uncle, Elise was a resolute woman who wasn't chary of dishing out punishment when necessary. Gerald and I got on well with her and felt at ease in her company.

The eldest of the children living at home was Pearl, a warm and considerate person who took the role of big sister to the whole family. Her gentleness made it easy to communicate over many issues, including concerns over our separation from our parents and the prospect of travel to the UK. Ta Ta was younger than Pearl and very energetic. Soon after our arrival in Spooner's Hill she started seeing a young man whom she was later to marry. I saw the process of courtship from a whole new perspective, was very aware of this handsome young man who regularly came to the house, waiting patiently outside the building for Ta Ta to appear. He was very fond of her.

Ta Ta regularly joined Gerald and me in our adventures. Not long after our arrival, the three of us were playing in the derelict house on my uncle and aunt's land when Gerald decided play a practical joke and frighten us, so he shouted, 'Centapee!' In some ways the incident had an echo of the incident with Mrs Gayle and the 'ghost', because in her panic Ta Ta dislodged some glass shards from a broken window. A piece fell and gave her a nasty, deep cut on her foot. There was a lot of anxiety over the injury, but no bitterness towards Gerald, either from Ta Ta or from the rest of the family.

Living in my aunt and uncle's home taught me how myths and prejudices are created in families and, through them, whole communities. In my parents' household Elise and Samuel and their family were regarded as different, less sophisticated than we were, and we were seen as a cut above them. When I came to know them, it was at once apparent that much had been myth, driven by a desire for self-aggrandisement: subtly putting down these other people in order to boost my parents' self-image. I soon realised that my uncle and aunt's family were just as sophisticated as my own, and as worthy in every way. They had much to offer that my parents lacked; indeed, being in their household greatly enriched my life.

My mother had kept chickens and one or two animals, but Spooner's Hill was effectively a small farm, with not only chickens but also a couple of cows and some pigs, sheep and rabbits. There was also a donkey and cart. I loved the early-morning call of the cockerel, the grunting of the pigs as they slurped their swill, the heady mix of cow manure, bails of straw, rabbits in coops and bleating black-belly sheep.

I enjoyed feeding the animals slips, the foliage from sweet potatoes, and hay. The cows lowed their deep bass notes as they fed, and the horses whinnied with excitement before gorging themselves on a cocktail of oats and molasses pap. I loved the smell of the cow-pen and even the pigsty, the cushion of warm hay on which the pigs slept, emitting a pungent and evocative farmyard aroma. I watched my aunt milk Rose, the cow, listened as the fine jet of white fluid speared into the empty pail, Aunt Elise's expert hands releasing the milk from the bulging udders in a steady pulling rhythm. The pens, the potent smell of manure and hay, the call of the animals, were the cornerstones of an inner freedom unique in my experience.

Many years later, as an art student in Britain, I saw a Bonnard exhibition at the Royal Academy and was enraptured by a landscape which evoked memories of my aunt and uncle's life, especially the smell of damp cow bedding, tilled soil and the rich aromas of country living. The painting came alive for me in a way rarely experienced when I stood before any work: it evoked wet manure and shimmering corn in the fields, lowing cows and pails of fresh milk. I was transfixed by it, by the feeling of summer heat folded into the paint. I thought of days in Barbados so hot that each step required a special effort, of Sam Sam moving Rose to the shade of a tree to keep her cool, her distended udder bulging beneath her.

At Spooner's Hill I was for the first time surrounded by young women, an entirely new experience for someone brought up in a family of boys, and they treated me like a brother. I discovered girls' playful ways, painting their nails with sticky dyes secreted from berries, or pasting coloured substances on their lips for play. I saw them weep with pain while having their hair combed and plaited, I smelt the sweet aromas that filled their world, saw the layers of nylon, lace and cotton that framed their stylish appearance on Sundays. This new and full environment stretched my senses to a degree I had never expected.

Grazettes plantation began at our doorstep. When the cane was mature, it was like an impenetrable forest of stunted trees, full of menace at night and of enticing challenges by day. I had dark imaginings of 'outmen' and duppies in the fields at night; the whole scene was a no-go area. But all this changed when the cane was cut. Men blackened by exposure to tropical sunlight attacked the cane with cutlasses, the remaining plants towering above them. When the work was done we got wide, sweeping views across the stripped fields: how different the landscape was with its subtle undulations and fertile brown soil.

A couple of times I went with Samuel in the donkey cart when he was working on the plantation. I loved travelling in the cart, the bumpy ride and the ease with which the donkey pulled us along, the crunching of the metal on the tarmac streets. The instruction to 'Gee up' was given by a flick of the reigns or a sucking of Samuel's teeth. All this was another rich new experience, which I lapped up willingly. We collected slips for the rabbits and the cows, vegetable waste from recently lifted sweet potatoes, which would otherwise have been thrown away.

Gerald, Sam Sam, Darnley and I roamed the fields of Grazettes for whatever we could find. I loved the mature cane that towered above us as we searched for a centipede, a ball or tid-bit left behind by a passing traveller. But the fields could be scary, too, if only initially, for when walking a little way in it was easy to become disorientated. I remember the panic that welled up as I ventured in, the scampering back for a sight of home or a familiar tree before finding the courage to have another try. As we ventured further, there were often traces of other visitors, a coiled cone of human excrement, myriad pieces of garbage, a used condom.

In the privacy of the canefield boys talked about sex, sometimes illustrating a point by exposing their genitals, their foreskin pointed like the proboscis of an Amazonian tapir. There was talk of 'fooping', 'tuckers' and nature. My initial education about sex came by this means, in the company of older boys exchanging ideas and fears, prejudices and hopes; strangely allusive conversations delivered with apparent confidence by very young people blindly searching for answers. Their misguided pronouncements on sex became my certainties, forming a notion of human sexuality which it took years of re-education to unpick.

A year earlier at Station Hill, while we were exploring shrubs and outcrops of cane with a group of other boys, someone had managed to ejaculate, and he called us over to witness the milky white sperm that smeared his penis. We gathered round him and saw the fluid, but couldn't connect it with the testis or urethra, refusing to accept it could have come by the usual route through the penis, and believing instead that it had materialised like sweat from the helmet of the boy's genitals. I was so astonished by the trick that I ran home and told my mother about a boy who could 'squeeze milk from his tucker'. She was washing at the time and continued as if I hadn't spoken, unable to respond because she wasn't prepared for the subject. I didn't get an answer from her then or on other occasions when the subject was broached.

But there were other ways of learning about sex. I had often seen animals mating – chickens, dogs, cows, horses, pigs, goats. On street, backyard and grassland I saw dogs locked together, and witnessed their frustration as the male sought release that wouldn't come, its penis fixed in the bitch's body, making to twist and turn on her, the two sometimes pointing in opposite directions. I watched agog as mares were mounted, the stallion's member stout as a man's arm and stiff with desire. I saw calves come into the world, my uncle sometimes acting as nursemaid, pulling at the slight form, and releasing it from it's mother's tortured body, then the parent's licking and tending of the newborn.

I knew about human sexuality, but couldn't make the leap

from what was going on in the animal world around me to what people do, perceiving human life as distant from animal existence and on a different sexual plane. The link between the two couldn't be made; my Methodist upbringing creating a barrier between us and them. No responsible adult talked about that 'dirty subject' to or in front of children. So children learnt from each other in roundabout ways and canefield conversations.

My uncle's smallholding included a kitchen garden, in which he grew a rich assortment of vegetables: beetroot, carrots, eddoes, yams, sweet potatoes, onions, shallots, spring onions, lettuce, cabbages and herbs. I was filled with wonder at the full ripeness of mature cassava, yam and sweet potato, the fresh succulence of the bulbs when washed and peeled. Pigeon peas were picked from vines in the garden for rice and peas. We cut ripe breadfruit from our own tree, and watched the white milk ooze from them. They were wonderful when mashed for breadfruit cou-cou with chunks of meat lodged in them. And Samuel often brought home from Grazettes an arm of bananas, to be stored until ripe.

Most importantly I developed a feeling for animals, not only for my uncle's livestock – I milked the cows, with their sticky waxen teats – but for wildlife. I trawled the fields for centipedes, earth crabs and lizards. We played tag in the canefields, games where the sense of hearing was paramount in the dense obscurity. As I waited silently for movement on the dry, trashy floor, which would indicate the presence of my hunter or prey, my eye was sometimes caught by a centipede lodged between the leaf and stem of a plant, its legs radiating from its segmented body. Then I would instantly move away – anywhere, so long as it was away from that hated and feared insect. If I was the quarry, there might be an explosion of excited voices and a rustling of cane trash as the hunters descended on me. I made many fascinating discoveries in the canefields. The eggs of a wood dove, for instance, provided endless interest through their mystery and beauty.

Lizards often sprinted across the garden in search of flies and other prey. Some were large, more than twenty centimetres long; they constantly ducked their heads to appeal to a mate or signal to their kind. Gerald taught me to make a loop from the spine of a strong grass to lasso them with. I would creep quietly to a lizard and gently inveigle it into my trap. When it was caught I would give it to Gerald and his 'big' friends. A whole battery of stones, pebbles, twigs and lumps of turf would go crashing around the poor animal. Fortunately, they usually missed, but occasionally we did score a hit. If the animal was merely stunned, which was what we preferred, it was subjected to awful treatment. A favourite pastime was to cut off the tail, which continued to wriggle from side to side, sometimes more violently than when it was attached to the lizard. I could not for the life of me understand this, and demanded more lizards so the experiment could be repeated.

Doctor boobies (humming-birds) sometimes visited the garden, darting into the cup of a flower, withdrawing and gently positioning themselves again at its centre, extracting the nectar so important to their survival. They are delightful birds, which I cannot remember ever terrorising: I was simply too enthralled and admiring of their beauty and genius.

One day Sam Sam and I used my uncle's donkey cart to collect slips from a distant field. Part of the route took us by a nearby quarry. Sam Sam couldn't resist pushing the donkey for speed and fun, the two of us rattling about in the cart. As we approached the quarry, the donkey bolted to avoid a snapping dog, the wheel running for a second or so along the edge of the deep pit. We were perilously close to death. The moment made me aware again of the fragility of human life, the thin divide between survival and death, success and failure. It made me reflect, too, on the wisdom of placing the responsibility for one's survival in the hands of another.

I remember the exciting panic when playing cricket or exploring in open places and fields, ignoring the gathering threat of rain in dark clouds and freshening wind and the distant jingle of raindrops, like the chime of a million tiny bells, seconds before the deluge. Then the race for cover, every manjack for himself. Running to beat a tropical storm was deliciously scary, the biting wetness of drops striking the body now here, now there, in twos and threes before you were drenched from head to foot. Within moments there were rivulets streaming everywhere, the raindrops exploding like tiny bombs in the film of water that covered the land.

Running at such times was not unlike chasing over the prostrate form of a giant torso, and gave one a feel for the profile of the land, its curves, undulations and troughs conveying an extraordinary sensuality in their gentle rise and fall.

We played games in bamboo groves enjoying the shimmering sound of their long, spindly leaves in the Atlantic breeze. By night we pelted bats as they steered their convoluted paths across the sky, not suspecting that their inbuilt 'sonar' made a hit impossible. We watched doctor boobies dart and freeze in mid-air, their wings a blur of motion as they took nectar from a flower.

The nearby canefields where we often played were surrounded by fruit trees which proclaimed their bounty in a giddy array of leaf, bark, vivid colour, succulent fruit and sweet aromas. Walking through pastureland, climbing trees and damming streams, one made discoveries about nesting birds, and about centipede, mongoose and wood dove, which would not have been possible by other means. All this was in an environment of sugary sap and cooling Atlantic breezes. It was idyllic. When we explored distant fields of succulents and strange trees with peculiar-shaped leaves, we saw rare birds in brilliant colours, sometimes with long, probing beaks; or mature caterpillars of enormous girth, their presence instilling fear of the unknown. We picked cashew nuts and plums, nicked guavas and sucked ackees. Every variety of mango from the giant to the small, green to brilliant red, grew in those fields. This Caribbean pastoral made a big impact on me, despite my previous exposure to the natural environment. Life here was of an entirely different order. It is a period I shall always value, one which filled me with awe at the complexity and fecundity of nature.

Came December 1956, and we were all busy with Christmas preparations. We cleaned the house and spread marl. The house was decorated with bows of coloured paper alongside lengths of coloured ribbon, crêpe- and tissue-paper bunting. We received letters and cards, and everything was made ready for the festival. Pots of rice and peas were cooked on Christmas Eve and blocks of ice for cooling drinks brought in from a local store.

My uncle killed a pig on Christmas Eve. He woke early, and

when the house was still asleep he took the animal from its pen. I was awake, and observed the slaughter by peeping through a chink between timbers. My uncle had a sickle prepared by a blacksmith, its blade beaten straight like that of a sword. I couldn't work out why he wanted something like that. The pig was taken to a table my uncle had prepared in the yard, and its feet were bound; then Samuel lifted it onto the table. Throwing his weight across the animal, Samuel quickly strapped it down, finally disabling it by strapping its snout.

A bucket was placed on the ground beneath the pig's head. Samuel took the sword and pushed it into the soft, fleshy part of the throat, which was not unlike a fat man's unshaven throat. The pig squealed and thrashed about desperately. The sword went in several inches, but the animal only became more frantic. Samuel withdrew the sword; there was some bleeding but not much. Once more he fed the sword in, and it travelled about a foot into the pig's chest. Samuel withdrew the sword, and this time blood poured from the wound like water from a tap, forming a jet from the animal's body into the waiting pail.

The pig continued to squeal and thrash about, but within a few moments its movements became less violent. It twitched, then stopped moving and was silent. Samuel untied the body and took it over to a cleared area in the garden. By now the whole house had been awakened by the noise. Aunt Elise was already preparing for the next stage of the butchering. She boiled several pails of water, which was poured over the carcass. Sand was rubbed into its hair. I remember smelling the scalded skin and watching with amazement as the black hair peeled away and fell in great clumps onto the floor at my aunt and uncle's feet. I knew there was white meat beneath the animal's black hair, but seeing it so white when shorn of its black hair was still a surprise. Samuel butchered the pig, sharpening his knife and cutting down the middle of the carcass, removing the intestines, which were different pastel shades of pink, grey and green, reflecting the different stages of digestion of food.

I was transfixed by the knife and the savage slice that had killed an animal I had fed and watered many times, an animal whose pen I had regularly washed down while the pig rummaged in troughs of swill, its coiled tail fanning with pleasure. I remember, too, the heart with the jagged wound in it, the kidneys, lungs and liver, how everything seem to come tumbling out of the guts of the carcass. We were given the bladder, which we inflated later that day and used as a football. Gangs of children descended on us and we punted the tough and resilient bladder from pillar to post.

Scales were set up in the back garden. Elise and Samuel removed the bits that would be used by the family. Liver – called 'harslit' in Barbadian dialect, from the English 'haslit' – is much prized on the island. It was cooked that day. Though I found the whole killing process distasteful, I ate the meat and appreciated its freshness. People came from some distance around as the rest of the pig was butchered: head, chops, joints, rib racks, intestines and blood for black pudding, the trotters for use in souse to accompany black pudding or for soup. We kept enough meat to ensure we had plenty for Christmas, and the whole of the rest of the carcass was sold to grateful customers.

Christmas wasn't the only time animals were butchered. There were regular kills of sheep, goats or pigs, slaughtered by neighbours and disposed of by midday.

We didn't receive many letters from our parents. My mother, being semi-literate, would have found it difficult to write but my father wrote copiously to other adults and must have written to my uncle and aunt, sending money for our care and keeping them informed about what was to become of us. Children at that time simply weren't taken seriously as people who had values and opinions and who needed to be informed. Our life at Samuel and Elise's was almost separate from our parents' as a result of this lack of contact. When at the Innises', we hadn't been communicated with and were informed of the move by Harry and Violet without any mention of letters from my parents. It was a strangely disjointed world, where children had their place and didn't concern themselves with adult business, even when that business was our welfare.

Gerald, Sam Sam, Darnley and I made a cricket wicket on a piece of waste land. We made a roller from a length of metal pipe from an old stone building, and filled it with stones and cement to make it heavy. We rolled the wicket by balancing on the pipe and walking it down the batting surface. Only one end of the wicket was used for batting, so that was the end we rolled. The surface was built up with soil and trash, which bound it together and in the batting area was some six inches thick. When the surface had been prepared for a match it shone like a glass.

Most evenings after school and on Saturdays there would be a gaggle of schoolboys milling around the field, swarming after a ball. We honed skills in defensive play, executed perfect square cuts, glanced leg breaks to the square leg-boundary. Over time the playing-surface was improved. Buckets of earth were taken from the nearby canefield and laid in the centre of the strip to create a built-up wicket. The dampened surface was then rolled until it was flat and hard. The level and quality of play rose. Saturday afternoons were a time of fun and excitement as we played against children from outlying districts. Some years later I heard that the ground had developed into a successful lower-level club side. And it all started with four boys and their passion for the game.

I cannot help feeling that that time with my uncle and aunt and my cousins was of enormous importance to my development, especially to my love of art and my desire to become an artist. Spooner's Hill brought out the creative side of my personality in a way that nothing else had until then. I was happy there, and took a closer interest in the natural environment than had been possible in Station Hill. While Fairfield taught me a sense of family and community, Spooner's Hill brought home to me the beauty and significance of the Barbadian landscape.

PART II

—

BRITAIN

Fig. 6 The author at an Award-winning
ceremony in 2002

(Photo: Frank Manning of Manning Photographers)

IN 1957 MY PARENTS FOUND THE CASH to send for my brothers and me, and berths were booked for us on an Italian liner, the *Serrienta*. Gerald and I had grown fond of our aunt and uncle and our many cousins. There was a great deal of respect on both sides. The opportunities they provided us with, the sheer generosity of spirit, the firm moral guidelines and, equally importantly, the opportunity to grow and develop in a new and secure environment: all these things meant much to me and remain cornerstones of my life. My aunt was very moved and expressed her affection openly and without inhibition; Uncle Samuel remained his upright self. I was also sad to be leaving Sam Sam, Darnley and my other cousins. Gerald and I had a great deal to thank them all for. They had taken us in and treated us like true family. I knew I would miss them.

But unlike Levi, who knew no family but the Innises, Gerald and I related firmly to our parents as our guardians and were eager to be reunited with them. Gloria, then my eldest brother George's fiancée , was in charge of our small party. She had with her her daughter Pat, then a toddler, so she had her hands full.

The Atlantic crossing took eleven days. Gloria, Pat and Levi shared a cabin, Gerald and I shared another. When he arrived in Britain Levi was still traumatized by leaving the Innises and he took considerable time even to begin to settle, so he may well have been fractious and difficult on board ship, though I have to admit that I was so caught up in the overwhelming experience that I cannot remember. Perhaps he was in fact reasonably well-behaved, if only because he knew Gloria and was himself excited by the experience. None of us was seriously seasick, but people around us sometimes were, vomiting when the ship pitched or rolled and generally being under the weather.

The Italian crew did their jobs and left us to fend for ourselves. We were given anchovies, which I disliked, but we also ate minestrone soup and drank non-alcoholic wine for the first time. We had garlic sausage and ate European apples; I have not tasted better since. We were not used to eating formally with large groups of people at table, and the formality of it, with white men ladling out soup and laying the table, was something I was wholly unprepared for. Nor was that all. White men worked at menial tasks like cleaning the decks, polishing furniture and touching up the paint-work. There was a constant smell of paint, which is an abiding memory of the whole voyage.

Much of my time was spent running around on deck, often barefoot as we played in Barbados. But the decks were covered in black grime, which worked its way into the soles of our feet. Even Gloria, still in her teens, had blackened feet; it was many months after arriving in Britain before the stuff worked its way out of our system. I enjoyed going on to the top deck and observing the upper-class white people swim-ming in the two pools, the way they dived and plashed around. But I couldn't swim; none of us could (an early frightening experience at the seaside scared me away from water for years). This was the first time I saw white people sunning themselves in deckchairs to acquire a tan. Barbadian black people never, ever, did that. Much of our time was spent in the shade, the strong rays of sunlight being uncomfortable and at times even unpleasant. I couldn't understand how they could put up with the discomfort of the intense sunlight.

I left Barbados in a thin see-through nylon shirt – my best one, with a sailing-boat motif on the pocket – worn over the ubiquitous vest, and of course I was in short trousers. As the ship sailed north the weather gradually got cooler. I cannot recollect any rain, but some evenings after the first two or thee days were decidedly chilly. In Barbados around Christmas and into January and possibly February, the temperature fell a little and one needed warmer clothes (most people wore sleeveless sweaters), but this was cooler than anything I had known before and we had no sweaters to hand. Of an evening, to keep warm we stayed below and played in the cabin. Gloria, older and wiser than ourselves, kept her own company. She checked on us but spent time with people her own age.

I enjoyed walking on deck, peering into cabins, whose doors were often slammed on me, and getting to know a few other black youngsters like myself. Best of all was standing right up forward, feeling the ship's diving rhythm as her bow plunged into the sea. I stood there for what seemed like hours at a time and was never challenged, a surprise, given the potential dangers. The captain and crew must have seen me there, my head bent as I looked down into the depths of the water and drank in the sensation of the ship's pitching. Occasionally spray whipped up and sprinkled me, but there was no challenge, no enquiry why an eleven-year-old was allowed to stand in such a dangerous place without adult supervision. Often dolphins escorted the boat, plunging in and out of the water, for mile after mile. Sometimes in those early days we saw flying-fish, winglike fins outstretched as they glided over great distances after shooting out of the water.

After eleven days at sea we arrived in Genoa. Gloria had the responsibility of shepherding us through customs and immigration and she was magnificent in her maturity and care, despite the responsibility of tending Pat and Levi. We have much to thank her for. That she coped at such a young age, not to mention her selflessness in agreeing to take on that responsibility, is something for which we are still grateful. After passports were checked and the necessary documents stamped, we were bundled on to the train to Calais, my first train journey. The trip went well, the richness of the experience after the Atlantic crossing being an effective opiate. In Calais we boarded another ship. It was the cross-Channel ferry and would carry us to Dover. To England, where our parents were waiting for us.

Crossing the Channel posed few problems after our journey on the *Serrienta*. We took an evening ferry, remaining below deck to keep out of the cool wind. The pounding of the engine reflected our mounting excitement at being with the rest of the family again. My mind was a jumble of memories and images, the immediate reality so vital and varied as to suppress many thoughts of the past and even the future. We were tired and unwashed, piled one on top of the other for comfort in this new and challenging environment. Levi was clearly nervous, but being with Gerald, Gloria and me made things easier for him. We cast our minds forward to to seeing Mama and Daddy in a few hours' time, wondering what it would be like, how much they would have changed. It was a strange period of waiting, expectancy and nervous tension.

There were a lot of white people aboard the ferry, but those nearest us were black, Caribbean people like us making a new life in Great Britain. The white people kept themselves some distance from us. We were scrutinized and we in turn eyed them, if only to establish the ground rules in this stand-off. The drone of the ship's engine was a constant companion. We slept and dreamt, then suddenly we were there, at Dover. As before, there were many checkpoints and lots of British officials with tense faces, focused on the business at hand, speaking to their interviewees in their formal, clipped accents. Again, Gloria did all that was necessary. A porter helped with the luggage, but we were loaded down, very tired and stressed by the journey.

Before long we were boarding another train, this time heading for London. I nodded off, and seemingly within moments we were pulling into Victoria Station.

We arrived late in the evening. It was dark and cool. There were masses of people, both those arriving and those waiting to greet them. Daddy suddenly materialized before us. It was good seeing him. He was wearing a felt hat as always, and he greeted us with a smile and an embrace, before asking about the journey. He tried to take Levi, but Levi clung to Gloria, turning his back on my father as if he wanted to bury himself in her skirt. Gloria was, of course, holding Pat and carrying luggage. I could see tension in Daddy's face: he wasn't used to being rejected by his children. Passengers milled about everywhere; there were families embracing and people weeping. I recognized the lilting cadences of Barbadian accents as families and loved ones were reunited. We walked from the platform and Daddy took us to the steps outside the Barclays Bank in the station. He gave us a hot drink from a flask. There in the midst of teeming humanity, we tried to orientate ourselves after all that had happened in the last fortnight.

My father wasn't one to show a lot of affection, so words didn't flow at this reunion. There was just a quiet satisfaction that we were together again as a family. I was keen to see Mama and George, keen to make the family complete. In the meantime, Levi was wailing. He wouldn't be coaxed by my father, refusing to have anything to do with a man he saw as a stranger. I knew Daddy was an impatient man, certainly with children and especially with his own. I looked from him to Levi, waiting so see how long he would tolerate Levi's resistance. It was only a matter of time before matters reached a crisis.

My father had been brought to the station by a friend who owned a car. After loading up, we set off on the journey to Oxford. I tried to see what I could of the streets of London, sometimes getting fleeting glimpses of brickwork, shop fronts and awnings, but there were many high buildings and it was grey and murky. Indeed, almost everything was submerged in a dull gloom at odds with the mental picture I had built up of the great city. This was just twelve years after the war, and its impact on how people lived passed me by.

After working our way through the streets of London we reached the A40 to Oxford, but my father was asking questions about the journey and various people back home. I cannot remember much of the journey to Oxford or indeed what was said. That whole interval, like the landscape that surrounded us is a vague memory. My head was full of new experiences, and I was dizzy with tiredness.

We arrived in Oxford in the soft light of an English September early morning. My mind was in such turmoil I couldn't think of the house or the area, couldn't be impressed by the streets of Cowley. We parked outside 450 Cowley Road, my parents' home. I remember looking up the curving path to the front door. Mama came to the door as soon as the car pulled up, and hurried to the front gate. She was wreathed in smiles and I heard her say, 'Thank God, wunna get down safely, thank God.' My father took Levi from the car but Levi didn't want to go with him. He became almost hysterical, screaming and kicking, and kept saying that he wanted Harry and Violet, that he wanted to go home. When my father reached the front door, Levi had the presence of mind to jam his legs against the doorposts, his final act of defiance at being introduced to his new home. It must have been a thoroughly unexpected and deeply worrying, if not embarrassing, scene for my parents. The noise would have carried some distance and it was evident that Levi was deeply distressed. My father managed to manoeuvre himself and Levi into the hall. Levi wasn't responding to Daddy or my mother. By now he had even forgotten that Gerald and I existed, not to mention Pat and Gloria. His hysteria continued for a while. Harry and Violet Innis were his family: they loved him and he them. The journey to Britain was for him akin to a kidnapping. He wanted to go home. But eventually, from sheer exhaustion, though he still couldn't relate to the strange people around him, he grew quieter.

This difficulty aside, Mama couldn't contain her joy, babbling on and commenting on how much we had all grown, and what a big man Levi was. She was very much the woman I had last seen at the Careenage in Barbados, as loving and as caring as ever. I was glad to be here at last, delighted to be with my parents again. Being with them was like being in a dream. Though I had greatly enjoyed being with my aunt, uncle and cousins, I had never forgotten my own parents. In the days ahead, I spent a lot of time getting to know them again, reforging links and tapping into old emotions.

There was one major surprise for us: we had a new baby brother, John, just three months old. My parents had kept his existence from us, had never even hinted that Mama had been pregnant and given birth to a son. John was fair in complexion and very beautiful. Gerald and I were delighted at having a new brother. We played with him for hours and tried to make out his personality by staring at him. I held him and liked to be present when he was bathed. He took after our mother in appearance, and she was clearly delighted at having another child.

My father took things in his stride, not revealing his feelings. We were too nervous of him to talk much about John – or about anything else, for that matter. We were tutored to obey instructions and not have a point of view. The tenseness I felt in Daddy's company was the only way I could relate to him. It was a relationship that fed on fear. Within me there was a joy at seeing him again, but my feelings remained bottled up, unexpressed by reason of my conditioning. It was a respect that defined itself by distance, a permanent keeping out of reach of a man who, when riled, would lash out and catch the unwary, so you kept your distance and said as little as possible. Even now, in the early hours of our reunion, the familiar positions were being re-inscribed.

Levi knew nothing of them so he soon incurred my father's impatience and angry determination to maintain his authority over his household. Levi, more than any, other was to pay a high price for challenging the rules that my father decided we should live by. In that regard he was the first casualty of the move from the Barbados to Britain. The damage began the moment my parents boarded the ferry at the Careenage, and it was crowned, on our reunion, by the family's inability to heal those members most in need of healing.

The family house was a two-storey 1920s four-bedroom, semi-detached one. It had two sitting-rooms, one of which was rented to Gerald and Elaine Skeete, a Barbadian couple. George and Gloria occupied one of the bedrooms, my parents and John another; Gerald had a small room to himself, and Levi and I shared the fourth. There was in the sizeable garden an old apple tree which still bore fruit, and, on the other side of the path that ran down its centre, a plum tree. The Granny Smiths weren't particularly sweet, but the difference in texture from apples I had eaten aboard ship, not to mention the different fruit I had eaten in Barbados, made them special and unusual and of great interest. Blackberries grew profusely in the garden, and we plucked and ate them with relish because of their novelty value. My father had planted potatoes. In Barbados we called them English potatoes, so it was strange seeing them grow in their natural habitat; everything about the garden had a unique and special value for me. There was, too, a greenhouse in which my father grew tomatoes. I had never seen a glass building before, and was concerned about breaking the glass and upsetting him. There was a small garden shed, which I explored for whatever there was of interest.

Across the road was the bus station. I watched the lumbering double-deckers leave to take passengers across the city. The giant buses were fascinating because of their size and the fact that people could sit on two decks on a vehicle which worked the streets. Several West Indians were employed by Oxford Transport, and we watched them leaving the station on their scheduled routes. Their position within the company was an issue of some debate. None of them was allowed to drive a bus, though several with experience of driving buses in the Caribbean had applied for training. Black people were restricted to working as cleaners or conductors. The job of driver implied higher rank, as the drivers commanded higher pay and greater responsibility. It was a few years before Frank Downey, a Barbadian, broke the mould and became the first black man in Oxford to drive a bus. His appointment raised his status in Oxford's small West Indian community, almost level with that of with that of a professional person in the

Caribbean. His effectively was a middle-class presence, and he an achiever who had successfully challenged the white system in a way that others had not.

In time I ventured further afield, visiting the local park with Gerald. I shall always remember the distinctive smell of ash, horse chestnut, cherry and other leaf-fall smoulderings in the heavy autumn air, emitting aromas unlike anything I had encountered in Bridgetown, where the atmosphere is less humid. There were walks by the Cricketer's Arms, the nearest pub, and we visited Florence Park. We also took bus trips into Carfax, the town centre. I saw the university for the first time, and was impressed by the ancient architecture, the ornate metalwork and the teeming crowds.

The taint of war was still in the air, if in a very reduced way. Many people lived modest lives, and soldiers were seen in uniform. Army trucks could still be seen on the streets, and there were barracks and rifle-ranges in various places. Occasionally a procession of vehicles would thunder by, often towing tanks and other heavy weaponry. Yankee sailors and airmen frequently came into town, where they stole the hearts of the local women – to the chagrin of the local youth. But there was no clear sign of war damage. The infrastructure of Oxford was undamaged; the war had left no permanent physical scars on the city. The influx of black immigrants in the big wave of immigration was arguably as traumatic a challenge to the sensibilities of the locals as all that had happened since 1939.

That first year we travelled to the coast where I saw pill-boxes, once used to defend the coast against potential invaders. The way they crouched among the sand-dunes, the narrow slits through which the soldiers would have fired at the enemy, and their sturdy walls sent my imagination wild. I withdrew into my thoughts, imagining the Luftwaffe flying overhead and daredevil British pilots doing battle against them. Some evenings, searchlights played in the sky in scissor-like movements as they sought a non-existent enemy. Sirens on the nearby factory roof screeched their alarm, reminding us that we shouldn't be too complacent and that the state military machinery was still ready for battle, twelve years after the enemy had been vanquished. But these sounds and sights, the culture of warfare, fired my imagination about a conflict out of my reach. Within a couple of years George was conscripted into the Royal Electrical and Mechanical Engineers regiment, REME, in Taunton (Fig. 7). I tried on his woollen uniform and it threw me into spasms of itchy discomfort, reviving memories of childhood ordeals.

Fig. 7 George in his REME uniform

If John was the biggest and most welcome surprise on our arrival in Britain, television was the next best thing. I had never heard of it before, had no concept of images being broadcast by such means. For days we watched everything on 'the box', *The Black and White Minstrel Show, Double Your Money, Dixon of Dock Green, The Billy Cotton Band Show, The Perry Como Show, Quatermass and the Pit,* several variety programmes, comedy shows, games shows and many others.

I had seen my first films in Barbados: on special occasions we went to see a Western or detective movie. Laurence Olivier's masterful rendition of Richard III encapsulated the power of cinema for me, even at that early age. His depiction of the dismounted king offering his kingdom for a horse gripped my imagination. I tentatively engaged with the meaning of so much being offered in return for so little, and was able to make that first connection between what we aspire to and what has real value when we are stripped of the mask behind which we hide.

But television was a whole new experience: cinema at the turn of a knob. I watched it for hours. There was only BBC television then. The pictures were in black and white, and they were not sharp, particularly when compared to today's digital imagery.

Our television diet also contained a lot of British and American films. Whodunits and Westerns were favourites, alongside cartoon shows. Each Sunday afternoon a feature film was broadcast. Fred Astaire, Ginger Rogers, Errol Flynn, Alec Guinness and many other stars featured in a series of fine and not-so-fine movies. Through Astaire and Rogers we were introduced to the musical, a genre which went down well with the British but to Caribbean people was an acquired taste. We enjoyed the dancing of Astaire and Rogers, and my mother resonated with their romantic story-lines. Films or programmes with a black – or as we said then a 'coloured' – presence were of particular interest. Inevitably in such material the black people were in menial positions, working as bootblacks, servants or two-bit musicians. Willie Best was a clear case in point. He often played the part of the terrified simpleton who couldn't cope with machinery and the wider refinements of life in the white man's world, so he lived in a permanent state of wide-eyed, quivering fear. Stepin Fetchit took similar parts in many movies. Even Louis Armstrong, despite his obvious genius, came close to buffoonery in a series of questionable parts. Africans were depicted as spear-chucking savages, with shiny faces and wild, staring eyes, which further extended the distance between myself and them as people. The black man was represented as full of superstition or confusion, and lacking the resolve of the white man, who was prepared for any and every eventuality. We saw black men dancing for white guests and serving their families. Black women like Louise Beavers, headscarves knotted on the forehead, always did as they were told, and spoke with wildly slurred accents. We never saw black people in positions of authority. The subject of such representations was not debated within the family, but we were all trying to make sense of them. These, after all, were black people who were not black. We might as well have been watching Martians or other characters from some science fiction.

Occasionally, however, we saw and heard Paul Robeson making wonderful music with his rich, sonorous, bass voice. We warmed to him in *Sanders of the River* because of the dignified character he played. I responded positively to Robeson's extraordinary talent.

I liked action films, particularly westerns and war films. However, I was disturbed by *The Dam Busters*, in which the leading character had a dog called Nigger. I found this deeply offensive and it coloured my view of the film and, indeed, the actors who played in it. By regularly seeing films of this sort, in which black people were poorly represented, I began to withdraw from some aspects of television, sensing the racism that was implicit to it.

The Black and White Minstrel Show was a popular pro-gramme which I couldn't make sense of. Minstrelsy was a genre I had not met through cinema in Barbados. We were all bemused by it. My mother often remarked on the quality of make-up, but there was clearly a deep-seated disturbance there that we couldn't define. We knew the male characters were white men dressed up as blacks. Gerald was particularly disgusted by their make-up, in particular the way white paint covering their lips extended out on to their faces, making their mouths look huge and grotesque. As a Barbadian I wasn't fully aware of the 'Coon' culture from which the show was derived, but I sensed the derogatory nature of the material.

In a similar vein I found the Tarzan series profoundly dis-turbing. I deeply resented the notion of a white man going into Africa to dominate and teach blacks about their environment. Though I hadn't yet acknowledged my African heritage, this material clearly articulated an assumed lack on the part of Africans and I resented it. I could see that it was meant to make white people look great.

Our viewing was done in the back room, which doubled as the family living-room and dining-room. It was very uncom-fortable. The floor was covered not in carpet but in linoleum, which suited our erstwhile Barbadian environment but was thoroughly unsuited to an English living-room, particularly in winter, when the body craved the warmth of snug carpets.

There was no sofa as it was felt a sofa would soon get damaged. The only seating was straight-backed dining-chairs. And of course there was a large dining-table. My father had a seat at the corner of that dining-table where no one else sat, at least not while he was in the house. Of course it was bang opposite the TV, so he got the best view of it. If one of us was sitting there when he came in from work, we had to vacate the chair at once. That was where he conducted his business, counted Partner money, and filled in pools coupons.

By saving the 'good' furniture for guests in this way, we rarely sat on a settee in the early years except when, for a few minutes, we were invited into the front room to join a special guest or when we were allowed to play music on the radiogram (this changed later, when we started playing music regularly). Only close friends and family members were allowed in the back room, because it was considered that it didn't show us at our best, lacking the 'refinements' of the front room.

The front room was a hallowed space in the West Indian home, a place where children, when they were allowed in, had to be on their best behaviour. We always took our shoes off at the door so as not to damage the carpet. This was a room for guests, an environment where the family was, so to speak, on display; the décor therefore had to reflect the taste and discernment of its occupants. Almost every West Indian front room was pile-carpeted, the carpet usually heavily patterned with floral motifs. There was, of course, the never-to-be-neglected radiogram. Radiograms were a revolution in sound systems. They were all large, and some had a built-in drinks cabinet and a compartment for glasses, as well as a section for magazines. There were doors, and even drawers, which added to the complexity of the system and made it seem special. There was of course a radio. Most housed two speakers, one to either side, which produced a stereophonic effect. That simple change from the single speaker on a record-player was extraordinary. No self-respecting family would be seen without a radiogram which had this feature. It was a sign of success and taste, of well-being and affluence.

Front rooms often contained drinks cabinet. Made of timber and and glass, they were fairly substantial pieces of furniture, standing about four feet high and more than three feet wide. Each contained three or four shelves which were covered with lace or a cheap imitation, on which the glasses were placed. The glasses themselves were usually decorated with gold and other patterns. A thick frilly nylon covering was placed on the cabinet. Photos of family members were placed on this.

Most front rooms were decorated with richly patterned wallpaper, often with a floral motif. We had a number of framed religious images on the walls, and a few photographs mounted behind glass, with decorative coloured edges. Our ceiling was finished with artex in a scalloped pattern. Curtains were in two layers, an outer, heavier fabric with a showy design, and, on the inside, a lacy, frilly hanging. These were often tied with a neat bow to add to the decorative effect. We had a piano, on which my mother put framed photographs of the family. The sofa and chairs, usually a three-piece suite, were similarly decorated. Each cushion was edged with a cord which echoed a colour in the patterns. There was also a glass coffee-table with a chequer-board inlay. It was never used for chess, draughts or any other game; it was just there, and added to the decoration. The whole environment was a mass of floral patterns, frills and lace. Even the lighting was from a decorative chandelier. This in my experience was a typical West Indian home, in that it emphasised decoration at the expense of form and line. My father being the sole bread-winner, there was a perception that we couldn't afford to replace the furniture, so it had to be protected at all costs. You were always careful and you could never be free in a space regarded as so special. You learnt to hold things back, but you could never relax.

In both rooms, we burnt coal in a grate to keep warm. In the living-room we also regularly used a paraffin heater, which often gave off fumes as the wick needed regular trimming. Many West Indians had died in house fires caused by the misuse of heaters like ours, and we were given stern warnings about it. In fact, paraffin heaters and the fires they sometimes caused had become associated with immigrants and their poverty in Britain. The fumes eventually became part of the Caribbean culture for many people, just as the smell of burnt hair was an integral part of a woman's toilette.

Levi was still unable to settle down in his new environment. He cried a great deal and was fractious. He didn't sleep well and didn't respond to my parents' approaches. The impasse reached a head when Daddy, losing patience with him, applied the disciplinary measure he regularly used with brutal effectiveness. He shouted at Levi, who only became even more hysterical. My father's shouts were very frightening: you could feel the threat of real violence in his voice. This, coupled with a hard and uncompromising glare of deep anger, ensured he got the response he demanded. Living in fear of him, always expecting a beating for any misdemeanour, for your own survival you learnt to live within the rules he laid down. Levi had yet to learn this reality, and got a sharp slap as an accompaniment to my father's rough words. Levi stifled his emotions and soon quietened, but his shock and distress were long-lasting.

From then on the relationship between him and my father changed. The crying and wailing certainly diminished, but the resentment and distance from my father increased. To be fair, my father must have found it difficult to take to a son who resisted him so totally, and he could never adjust to that reality. All possibilities of a loving and close relationship between them dwindled; there was deep mutual mistrust. Levi's repression, the retention of thoughts and emotions he could not express, were manifested in what might be described as aberrant behaviour.

My father has never been noted for thinking through the possible effects of a particular line of action. Locked into his head are norms of behaviour alongside which everyone is measured, and where children are concerned he pursues these norms irrespective of their possible consequences. In his view, children should be totally obedient, seen but not heard: parents are adults who know best, their views the final word in any dialogue. A questioning child was therefore an unruly and 'hard-ears' one who needed to be disciplined. Discipline took one main form: severe beatings or the real threat of them.

Our migration from Barbados to Britain hurt many people and damaged the lives of others, especially within the family. Levi was psychologically scarred by the separations, which occurred at times when he was still forming a sense of self, still identifying individual adults as stable anchor-points in a complex and challenging world. When those anchor-points became shifting and unstable, it left him traumatised and deeply insecure. His distress when he arrived in Britain was a cry for help, not the sign of an unruly and inherently awkward child. That he was treated as such was a betrayal of his need for succour and support at a time of fear and confusion. That his needs were not met at that crucial time remains an issue of regret and sadness. This dislocation, the unhinging in African Caribbean familial relations, must have been experienced by many migrating families from the region after the war and may well have an echo in the lives of migrants everywhere.

Within a few weeks places were found for Gerald and me at Cowley St John Secondary Modern School on the Cowley Road; we hadn't taken the eleven-plus exam and so were not eligible for grammar school. Gerald, at the age of fourteen, had only a year to go before he was required to leave. I was eleven and had my full secondary-modern school career ahead of me. The school was small, with two forms of thirty pupils aged between eleven and fifteen, and its total number of pupils was under 280. The facilities consisted of a small, older building, which housed the tiny assembly hall, a few classrooms and the headmaster's office, and two more recent two-storey buildings, where most of the classrooms were. There was a bicycle shed and a separate small building for the toilets. There were poor sports and play facilities. The play-ground was no bigger than the average gymnasium, and two hundred and seventy boys kicking a football around it during mid-morning break and at lunchtime was at times quite hairy, though in winter it made an excellent skating-rink.

The classes were divided into two streams, A and B. The A stream consisted largely of more able students, while in the B stream were the slow learners who needed remedial support, a few children who couldn't be bothered to stretch themselves academically, and a few misfits who posed real challenges for the staff. In my first week I was tested for basic numeracy by the headmaster, teacher, Mr Clibborn, a thick-set, stern, elderly man who was clearly disturbed by my presence. He walked into Mrs Harris's class in the old block. Immediately all the children stood up without being asked, and he told us all to sit down. He stood by Mrs Harris's lectern, leaning his weight on one leg and resting his hand on her desk. I was horrified by his heavily stained pipe-smoker's teeth and by the long dark hairs that protruded from his nostrils, echoing the bushy mass of his eyebrows.

'Dash, come here,' he said.

My heart missed a beat. Why did he want to speak to me? I hadn't done anything wrong, and all I wanted was to be left alone, become invisible. I walked up and stood before him; you could hear a feather drop. Everyone was afraid of him because he was cane-happy, but they were keen to see what would happen next.

'What is two and two?' he said.

'Four, sir.'

'What is four and four?'

'Eight, sir.'

'What is eight and eight?'

'Sixteen, sir.'

'Very well,' he said, 'go back to your seat.' With that he turned on his heel and walked out.

That was the only testing I ever received at Cowley St John, apart from the normal end-of-year exams that everyone took. It wasn't a diagnostic exercise, intended to determine the level of support I needed, or even to assess my level of intellectual ability. It was meant purely to satisfy himself and his staff that I was sufficiently numerate and educable to be accepted into the school. I was being singled out for reasons of which I was fully cognisant but which I none the less found painfully upsetting. Though all I wanted was to merge into the fabric of school life, the staff's preconceived idea of 'the black pupil' went against me. Walking back to my seat after Mr Clibborn's examination was like being in a dream, so deep was my humiliation. Somehow my legs took me there, but I swear they were not under my control.

One evening we spoke about the journey at sea and the differences we had noticed between Barbados and Britain. My father talked about his and Mama's experiences when they first came to Britain. Their voyage, he said, had been difficult. My mother was violently seasick for the first few days, and he had to support not only her but a family friend who was also aboard. 'Man, de boat was a roun'-bottom one, and it use to role from side to side and you mudder couldn't take it. I use to take she and Applewhite wife Jean to de toilet at de same time, one on one hand, de other on de other hand, and they would be sick, vomiting. Day and night I had to take them to de toilet. We spen' Christmas at sea, before we arrive' at Liverpool. A white man who advise me to go to England give me warm close; he wife give ya mudder some close too. Widout dat I doan know what we would ha do when we get to England, because it was freezing.

'Anyway we took a train dat was suppose to take us to Abingdon where we were to work in a big hotel there. We travel from six in de morning till eight at night with nothing to eat or drink. Nobody won't tell us where to go or what to do. We ended up in some village miles away from de place. Den we talked to a white man an ask him how to get to Abingdon. He ask us how long we travelling and we tell him since six in de morning. He was so angry and upset for us dat he gave us bars of chocolate he had on him. Den he took us in his car to Abingdon and de hotel.

'After we had been there a few weeks dis white man from Poland insulted you mudder about she colour. I got so angry I picked up a kitchen knife and went to kill him. You mudder leapt on me arm and was screaming. Den de man ran and I broke away from you mudder and chase him all over de hotel until he manage to get away. De police came and said they should arrest me but they understand de problems some a we black people having with people, so he said he would let me go.

'You mudder and me left there and went to London. We walk all roun west London, Notting Hill, den we went to an area where a white man tell me some black people living. We press somebody doorbell and dis Barbadian fella open de door, somebody from Fairfield. I couldn't believe it. He took we in and told us we had to be quiet because if de white man find out we staying there he would be evicted. He had to work in de day time and we stay there and sleep in his bed when he out.'

I asked my father how they managed to find the deposit for a property within two years of being in Britain. He tells me that he did several jobs. 'I worked for de Co-op as a milkman. At de end of my shift I cleaned de floats; at nine in de evening I ran to local restaurant where I cleaned dishes till two in de morning, then I went home and got up at six and started all over again.'

At first I found school challenging in many respects. Most pupils showed an active interest in my colour: some thought it might rub off; others asked very personal questions. As a result, I became painfully self-conscious. Changing for PE was a problem, eating in public an ordeal. In my everyday contact with white children they behaved absolutely like children everywhere, but there was a schizophrenic split in my view of them as somehow part of something other and possibly superior, though that something wasn't evident in my day-to-day relationships with them. This confusion immersed me in self-doubt. I never ate meals at school, preferring instead to make the one-mile journey home for lunch. Despite the inconvenience, it was preferable to the nudge and wink of the dining hall.

For all that, like so many children who face humiliation or even bullying, I found the strength to go to school, turning up each day without fail. Many children still face surviving bullying and exclusion in school on the grounds of their presumed sexuality, body shape, colour or pitch of voice. We throw a protective band round children to keep them safe as we try to induct them into the ways of the world, but many face the daily grind and threat of exclusion and hate silently and alone.

The boys were fascinated by my hair and constantly ruffled it. But their good-natured curiosity left me feeling untidy, ugly and very irritated. Black people have a thing about their hair. Much trouble was taken over dressing it and placing every strand in position before leaving home. Some black people straightened or conked their hair, so as to bring it closer to the white model with its sheen and flowing locks; but the vast majority saw their hair in its natural state as something very important to their sense of dress and style. In spite of that, feeling constantly in the spotlight, I was unwilling to comb or dress my hair in public, for fear of catching the comb in it. That didn't happen to white people's hair, so I didn't want them to see it happening to mine. I was measuring my life against theirs and didn't want to appear different, and awaken yet more curiosity. Stubborn combing associated with black hair dressing was a cause of embarrassment. This was part of our secret. In Barbados, very short 'peppercorn' hair was frowned on because the tight little balls were far removed from the straight flow of European hair.

If the children's mindless curiosity was an irritant, the bloody-minded stupidity of the teachers made me boil with rage. One teacher, using me as a teaching resource, insisted that 'West Indians' lived in mud huts. Having my hair ruffled was one thing, but suggesting that Barbadians lived like tribal people in some village communities in Africa was the gravest insult. We had been brought up to believe that the traditional lifestyles of some tribal peoples of Africa – and indeed elsewhere – were utterly below everything we aspire to. People living in mud huts were seen as living at the lowest level of human life. Suggesting that Caribbean people were like that was too much to bear. I had to speak out. In my faltering Barbadian accent I blurted something about 'We doan live in mud huts, sir.' But he immediately rebuked me, insisting that his version was correct. I never forgive him for that.

The curriculum was basic. There were only twelve staff teaching the three 'Rs', PE, art, history, geography, music, metalwork, woodwork and general science. For us in the B stream it was dire. We did arithmetic, as opposed to maths. We didn't learn trigonometry or algebra. Instead we did long division, addition and subtraction: only what was needed for everyday life. We did only the most rudimentary science; chemistry, physics and biology were sciences I knew nothing about until after I left school. We didn't do English literature; teachers didn't introduce us to authors, either contemporary or classical. Music was a sing-along with the headmaster one lesson a week, to pieces such as 'Nymphs and Shepherds'.

I had always wanted to learn a foreign language, regarding that ability as a key indicator of a sound education. Besides, I wanted to unlock the mystery of another tongue, be able to converse with people from a different culture in their own idiom. In Barbados I had met men and women who had learnt Spanish or French while at Combermere, Harrison College Lodge or one of the other fine schools on the island. My ambition had been to go to a school like that, and take advantage of the fine teaching they offered. Attending a school which didn't set homework – not a single piece was set in any subject in the four years I was at Cowley – which set the level of mathematics below that I had been used to at primary school in Barbados, and not having the opportunity to study a foreign language were all a huge disappointment.

Mr Fisher, the science teacher, pointedly expressed the views of many staff when he referred to my class as 'dead-end kids', fit only for 'working in the local factory'.

My form mistress was one of the school's few female teachers, Mrs Harris. She was a stout, robust and bad-tempered woman, with large, powerful legs and a tough, no-nonsense approach to running her classroom. She wore the brown cotton stockings popular with the elderly and middle-aged women of her day, and looked the part of the schoolteacher as seen in countless pre- and post-war movies. From the outset I was made to sit at the front, away from the other children, and just a few paces from her desk. There was nothing between her and me but the polished parquet flooring. A short distance away on my right and at right angles to me was the rest of the class, some thirty-five children seated in pairs, their tables separated by gaps along which Mrs Harris patrolled.

That seating arrangement added to my unease, made me self-conscious. I could feel their gaze, the anonymity I craved compromised, rendered impossible. I was very conscious of my blackness, aware of every action I took. I couldn't sniff or cough without feeling someone's eyes burning into my cheeks; blowing my nose was a trial of courage and determination. Yet not wiping it properly, perhaps showing a bead of snot on removing my handkerchief, would have caused indescribable shame.

One afternoon in my second week at the school, Mrs Harris instructed us to take pens, rulers and pencils from our desks in preparation for a history lesson. As I lifted my desk lid and collected what was needed, the wooden ruler slipped from my hand and fell to the floor. This simple incident, an innocent everyday occurrence in almost every classroom, led to what was one of the most humiliating and painful experiences in my childhood. Watching the ruler fall was like a slow-motion scene from a movie, every millisecond registered, my panic magnified in dreadful anticipation. I froze in my seat, desk lid still open, my head out of sight of Mrs Harris. When the ruler landed on the parquet floor, the clatter reverberated round the room. Being painfully shy and nervous in this new environment, the last thing I wanted was to draw attention to myself. What I craved was to disappear, be rendered invisible. But I was under the watchful eye of Mrs Harris.

She represented all that I had come to fear in whites as figures of authority, and, worst of all, in her I sensed a loathing, a profound dislike of me, which undermined my confidence.

What followed surpassed my worst fears. I glanced over the rim of my desk lid, but Mrs Harris was already moving towards me. She fell on me in half-crazed violence and hate, hitting, kicking and snarling. She slapped my head, punched my shoulders and chest, kicked my bare shins. This was no mere scolding but a symbolic beating to death, an act of annihilation, a violation of my right to be. My Barbadian upbringing, my ingrained respect for teachers and awe of whites, combined to paralyse me, to make retaliation or even evasive action impossible.

Once the flurry of blows had subsided I cried uncontrollably, tears of humiliation and horror streaming down my face. The lesson ended and another came and went, but I couldn't follow anything, had no interest in what was going on around me. My conspicuous position under the gaze of the class and that fearsome woman was the final humiliation. I wanted to hide, become anonymous, but that was impossible. Yet crying brought its own humiliation. I felt ugly and weak, wanted desperately to turn off the flow of tears but hadn't the strength to control my emotions. There I was, a black boy from Barbados, physically isolated like an animal in a zoo, weeping uncontrollably. The conditioning to which I had been exposed from birth, the implied adulation of whiteness and rejection of blackness, the silence that overcame conversations when confronted by any criticism of the white world, began to take on new meanings. Reverence for white people was so firmly inculcated in us that it was difficult to equate the harsh reality of racism with a myth engendered by years of brainwashing. Mine was not the type of family where such issues were debated: we children did as we were told.

My father's inapproachability, combined with his irrational response to any slight, made it impossible to tell anyone what had happened. I was afraid he would do something rash. Memories of Errie Pa's execution, and the effect it had had on all of us, flooded back. I didn't want my father facing a murder charge as a result of punishing Mrs Harris. When angered, he was capable of violence, as the incident with the Polish man showed. I had visions of Daddy going to the school, losing his temper and attacking Mrs Harris – he might quite literally kill her. I couldn't risk that. I couldn't even tell Gerald, for fear he would tell Mama. She would certainly tell my father and the result might be disastrous. The only course of action was to keep everything to myself.

I sat through the afternoon lessons like a loyal but brutalized puppy, still strangely respectful of my teacher, as I had been brought up to be. By the end of the day Mrs Harris was worried: I was still weeping inconsolably. She found a handkerchief, wiped away my tears and begged me not to tell my parents. Her fear was palpable, and I was confused. But she needn't have worried.

The day after my beating I was back in school as usual. Though she tried not to show it, I could tell Mrs Harris was relieved that the matter had apparently been taken no further. Our relationship settled into one of tolerance; she tolerated me and I despised her while accepting her authority. I did my work and kept out of trouble. But there were difficult moments with other staff.

Though pretty much accepted by my fellow students, I still had to go through a period of some trial. I remember a science lesson one day when I became aware something was going on behind me, perhaps, people gesturing or smirking. I tentatively looked round and saw a boy on his knees behind me, sniffing my rear end, presumably to establish whether I smelt like other children. It was a shocking experience. Occasionally children in the playground called me 'Sambo' or names like that, but it was rare. They were often told off by others. Within weeks of my arrival my fellow pupils grew bored of examining me – at least directly – and got on with normal school life.

We rarely went out as a family, and our circle of friends, though wide in terms of numbers, of people we knew, was narrow in terms of close friendships. The regular Sunday visits to church that had formed a cornerstone of our lives were no more. We weren't attached to a church, because many black people had experienced overt racism and downright hostility in church, diminishing the appetite for church-going, and the concept of the black church did not yet form part of the lives of people in Oxford. My father did join a congregation, but my mother didn't. On arrival in this country, we were not pressed into making church visits by my father, and so we simply didn't go.

This was a particularly trying time for my mother. People came to our home, usually visiting my father to pay their subscription to the Partner savings scheme, to sing in his fledgling choir, to have their hair cut or whatever, and Mama made them comfortable, serving drinks and preparing food. She had no role outside her family responsibilities, had no friends, and was too conscious of her origins to be able to socialize and build a new life in Cowley. Apart from her visits to the shops, she went nowhere. Like Levi, though in a different way, she had become a victim of the move from Barbados. The lively, socially active and successful woman had become a drudge, confined to her home, needing help to break out of that narrow environment but receiving none. Life was very much a case of each for himself – if you hadn't the confidence, experience or personality to make new contacts and create new environments, you simply weren't supported. It was a brutal reality. I watched my mother, the woman whom I most loved and admired, gradually diminish as a person. The process of social and psychic erosion had started.

I was beginning to think that my father's obsession with the church was to do with looking after his future with 'God', his own survivability in 'Christ'. It was a form of belief centred on the perpetuation of one's own existence. As such, religion, certainly as it was practised around me, was deeply selfish. This I found difficult to square with the notion of family, seen in the context of what I experienced at home and the questionable attitude to Christian worship. As black churches began to be established, and my father became a member of one, strange people of whom we knew little came to our home: women in nylon wigs and dark coats and men in three-piece suits and well-polished shoes with hankies tucked into their top pockets. My father held forth about a text from the scriptures, leading the visitors in 'prayer' and chanting hymns.

We sat elsewhere in the house, listening to this and putting up with it because we had no choice. My mother spent much of her time scuttling around in the kitchen, conservatory and back living-room, and acting as cook and waitress. There was a real dislocation between her way of life and the life my father built for himself. She merely hovered in the margins.

On the Fifth of November my father and George let off fireworks in the back garden. No bombs for chucking here, nor crab-oil explosives. Everything was neatly packaged in pretty paper: catherine wheels, bangers, sparklers, and of course rockets. Not that we children were allowed to touch them. It was a disappointing display, particularly when set against what we were used to. But the fireworks we used back home would probably not be allowed in Britain. Still, I loved the way the sky came alive with exploding rockets, their whiz and bang. Other huge fireworks left showers of sparks or disintegrated into intricate patterns. But they were in other people's gardens, and I missed the hands-on fun of bombs and crab-oil explosives. Guy Fawkes nights in Barbados were much more communal and street-orientated. People played with fireworks in the streets, not in their back gardens.

Oxford in the late 1950s was a city which lacked comfort, a place mired in work, toil and greyness. I found Cowley in those first winters bleak, cold and dark. Living under a canopy of cloud for days on end, untouched by sunlight, was a reversal of everything I was used to and regarded as central to life. We settled in the autumn evenings around the coal fire in the living-room, paraffin heaters doing their work in other rooms. Journeys out were few, just those to the shops in town, or the occasional trip to the corner store; life was bounded by the cold weather and our alienation from British society. We got used to people in overcoats, new to us, which shrouded the body in a way wholly at odds with what we had been used to the Caribbean. The dampness caused by boiling kettles, poor ventilation, steaming baths, the extensive use of paraffin heaters, cooking, and trapped carbon dioxide, formed streaming tear-trails on the windows, blocking out the wider world. This was indeed a new world.

Getting into bed took an iron will. My loathing of moist environments, engendered by Mama's ointments and flannel vests, was sorely put to the test, the dampness from the atmosphere trapped in cold, cheap, cotton sheets adding to my distress. Gerald always filled a hot-water bottle, which I could borrow after he had finished with it, but this was only partially satisfactory and the worry about it bursting and flooding my mattress added to my alarm. We warmed our pyjamas in front of the paraffin heater at night, careful not to let legs and sleeves catch in the grille and take fire. Then we took a deep breath and jumped into bed, where we remained still until our body-heat created a warm area. Bedtime wasn't an experience to look forward to.

That autumn I played rugby for the first time. To a Barbadian boy weaned on cricket, football and rugby were of little interest. I was slightly familiar with football, but had never heard of rugby before. Playing it was one of the worst experiences I have ever had. Stripped to light shorts and a thin shirt, I was frozen for much of the time and wanted desperately to be off the field and at home. Worst of all, I couldn't follow the game because no one bothered to explain the rules: why the posts were so high, and about getting the ball from one end of the field to the other. Even the shape of the ball was bizarre.

One cold and very damp afternoon, during a match the ball was thrown to me. I managed to catch it and started running back towards my own line until someone told me to run the other way. I ran like hell, but I was never the fastest sprinter and in a moment about six large bodies fell on top of me. By then I had lost the ball but my head was stuck in the muddy field. In the tangle of bodies, a boy stepped on the side of my face with his spiked boots. The pain, cold and confusion were overwhelming. I managed to pull myself up from the ground but by then everyone else was at the other end of the field. That experience sealed my dislike of rugby for life, certainly as a sport in which to participate.

That first winter we suffered other indignities. I hated long-distance running anyway, but cross-country running in winter, when the ground was frozen underfoot or, worse, thick mud, was particularly unpleasant. The field where we ran was on a slope. Water ran down it and collected at the bottom, where it lasted right through the winter – we had to run through the mud and grime. My hands were always cold, sometimes so cold that I couldn't bend my fingers or do up my fly. Having a pee after a game therefore became an ordeal, as I tried desperately not to wet myself on account of my inability to get myself sorted in front of the bowl. The need to use the loo was partly psychological, gaining in strength the closer I got to a relief point. Standing close to a urinal, being right there without being free to pee, was unintentional torture, self-inflicted and painful. Doing the buttons up again on my trousers and duffle coat was unbelievably uncomfortable. The pain from my frozen fingers was not unlike a mild electric shock, and the harder I pressed, trying to make my frozen fingers work, the greater the shock, which remained continuous with pressure. My heels, too, suffered from the cold, the balls of my feet sending controlled charges of electricity through my feet and ankles with each step, and my toes losing all feeling. By the time I got home I was like a solid block of ice.

Mama often helped, if she was free, by undoing the buttons on my duffle coat. I then slipped out of it and made my way to the fireside. She never failed to remind me to keep my hands and feet a safe distance from the fire, for fear of developing chilblains, the plague of our lives. And in truth the temptation was to plunge my hands right into the glowing embers. My father said that when he arrived in Oxford he knew people who went out in the cold without gloves on, and then when they got home warmed their hands too close to the fire. The result was chilblains, caused by not letting the blood vessels adjust to the change in temperature and leading to tiny ruptures in the veins. The chilblains itched unbearably. He said some people suffered so badly that they used to run outside and put their hands into the snow to stop the itching. I sat on my hands and crept my feet as close as I dared to the fire without overstepping a by now deeply instilled chilblain threshold.

That winter I saw my first snow. There was a lot of it, and we made and threw snowballs. But snow was no big deal, much less so than the fog that periodically engulfed Cowley. Nothing had prepared me for the mystery and utter beauty of fog, the way trees and buildings dissolved into nothing. We walked in the streets in the fog and occasionally went to Florence Park, where I was spellbound by the trees and the way they disappeared. But alongside this beauty were the casualties it caused on the roads. For the first time I heard of multiple pile-ups and the carnage they caused. This side of travel and life in Britain was thoroughly unexpected. My mind was being stretched to accommodate a whole new range of experience, which in Barbados simply wasn't possible.

My family was settling into a new routine. Levi was at Temple Cowley Primary School, and George was working as an electrician. Mama was a housewife, while my father continued with the Co-op milk company. He was also banker for a Partner scheme, which attracted other visitors. This was a method of saving which greatly supported people on modest incomes and enabled them to save and make headway in Barbados in the first instance and later Oxford. People paid in a set sum of money each week to an individual who acted as banker. That money was then distributed on a weekly basis to everyone, including the banker – who got not a penny more than anyone else – and then the whole thing started again. By this means, people were enabled to save money to pay passages for relatives coming from the Caribbean and support them during difficult times, and to pay for badly needed furniture, cars, and so on.

There was also a half-hearted attempt to revive his interest in choral music. Some friends and neighbours became involved, but the lack of a central church put paid to that idea and interest soon petered out. This attempt to create a community activity also suffered from the new society to which we were having to adapt, which was very different from the small, settled close-knit community of Fairfield or Spooner's Hill. These West Indians were from different islands, with different lifestyles and traditions. Moreover, their homes were spread over a much wider area, so they needed easy access to transport for meetings.

Daddy also cut men's hair, and that brought lots of people from around Oxford to our home. I remember groups of men sitting in the conservatory waiting their turn, and the Caribbean penchant for stories and tall tales became evident. But here in Oxford there were not only Barbadians but men from St Vincent, Jamaica, Trinidad, Grenada and elsewhere. I met West Indian men customers, and indeed a few women, but not a single child my age. In fact, throughout my four years at school I never met another black youngster from my age group. The family offered much that was nourishing and stable, but couldn't fully compensate for this lack, particularly with the constraints of the testing white British environment.

This caught us all by surprise: as parents and children, students and workers, and, collectively, as new immigrants to

Great Britain. It may be that much of the psychological disintegration that many Caribbean British people experience today in Great Britain is partly due to the inadequacies exhibited by many of our people in coming to terms with these very real challenges, challenges for which we were not even moderately prepared.

Cowley St John put a cap on my learning as it did on the learning of other children there, particularly those in the B stream. Effectively, the school challenged my self-worth. I knew I was being undereducated and, as a result, would have to fight hard to achieve success. Instead of a proper grounding in English grammar, for example – the use of nouns and pronouns, the conjugation of verbs, correct syntax and so on – it was felt we needed only the most basic grasp of the language. There was no nurturing, no introduction to new layers of learning which would have moved our thinking on in a structured way, no follow-up, no extension, no expansion of an idea or concept, just a shutting-down of potential. I raged at this betrayal, this diminishing of me, the impact it would have on my future. And there was no possibility of talking it over at home. I really don't know which was the sadder, which betrayal the more outrageous.

I regularly found myself walking with children who attended Cheyne Grammar School. It was just a half-mile from Cowley St Johns, but the difference between the two was marked. Whereas my school was situated on the main road of Cowley and had not even a single tree in its grounds, Cheyne was set back from Cowley Road up a long, leafy lane in a comparatively secluded and private spot. The uniforms were much more attractive, consisting of stripes against a pale background. All the children had satchels, in which they carried their homework and books. I walked with Cheyne pupils, feeling the great gap that separated us and our different life chances. I felt humiliated and envious. I desperately wanted to be treated like someone special, as they were, to wear a uniform like theirs, to carry a satchel fat with books, to be respected and admired for being the schoolboy success that I wasn't. I was growing aware of the politics of schooling, and I agonised privately over the inequity of it.

To this day I balk at the whole idea of grammar-school education, because there are bound to be many children who, like me, feel excluded, failures merely because of the school they find themselves in. Many years later I was a head of department at a school where a former Cheyne student was also head of department. We sat together at meetings, chaired by the headteacher, and I couldn't help thinking about the past and seeing it in the light of the present.

More painful than the frustration of being subjected to a substandard education was the treatment meted out to me by Mr Shirley, the PE teacher at the beginning of a lesson on the school hall one afternoon. We did PE in the assembly hall, which was equipped as a gym. Our class vaulted and worked on the pommel horse. Exercises of that sort were for me comparatively straightforward, with my street gymnastics background.

One afternoon, however, as my class dutifully sat in rows in the hall, waiting to be told what we would do during the lesson, Mr Shirley walked down the row and stopped in front of me. He was carrying the heavy medicine-ball we were to use during the lesson. As I sat at his feet, he threw the ball on to my head. Pink, blue and yellow stars flashed across my vision. After keeling over to one side, I picked myself up and sat with an expression which flicked between an embarrassed grin and a sob. I just managed to control my emotions because I didn't want to appear wimpish. But I knew that I had been the victim of racism.

As an eleven-year-old, I brooded on this inequality, and grew more and more anxious. Instead of turning in on myself and allowing myself to be defeated by exclusion, I vowed to overcome my serious social and educational disadvantages by self-education.

Life at home went on much as before. When allowed in the front room, we were sometimes given permission to play music on the radiogram, pieces by Cyril Diaz, Lord Kitchener and Mighty Sparrow – Trinidadian music we had been brought up on. Our collection of vinyl records was growing, thanks to George and my father who bought gospel music, recordings by Bing Crosby and much else. My father fancied himself as a pianist and bought a piano. We were allowed to play it: despite the fear he instilled in us, when it came to education he encouraged us to develop new skills and explore new ways of self-improvement. Within a week I was picking out simple tunes such as 'God Save the Queen', 'Little Brown Jug' and 'Home on the Range'. It was an opportunity to learn something I could have learnt at grammar school: to play a musical instrument. I usually played in the key of C major. My father bought a few chord-books, and I began to play basic chords, like C, D, B minor, F and a range of minor chords. Soon I could play other tunes, too, and I was greatly encouraged by everyone in the house and praised for learning as much as I had as quickly as I had. Before long I could play a simple melody together with a basic major-key chord pattern, usually still in C major.

As I became more proficient, my father sometimes accompanied me on his acoustic guitar. He hummed, as is his wont, and I played the rhythm and picked out the melody. Then Gerald started playing the mouth-organ. A whole knot of family members used to come and listen to our playing and join in, my mother enjoying every moment. These were among the most enjoyable times I spent in Oxford, and they even brought some freshness back to my mother's life. The issue of formal lessons was never raised, and I was too afraid of my father to ask for them. But I was keen to learn to sight-read.

Apart from the rental money from letting our front room, my father's was the main source of income. George brought in a salary but he had his own responsibilities. My mother was managing the household on less than ten pounds a week. From that she was able to set money aside for birthday and Christmas presents and for her own clothes.

That Christmas, we got the same types of gift we always got: underwear, push-along cars, toy pistols and so on. We were happy with them because they were all we knew and we expected nothing else. My father worked all the hours he could. We went nowhere. Mama didn't visit friends, as she didn't have any. My father had his own life and it was lived largely in the church or with his network of friends. His life sometimes spilt into the home with the appearance of his hymn-singing friends. The tradition of marking Christmas by a church service, the early-morning visits of singers and musicians, the tots of grog, was gone for ever. All we had was our television and a warm fire, apart from each other's company – my mother's and brothers', that is. Some visitors came round and were very welcome, my mother providing drinks and the traditional fare of sliced ham and hot pepper sauce. But that was it.

After Christmas and as we moved into the new year, 1958, life settled back into its narrow rhythm. Once a week my mother and I did a 'big shop' in Carfax by bus. Sitting on the upper deck, I gorged myself on the complex beauty of the Oxford cityscape. The gothic buildings encrusted with grime but parading a heady mixture of brooding gargoyles, decorative friezes, finely worked iron balconies, high steeples, spires and fancy stained glass, a wonderful counterpoint to my Barbadian experience. The streets were a mass of heaving, swirling humanity, devoid of individuality, like a mottled sea sprinkled with beads of light. Magdalen College was a favourite place, just beyond the bridge, the beginning of another world from the working-class environment to which I was becoming accustomed (Fig. 8). I appreciated the antiquity of the university, the medieval architecture, the history. I yearned to be a scholar, was avid to learn, desperately wanted an education like that. I admired the students' striped jackets, Oxford shoes, fine tweeds and sweeping gowns. But I was aware of their haughty air, the conscious assertion of presence and power. Being a secondary-modern schoolboy receiving what I knew was a poor education hardly qualified me for acceptance to such a place, even if I had the intellectual ability – and that could not be taken for granted. So, given my Bajan admiration of learning and the special aura of academia, I was impressed by the university and its reputation as a seat of learning. In the summer, straw boaters were seen on college lawns, on the river and in the streets. The students, caught up in their own world, an inward-looking group seemingly oblivious of the city around them, punted on the Cherwell and drank quantities of champagne. We were invisible to them, the whole working class of a neglected city sub-stratum.

The rest of the High Street, All Souls and the other colleges with their tall steeples and fine metalwork were another part of that other world. I loved looking through the heavy gates, very much an outsider looking into the world of white people with money, influence and education, I wondered about their learning, what they did. I visualised them speaking Latin and reciting verse. From the upper deck of the bus I peeped into the half-open windows of Keele and All Souls and glimpsed

Fig. 8 Magdalen College, one of my favourite places

the very old wooden shelving, worn books, heavy volumes lovingly stacked, tantalisingly out there, yet almost within my grasp.

I wondered what sort of education those students had, and pictured well-laid tables and decorous table manners, ink-stained fingers and learned masters requesting answers about complex theories, equations, conjugations or verse. How I dreamt of that life: the beeswax polish and old stone floors, the way students, staff and visitors were swallowed up by the gloomy vestibules, the porters at their posts checking visitors for identification. But it was a world from which I would be permanently disengaged. I thought it would never be possible for me to enter an Oxford college to glimpse that other world from the inside even for a moment. In any case, before long the

1 *Dancing in the Streets*, c. 1961–2, oil on hardboard.
It was one my of first attempts at oils

2 *The Conversation*, 1963–4, oil on hardboard.
Playing and discussing music in our back room

3 *Dance at Reading*, 1964, oil on hardboard.
I painted it because I was so shocked to see a woman being sexually molested in public

4 *Mat*, 1976, a
collage with gouache
made from scraps of
paper found on the
streets of Seville
and North
London

5 *Mas*, 1976,
paper collage
and water-
colour. It
derives from
a photograph
taken at the
Notting Hill
Carnival

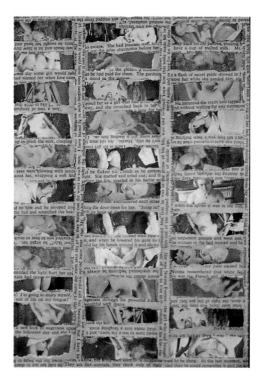

6 *Dam*, 2001,
paper collage.
I made it after
seeing the
prostitutes in
the Dam area
of Amsterdam

7 *Ibou*,
completed
2002,
reworked
paper collage
with gouache.
It came togeth
almost acciden
tally, from bits
I'd thrown on
the floor

8 *Great
American
Pin-Up*, work
in progress,
paper collage
inspired by the
horrors of
lynching in
the USA

bus was pulling up in Carfax and I was back in my own world.

Oxford market was a fascinating place, a show of plenty, the like of which I had not seen before. I enjoyed the displays of food, the hams and the smell of raw meat. Huge eviscerated hares and pheasants in full plumage, strung up by their legs, their eyes fixed in the glassy, unfocused stare of the dead. Other fowl were displayed alongside mountains of eggs in boxes. I wondered how the butchers could possibly shift it all. There were stacks of pies, bacon and strings of sausages. Then there was black pudding, so very different from the Barbadian variety I much preferred. I cannot describe our disappointment on first eating British black pudding. It looked the part, was the right shape, but totally lacked the flavour of our own. Elsewhere there were mounds of apples, especially Granny Smiths and Cox's, and pears, plums and peaches. Such fruit I had not seen before the *Serrienta*, but it was now part of my life.

I loved the excitement of being 'in town', the cheek-by-jowl nature of shopping there, the shopkeepers and stall-owners with their peculiar ways and idiosyncratic language. Each Saturday and Sunday morning, Mama cooked a breakfast of bacon, tomatoes and eggs bought at the market. I really enjoyed them. I became expert at selecting cheap but good cuts of bacon with her. She loved bartering, and the way the shopkeepers who knew her well called her 'ma love' and 'darling'; she flirted with them a little, too, and found that sort of affectionate treatment touching. I liked the world of the stallholders, the culture of their trade, the hustle and bustle, the no-nonsense way in which they sold things.

Sometimes she bought offal, too, tripe for soup and liver. Tripe is probably an acquired taste – it certainly has a character all its own – but we used it a lot in the Caribbean. I liked it at times but must admit to not loving it. We bought bloomers, large loaves which we carved into thick slices and ate with bacon and eggs. It was delicious bread, much nicer than ordinary sliced bread. Pickled onions and gherkins added to the rich assortment of smells and tastes and were delicious with ham.

I looked forward to going there with my mother as much for the dimension it brought to my world as to give her a hand with the shopping, which I realized was an important contribution to her workload. These regular visits to Oxford city centre clearly indicated the differences in wealth between Barbados and Oxford. We had eaten well back home and had enjoyed fresh produce, but there hadn't been the quantity of food, the variety and all-round indication of affluence.

We still ate a lot of traditional Caribbean food but Mama also gave us pies, which were a quick and filling meal. In England we started eating evening meals. In Barbados we didn't have heavy meals at night, our main meal being at midday. When I started school there, Mama had continued the habit by bringing our meals to school in a basket. We had a light supper when we got home, but not a large, late-evening dinner. Eating late at night in Britain was a whole new experience.

In February, seven members of Manchester United football team were killed, and several others injured – the great left-half Duncan Edwards died of his injuries later that month – in a plane crash at Munich. (I had become much more knowledgeable about football from playing it at school but I still wasn't fully acquainted with the rules, and some aspects of the game such as the off-side rule and the finer points of taking a throw, not to mention skills such as dribbling and volleying, were beyond me.) I remember watching the TV and thinking about the people trapped in the plane, the near-destruction of what was said to be a wonderful team. Names such as Dennis Violet, Bobby Charlton and Nobby Stiles were mentioned and, of course, Matt Busby. They had previously meant nothing to me, but from that day I followed Man United and the people involved in the accident, and became a keen supporter.

As the winter drew on I travelled more extensively around the Cowley area of Oxford. Autumn held endless fascination. Never before had I seen such a wide range of colour in leaves, the dappled greens interspersed with orange, yellow and brown as the leaves turned; a visually delicious tapestry that was new to me. At school during the mid-morning break and in the lunch hour we had conker fights, swinging at each other's best conker with all the viciousness we could muster in an effort to split it apart and thus win the bout. Some conkers had been specially treated with 'secret' fluids or chemicals; others were polished to a high sheen, presumably for cosmetic purposes. One friend told me that he pissed on his because urine toughened their skins. Others described weird concoctions which they thought improved the conkers' strength. I couldn't get into the pastime, finding it pointless and potentially painful, a badly bruised knuckle being a major possibility.

In the meantime other members of the family were faring well. George and Gloria were soon to marry. In his work as an electrician George had gained the confidence and respect of his colleagues. He had often wired complete houses on his own in Barbados, so the sectionalised work he was asked to do in Britain was straightforward and not particularly demanding. Gerald, when he wasn't at school, was chasing girls and being the extrovert everyone loves. Levi, on the other hand, was going still through traumas. His relationship with my father wasn't improving, simply because he couldn't respond in the way father expected of him, and he became difficult to manage. On the other hand, despite the separation of eighteen months, his warmth for Mama was soon rekindled. I think she felt guilty about Levi right up to her death. John, our new brother, had a very different relationship with Daddy. He, the youngest, arrived at a time when my father had become just a bit less severe, and in an environment where parental treatment of children came under closer scrutiny, so John was less affected by my father's aggressiveness. He was a beautiful child and we all enjoyed him, Levi included, though he was only a few years older. Patsy, Gloria's daughter, was also an important member of the family. Gloria and George had a room in the house and Pat slept in their bedroom. This was the only group of black children I knew throughout the remainder of my childhood.

We didn't have a summer holiday in 1958, my father regarding money spent on holidays as a frivolous waste. He did maintenance work in the factory during the holidays, on top of his regular job there. This pattern of year-round work continued for several years until I left Oxford. But on bank holidays we went out on drives with friends to the Cotswolds and small villages around Oxford.

I loved the Cotswolds, the neatness of the streets and quaint houses, and the dinky pubs, small places with aunt sally games at the side or the rear, and with swings for children. I loved the names like the Prince of Wales and the Dog and Duck or the Cricketers' Arms. The streets, particularly in Burton-on-the-Water and Stow-on-the-Wold, were like stage sets, unreal and different from the wide thoroughfares of Oxford.

The bird life excited me, the wagtails, tits and robins, and pheasants which burst out of cornfields in fright when we walked near them. Occasionally we saw swans nesting, but they alarmed me. I had never seen such big birds before, and I was thoroughly respectful of their power: nothing would get me to go near one.

We used drive around and look at people's gardens. Mama loved the window-boxes, which gave her ideas for her own. She loved the rose bushes and the flowering shrubs, tulips and hydrangeas, almost any flowering plant. What a pity she didn't get the chance to talk to the local people about how they grew their gardens, tended their climbers, propagated their shrubs; she would have valued that. She also loved the antiques shops. At home she had started collecting dolls, pots and cheap things. It was the way she gave vent to her creativity, alongside her gardening interest. But she lacked confidence, and her Barbadian dialect may have been a barrier to productive communication.

That year my parents bought me a new chromium-plated, standard Raleigh bicycle. It was a boy's bike, the first I had ever owned, and I loved it. I polished it after each ride and drank in the smell of the pristine rubber tyres. Occasionally I went out riding with friends from school. The tow-path by the river, near Donnington Bridge was a favourite place because there was no traffic and the wheels crunched satisfyingly on the gravel. My friends often did tricks, such as getting their bikes to skid by braking suddenly, but I didn't want to risk damaging my bike by doing things like that. They sometimes disturbed the anglers, who shooed us off aggressively. But if we were quiet and didn't disturb them, they sometimes let us see their catch, small fish held in a net at the water's edge. My Barbadian fascination with fish remained and I was always pleased when allowed to stroke one and feel the slithery smoothness of its scales. These anglers, sitting for hours beside the water, staring into its murky depths, were like no fishermen I had known. Most of all, I couldn't understand why they threw the fish back after a day's fishing. I had always regarded fish as food. Fishing for fun was a wholly new idea, which I couldn't begin to understand.

England was a land of grey, dark colours and mud, certainly in fields and embankments. But there was a beauty to the dark colours, a richness to the soil, which I enjoyed. And it seemed to penetrate much of the culture. The rowers on the Thames, backs arching, arms pulling at sculls which dipped and lifted, dipped and lifted, the boat creating waves as it cut through the water, were a pleasure to watch. Likewise the punters on the Cherwell, their poles sinking deep into the water before being lifted, often bringing up mud from the riverbed; above them a canopy of green leaves, and the water itself a muddy green on which surface ripples grew and spread into wavelets. We went to Iffley and heard the water rushing through the lock, witnessed the crash of the river to lower levels, in a roar of foam and spray. In Barbados there were ponds and swamps but nothing on this scale, and anyway we had been kept well away from the water for fear of drowning. Many days it was overcast and I was aware of the greyness, the greens and dull blues that were so different to the sharp colours of Barbados. But I took that difference in my stride, and loved it for itself.

A girl called Leila, who lived near Donnington Bridge, took an interest in me. I was painfully, paralysingly shy and had never had a real girlfriend to go out with, and she was white. My shyness made it impossible for me to speak to her, though I desperately wanted to. I tried to avoid making contact, but she was persistent. Leila was very pretty, round-faced and dark-haired. She told my friends of her interest and they told me. After a few weeks she started coming round to my home and ringing the bell. I hid in the conservatory and told people to tell her I wasn't in. After a while she stopped coming, but I shall always remember her beautiful face and mop of dark brown hair.

I was taken to the St Giles fair, the city's main fair, which takes place in the city centre. There were thousands of people there. The streets, normally busy with traffic, were given over to the event and there were dozens of rides, stalls and equipment. The noise was fantastic. The humming of the engines driving the wheels and producing electricity, the laughter and hubbub of voices made for a rich backdrop to the event. I was still quite small, and so at times was engulfed by people. Mama was of course as vigilant as ever and wouldn't let me stray from her side, so I had to bide my time until I was older before going on many of the rides. There were stalls advertising people with unusual qualities or strengths, there was the coconut shy, and toffee-apple sellers, the toffee giving off a delicious smell of boiled syrup. There were lots of youngsters and a few black people, including GIs from the American airbase at Upper Heyford. They stood out for their short hair and white socks: every American seemed to wear white sock and thick-framed glasses in the style of Ray Charles.

New horizons opened that year. My father invested in an *Oxford English Dictionary*, an assortment of trashy novelettes, and a new five-volume encyclopedia. Up to then the only reading matter to which I had had access was my father's Bible and *Daily Express*, a few copies of the *Readers' Digest*, and a very dated and musty encyclopedia in ten volumes. I had tried several times to read this last, but its poor condition, dull visual material and uninspiring text made it unappetizing. The Bible frankly didn't stimulate my interest, maybe because I always associated it with my father and his oppressive form of worship. At school we read only what was necessary for the class. No one in my family belonged to a library, and I certainly wasn't encouraged to join one.

The new encyclopaedia was therefore of particular interest. Each volume contained ten subjects, making fifty altogether. They covered a wide range of interests including accountancy, architecture, mathematics, English, electrical engineering, astronomy, art, and various languages including Russian, German, Greek, Italian, Latin, French and Spanish. I used these five volumes in my project of self-education. In the Anthropology section, I read about South American tribes which practised polygamy and polyandry, the first time I had heard of them or indeed these extraordinary social practices. I played around with mathematical formulae way beyond my capability, the section being for experienced mathematicians and people of much higher skill. I read about the pharaohs, the ancient Greeks, the Sumerians and the Romans, and was alerted to the wonders of ancient civilisations and the cultures that gave rise to the Parthenon, the Colosseum, the ziggurats and the pyramids. I was struck by the wonderfully sculpted head of Nefertiti, a colour reproduction of which occupied a page in the Egyptian section. I admired the queen's finely chiselled beauty, the elegance of her profile; never had I seen an object of such power and beauty, an image so refined.

Here, too, was my first exposure to people on the African continent achieving at the highest level in human civilization, though the implications of that took many years to become apparent. Egypt, as the encyclopedia presented it, was something separate from Africa, a civilisation apart. In the section on Botany, I learnt about soil structures, plant types and the impact river flows have on estuaries and surrounding wildlife. I learnt about life in the Alps and in the Nordic regions, as well as in African savannahs and the Sahara Desert. African civilizations and peoples, so long neglected in my world, were by this means tentatively addressed and shown to be rich, dynamic and full of wonder.

I tried to teach myself a foreign language from the encyclopedia. I started with French, but couldn't make headway because the spoken word was too far removed from the written text. Then I toyed with the idea of Russian and Greek, but realised very early on that self-tuition would be impossible. I took a brief interest in Latin, because I was aware of its relationship to English grammar, but soon gave up, thinking that a living language would be of greater value. Eventually I settled for Spanish, having had an introduction to very basic Spanish at primary school in Barbados and finding it relatively straightforward. I taught myself a few rudimentary sentences from the books, and was encouraged by recognising individual words when watching Westerns on television. The encyclopedia became my close buddy.

Another new venture was photography. I bought a Box Brownie camera from Boots, and took photographs of the family. The camera came with a detachable ultraviolet filter, which brought out the cloud forms in landscape shots. I shall never forget my pleasure when I took my first photos and had them developed. Walking into that shop, the smell of chemicals everywhere, and opening my packet of black-and-white photographs was magical. Pictures of John and Levi playing in the back garden, and a few of Mama, too. The ability to capture nature, and being the person responsible, invested me with a power I had never had before. By pressing a button I could create a world over which I had a degree of control. My control wasn't total, because I could never be certain of the outcomes, but that was part of its magic: the uncertainty, the challenge, the endless surprises.

From my pocket money, I managed to save enough to buy a tiny Perdio transistor radio. Turning the dial each evening and picking up stations in France and Spain was another form of magic. Most importantly, at night I didn't have to hand it over to anyone: it was mine, my choice, bought with my own saved-up coins and occasional gift of money. I was buying things and making things that came out of my own interests. No one else in the family took photos, and the radio was a similar gesture of independence. More especially, coming from a background where money was not plentiful and where the culture of sharing was dominant, I relished the autonomy that these simple pieces of technology brought me.

Christmas 1958 followed the usual routine. We had the usual meal, my father's dislike of turkey resulting in chicken, peas and rice with a choice of vegetables. My brothers and I were given practical gifts, plus what else Mama could afford from her meagre income: cap-guns, underwear, socks, toy rifles and comic books.

Not long afterwards we moved. My father bought a second house, in Annersley Road in Iffley, another Oxford suburb (Fig. 9). Our new home was a semi-detached 1920s bay-fronted house with a garage, and it was in excellent condition. George, Gloria and Pat lived in the Cowley Road house, part of which was rented to tenants.

One of our neighbours in Iffley took exception to our arrival. He was a very clean-cut, literally blue-veined, professional-looking man, who wore a tie even when relaxing in the garden. It was clear that he had a serious problem with our presence. He flatly refused to speak to us and would go indoors if we went into our garden while he was in his. If his family were with him, he whisked them away at speed, as if we were an obscenity from which they needed protection. Within a few months, he sold his house and moved, having never once spoken to us or even looked any of us in the eye. It was strange being hated like that. Having come from a country where strangers greeted each other in the streets, and where no one would dream of not welcoming a new neighbour by at least saying hullo, this was difficult to cope with. It is one thing reading about racism or seeing evidence of it on television, but quite another when it is directed directly at you. I often thought about the obvious distress we caused him. I wondered what he saw when he saw us, what he thought we would do to his family, or even in our own lives, which warranted his rejection. Seeing him hurriedly pick up his children and flee on seeing a member of my family was extraordinary. It made me angry but also embarrassed and confused.

Our first-hand experience of racism was as nothing compared to the riots that erupted on August 31 in Notting Hill Gate, West London. We saw news footage on television and I read about them in the *Daily Express*. My parents and family friends spoke of the riots, but Oxford was not a hotbed of insurrection and many probably found the problems in London slightly embarrassing. There was a view that the

Fig. 9 My mother outside our new house in Annersley Road

rioters might make life difficult for other black people, so there was a concern for the future. My father, though a Labour Party supporter, must have been influenced to some degree by the right-wing leanings of the *Express*, and seemed disinclined to speak on out behalf of the people caught up in the riots.

Apart from that, Oxford was very different from London, and though individuals suffered racist abuse there weren't enough black people in the city for them to be regarded as 'a threat', in the way black people sometimes were in London and other inner cities. The press's interpretation of the riots was such that many black readers, like their white counter-parts, were appalled by what was going on and simply wanted the problem sorted out as quickly as possible so that things could return to normal. We saw the issues pretty much as they were seen by members of the white community: a threat to the stable lifestyles everyone had come to enjoy and didn't want to see undermined. Being removed from the causes of the riots, we felt uncomfortable and concerned that they could lead to a wider conflict. There was real racism in Oxford. Some landlords refused to accept black tenants, a few churches didn't welcome black worshippers, a number of black people had real difficulty at work, there were occasional punch-ups, and so on, but people either swept it under the carpet or found ways of dealing with their situation. The riots threatened to bring everything to a head, and many of us were concerned.

My father passed his driving test at this time and bought himself a Morris 8. Initially we were happy to join the car-owning set but we soon came to see the Morris's shortcomings. It was a very old, uncool car, arguably the most antiquated I had seen on the roads of Oxford – even older than those on the streets of Bridgetown. The steering-wheel was massive, and the indicators were not lights but 'blades' which shot out from the side of the bodywork. Their shape reminded me of the sack beneath a lizard's neck. The gear-stick was a long, twisted length of iron with a knob at the end, like a piece of gate or garden fencing. The car had to be cranked before it could be persuaded to start.

To make things worse, my father wasn't a confident driver and took ages to park. The car belched out thick smoke and there was always a strong smell of petrol. I don't know where he got it from, nor the number of miles it had done, but it must have been several hundred thousand. One day it just wasn't there any more, and we were pleased to see the back of it. Eventually it was replaced by an Austin Cambridge, with which we were much happier (Fig. 10).

Fig. 10 My father posing with the Austin Cambridge

Wesley, one of Aunt Elise and Uncle Samuel's sons, came to stay with us in Annersley Road. His stay extended into weeks and months, but we didn't mind because he added a new dimension to our conversations, and family meant everything. Wesley, Gerald, Levi and I shared a bedroom. Wesley slept in a reclining chair, Levi and I had bunks, and Gerald slept on a single bed next to us. Wesley loved Gerald, resonated with his humour and sense of fun. Most nights he goaded Gerald into talking about almost any subject, knowing that his figurative speech and deadpan delivery would lead to outrageous comments or colourful observations. The most amusing moment came early in his stay and grew out of a ritual Gerald enacted every evening, switching off the lights and going to bed. From our earliest childhood, possibly as a result of my parents' stories about outmen and cut-throats loitering in canefields and breaking into homes, Gerald checked every nook and cranny in the bedroom to make sure there was no one lurking there who could harm him while he slept. In Oxford he kept up the ritual, often searching the ground floor, kitchen and living-rooms, just in case.

That evening we had all tucked ourselves up for the night when Gerald suddenly sprang out of bed, switched the light on, and began his routine of searching and poking around. Wesley, caught by surprise, peered over the side of his chair and saw Gerald, on all fours, investigating the space beneath his bed, lifting the bedcovers to get a clear view. Wesley wondered what was going on. 'Man, wa ya doing?'

Gerald heard the question but refused to be distracted, moving to the wardrobe and checking it thoroughly before feeling sufficiently at ease to switch the light off and return to bed. Wesley, conscious of the beautifully mad world that Gerald inhabited, persisted with his questions, occasionally giggling in expectation of a rib-cracking response,

'Gerry' – Wesley regularly switched between Gerald's two nicknames – 'wa ya do da fa man?'

'Wa I do it fa?' Gerald answered eventually. 'Boy, I always mek sure they ain' nobody in dis bedroom when I going to sleep at night.'

Wesley burst into laughter, farted very loudly and fell out of the chair.

Gerald instantly responded with 'Ya fart? If a eighteen-stone man stic 'e han' in ya neck during de night, ya more than fart, ya holla.'

Wesley laughed so much he almost passed out.

Gerald's timing, choice of words, ability to elaborate and extemporise, are always exquisite, and it is these qualities that make his witticisms so extraordinarily funny and warming. His humour springs from the everyday and commonplace. It is as much about language as the rhythm of a person's gait, the pitch of their laughter, or the curl of a lip. From his wit and deadpan delivery have arisen some of the most enjoyable and happy moments of my life. He gives his family and friends incalculable pleasure, and is a source of colour and fun for those who have the good fortune to be part of his life.

I remember a cricket match at Chinnor, where the newly formed Oxford West Indian cricket team was playing the village side. We were in the pavilion, enjoying some exhilarating stroke play from the West Indian side. During what was a very warm afternoon, Gerald began to show some anxiety, signalling his alarm in familiar ways.

'Wait, wa I see?'

Wesley, already giggling, as he could detect a good belly-laugh on the way, responded with 'Wa ya mean, Kites?'

Gerald, still staring at a distant spot on the cricket field or beyond it, his brow knotted with concern, began to rub his eyes. 'Man, my eyes mus' be playin' tricks 'pun me.'

'Why, wa happen, Gerry?'

'You can see wa I see?'

By now everyone on the pavilion was trying to see what Gerald was staring at.

Wesley said, 'Man, ah trying to see but ah can see nottin'.'

Gerald said, 'You can see de empire foot?'

'Wa wrong wid de empire foot, Gerry?' asked Wesley.

'Wa wrong wid 'e foot? Man, 'e foot so big 'e mus' be wearing coffins.'

Goodness knows the umpire did have big feet, but the way Gerald highlighted them was pure theatre.

In 1959 we went on an excursion to Margate. Daddy arranged the trip, hiring a coach and driver, collecting the money to pay for it, and generally getting the show on the road. We were all excited at the prospect of an excursion, a word full of potency for people in the Caribbean, to whom traditionally an excursion or outing is a key social event. On the day of the trip the bus was full of West Indians in smart casual gear, the women wearing colourful cotton dresses with floral and other patterns, and the men in baggy trousers and plain cotton shirts. Most people were couples, sometimes with young families, though there were a few single men. None of the children were my age; I had yet to meet a West Indian child of my own age. All the adults were in their prime, men and women between the ages of twenty-five and forty-five. There weren't any elderly West Indians in Oxford at that time, as most who settled there in the 1950s and 1960s were able-bodied men and women recruited to the British workforce.

The journey was long, compared to what we were used to in Barbados, but there was so much ribald humour and story-telling that the time flew by until we were at the coast. There was talk about the old days, cricket, the Russians and the bomb, and the bus rocked with laughter and bonhomie. It was strange hearing my father called 'Dashie' and 'Ernie' by other adults, so different was our family and its formal parent–children relationship. The man I so feared at home was a different person in society, affable and gregarious, willing to put up with aggressive attacks on his points of view in a manner utterly at odds with the person we knew indoors. It was a peek into the broader life of someone who had a major impact on the way I lived my life, the way I was formed. For the first time I was conscious of many new layers to to his personality and character. My father was a different man with his 'equals', especially outside the home, almost as if the walls of the family home imposed restrictions on his character, while on the coach he was more expansive and flexible. To me, reared to be totally submissive towards him, this affable side to his character was almost blasphemous. I looked at him two rows away talking to people, and expecting a violent retort to some detail of conversation, but one never came. Instead he rocked with laughter and acted in a perfectly normal and sociable way.

My mother had looked forward very much to the excursion, preparing the food – everyone, it seemed, had prepared plenty of food – and taking charge of the domestic side of the arrangements. She was protective and consistent in her treatment of us and in her dealings with adults on the trip.

Conversation on the bus skipped from one topic to the next. People argued about the different abilities of named cricketers and commentators, discussed the economies of Caribbean territories, and the West Indian Federation. Others denounced the communists. Some discussed the relative merits and demerits of Grantley Adams, Alexander Bustamante and Eric Williams, the great Caribbean leaders, arguing over who would make the best leader and who was the most dynamic. The intention of locating the capital of a federated West Indian state in Barbados triggered much debate, the

Barbadian contingent regarding this as right and proper on account of the the island's good communications and high standards of education.

There was much drinking of rum and other spirits but no lewd or improper behaviour. Though few were regular churchgoers, the underlying principles that had provided the moral foundation of their lives in the Caribbean remained fundamental to the way they conducted themselves in Britain. At the seaside we did the things the British normally do on trips to the seaside, except that few were willing to test the water, apart from paddling at the edge of the surf. The men played dominoes and my father collared a few friends to argue about details of the Bible, his favourite pastime. In the warm sunlight we spread ourselves out on large towels and blankets and enjoyed the food and each other's company. My mother fretted over our well-being and was concerned that we shouldn't get lost on the beach. However, some of us went into town, under the supervision of a few adults, had rides on the various funfair attractions, chewed toffee apples and ate candy-floss. The funfair was of course the big attraction for the children in the party; for many adults, too, it being a great spot for youngsters to find each other and forge new loving relationships. At the St Giles fair in Oxford there were rides, but these ones were much bigger, requiring nerves of steel and offering a challenge to even the toughest-spirited. I couldn't wait to get out there and try the big wheel, big dipper and countless other nerve-tingling attractions. I especially wanted to ride a bumper-car, even though I wouldn't be allowed to steer it myself because I always rode with Gerald, who inevitably took the wheel. That meant I was denied much of the fun of bumper-car driving. Instead, I suffered the irritating bumps and bruises, the unexpected thumps and half-spills, that you don't notice so much when driving but certainly do when a passenger. It was yet another frustration in a sibling pecking-order which reduced access to much that would have added to the quality of life. By the end of the day my insides had been churned, my body pummelled and my head left spinning on the beaches of Margate.

At school I had made a couple of good friends, Malcolm Kimber and John Jordan.

Malcolm was from a very poor background, the father a single, kindly but very elderly man who brought the boys up the best he could but who lacked, or hadn't the energy to acquire, housekeeping skills. Their home was down-at-heel and generally uncared-for, this mainly because of Mr Kimber's age – he was quite elderly – and the lack of adult support. I was quite surprised by the state of their home, hadn't experienced that level of poverty before – at least, not in Britain.

They kept pigeons, which Malcolm, his brother John and his dad raced from time to time. Malcolm loved the birds and spent many hours with them. He took me into the pigeon coop and carefully held the birds so they wouldn't struggle and injure themselves, referring to this or that as a 'little 'un' or 'chick', when in fact they looked adult to me. Malcolm was very fond of me and used to tweek my ear out of sheer friendship and comradely affection. I don't think that outside my family there was anyone more fond of me than Malcolm.

John Jordan was from a very different background. His parents were Scottish; his father worked in the motor factory and his mother was a housewife. They lived in an area bordering Blackbird Leys, which was soon to become a huge housing estate. John's parents made me feel very much at home, but there was a pristineness to their life, a hint of formality, which made me feel a little ill-at-ease. We were always given pretty little cakes and egg-and-watercress sandwiches on good china, the tea poured from a pot cloaked in tea-cosy.

Behind their home was a playing-field where John, Malcolm and I played with model aircraft and racing-cars made from balsa wood and cigar tubes and propelled by jet-X engines. John also had a petrol-driven model aircraft engine. We never managed to put it into an aircraft but we fired it up from time to time on a workbench in his back garden. We explored engines and talked pigeon-talk, kicked a football around in the winter, played cricket in the summer or went cycling.

I rarely invited John or Malcolm into my home, preferring to play out. My main concern was exposing the family to ridicule on account of how we lived. We hadn't yet found the confidence to be ourselves in the company of the British. Our house was fine in itself, but we were concerned about what we ate and how it would be regarded by others. I loved our food and wanted none other, but there was a suspicion that the choice of ingredients and the way the meals were prepared and presented wouldn't come up to English expectations. There was real embarrassment attached to eating Bajan because it had echoes of our African heritage. We were coy at showing our love of yams, green bananas, sweet potatoes and eddoes, and were most secretive about cou-cou dishes. Cou-cou is a near cousin of fou-fou and other African corn-meal foods, and is prepared with a wooden spoon, like many African dishes. Being distant from British foods, we were dis-inclined to have it scrutinised by a wider English public. The damaging effects of racism and the scarring it can leave on a people's self-esteem is no better demonstrated than in this type of self-subjugation.

At school, life became pleasanter with time. Besides Malcolm and John, I found other friends. Rodger Butler was from a very affluent background. He lived nearby in a large stone house with huge lawns. His family had a croquet lawn, and from time to time, some of us were invited round for a game. I had never heard of croquet before but found it easy to learn and straightforward to play. Rodger was very skilled, though, and what at first seemed an easy game turned out to be a little more difficult than met the eye. He used to bomb around the lawn at great speed, leaving the rest of us desper-ately trying to catch up. But it was nice going to a house like that and seeing the life of people who were well off. It was nice, too, having the refreshing snacks his mother provided while we sat outdoors enjoying the sight of the variegated shrubs and garden plants.

The school had more than its fair share of buffoons and in Michael Pipkin we had a natural comic and a genuine dare-devil. He was fair and fine-featured, with large, protruding blue eyes. He had a narrow attention-span but used the extra time that should have been devoted to study to devise elaborate schemes which might easily have got him expelled. Somehow that prospect didn't seem to bother him.

Because ours was a caning school, lessons were conducted in quiet. Students knew that if they misbehaved they would be punished, sometimes severely. But this seemed to spur Michael on to greater and greater heights of madness. A young woman came to teach English at the school, and one day Michael decided to use her as a prop. She was blond and thickset, with fat legs, which meant she often stood with her feet somewhat apart. She was also prim and proper, and wore boring tweed skirts that reached down to her knees. Essentially she looked a little frumpish. But I felt she was a good sort, whose philosophy was at odds with the tough regime that she was required to teach in.

Our desks were arranged in rows with spaces in between for the teacher to walk down. Michael's desk was directly in front of the teacher's and was jammed up tight against it – he saw to that for reasons I shall explain in a moment. Mine was behind his and a few places to the left. On the day in question there were a couple of absences, so places were left unfilled between myself, Michael and the teacher. I therefore had a good view of what happened.

It was a warm afternoon, and we were listless after the lunchtime break and not in the best frame of mind for work. Michael coughed in way we recognised as a signal that something was up. When we looked at him, he surreptitiously rolled his eyes in the direction of the desk, indicating the teacher's legs behind it. She was standing at her desk, feet apart, reading a piece of literature, her book held close to her eyes as if she was short-sighted. As she read, Michael slowly slipped down beneath his table and under hers. We could see what was going on but had to control ourselves so as not to give the game away. The teacher, being very inexperienced, didn't think to maintain regular eye-contact with the pupils, to gauge the 'feel' of the class, so she noticed neither Michael's disappearance nor the glances in his direction.

Michael carefully turned onto his back, slipped his head between her feet and looked up her skirt. Then he lifted his head, rolled his eyes at those with whom he could make eye-contact, and indicated by gestures the supposed massive size and shape of her genitalia. His mad act completed, he wound his way back into his seat, rolled his eyes in triumph and sat there as if nothing had happened.

On another occasion he performed a trick which, though amusing in many ways, made me feel ill for some days afterwards. The lesson was being taken by an experienced member of staff who was happy to use the cane at the slightest provocation, but that day he wasn't as focused as he should have been. Michael had an extraordinary ability to accumulate great globules of phlegm by drawing mucus from his sinuses. On the day in question, while the teacher was distracted, he screened his face with his hand and let a ball of phlegm the size of a marble roll slowly down his chin, then rapidly sucked it back in again. This went on for a considerable time, until he got bored with it. Pretending to work or pay attention while such subversion was going on required artifice and a capacity to maintain one's self-control in the most challenging of circumstances. I wouldn't have missed those moments for anything.

John Goodgame lacked Michael's mischievous appearance and talent for hilarity, but was just as daring. Whereas Michael was blond and blue-eyed, John was dark, and whereas Michael's humour came from his appearance and crazy pranks, John was insolent and uncooperative in a way that could undermine a teacher's authority. As a consequence, he was often in trouble and frequently caned. One day, during an English lesson, John had to read some text from a play. Being John, however, he did it with a flat voice and in a lackadaisical way, clearly showing his lack of enthusiasm. As part of the reading, John was required to make as if to kick something on the floor. The teacher was standing at right-angles to him, absorbed in following her own copy of the text. When John came to the kick, his black moccasin shot off his foot, did a few somersaults in mid-air and smacked the teacher squarely on the side of her face. The whole class exploded into hysterics. The thing was so neat, so precisely executed, that it could only have been deliberate. The teacher was shaken but, being a sensitive woman, she elected not to take the matter further. It would have been difficult to prove intent on John's part, even if she had wanted to report it to the headmaster.

But John got his come-uppance after he broke the window of a house near the school. The headmaster, Mr Clibborn, convened a special assembly and in front of the whole school slippered John Goodgame across the backside, with all the force he could muster. It was a nasty beating of real viciousness. John was never the same person after that.

In summer 1960 my father bought a house in Fern Hill Road, closer to the Cowley factory where he worked (by now the Cowley Road house had been sold). The new house was another 1920s three-bedroom semi with a garage, and also a large conservatory. I couldn't large understand why we were moving yet again and to a house which wasn't, on the face of it, much of an improvement on what we had before. However, it was here that the foundations were set for what would be my future career as an artist, and my work then developed rapidly.

By the age of fourteen I had gained a reputation in school as a painter. It just seemed to happen, yet we did not do art in the most propitious circumstances: one of the ordinary classrooms doubled as an art room and Mr Goodwill, who taught us English, doubled as art teacher. The room was badly furnished for art and we had to keep it clean for the English classes even though there was only one sink and few cupboards in which we could keep our work.

In my primary education in Barbados, art wasn't on the curriculum, so when I went St John's I knew nothing about art: I had never heard of a single artist, and had no idea what an artist did. Much of our work was on scraperboard, which didn't involve the use of colour but was entirely about drawing. My drawing skills were terrible at first – I literally reverted to schema (in this case, matchstick men) when representing the human figure – and I certainly couldn't compose a piece of work skilfully. In Mr Goodwill's class we were required to do only imaginative work, drawings from memory. We did no still-life and no work from a sitter, and landscape was never suggested. Contextual material in the form of other artists' work was never displayed.

In spite of these shortcomings, gradually, through exposure to the subject in the classroom, my skills began to develop and an interest in art as an activity began to stimulate my imagination. As we had to choose our own subjects and starting-points, I made scraperboard pieces of Oxford city centre, inspired by my trips to the market with my mother. Later, when we painted, these became more elaborate. I recreated the swirling masses of shoppers and ancient Cotswold stone architecture. I painted townscape after townscape, and gradually developed a facility for representing masses of figures in the street, using a pointillist technique. With each journey into town with my mother, I unconsciously imbibed details of architecture, the fine tracery of delicately worked wrought-iron balconies and fencing against solid stone forms, pots of flowers on balconies, the gnarled oak of medieval college gates.

With time, my reputation grew and my work was made a fuss of. I made a greater effort to study the detail of the city: the manicured lawns, flashes of capes and boaters, the way cyclists leant forward as they pedalled, the wear in the stone-work, a marquee in a college grounds. I painted to my heart's content, as there was no firm theme or project around which our activities were planned, refining my technique and creating a body of work with growing skill and assurance. I began to look forward to Friday afternoons in the art room with greater and greater excitement; I couldn't wait to get in there and settle into work. The smell of powder paint was as sweet as anything in God's creation, the clink of brushes in water-jars harbingers of deep pleasure. Watching an image build on the sugar paper, making decisions, being in charge, was most enjoyable. I lost myself totally in my art. By the age of fourteen my reputation for art in the school was established.

My mother was quietly supportive of my interest, and enjoyed my success at school. Positive reports reflected my achievements: my marks in art exams were always particu-larly high; comments in my reports indicated how well I was doing. Mama bought me artist's materials, initially cheap paints, then squirrel, ox-hair and other watercolour brushes. Few trips went without a purchase. She bought little sketch-books into which I put different images, branching out from my usual street scenes. She bought small tubes of watercolour. I remember gamboge, a dingy colour which I later discovered was made from cow's urine. There were alizarin and crimson, Naples yellow and Venetian red, colours of which I hadn't heard before but which extended the range of my palette and opened the way to new possibilities in painting. I didn't take any of these materials to school.

I started painting at home in the sketchbooks my mother bought me. I painted scenes based on my idea of Caribbean life, of moments in Spooners Hill; dancers were a favourite theme. The pictures were imbued with a West Indian flavour which spoke of a cultural heritage I remembered fondly, a heritage framing my sense of self. I began working on pieces of card and even sheets of wrapping-paper so as to increase the scale of my work. But I always represented scenes, markets, carnivals, pastorals. Though I enjoyed painting at school, the two great themes in my art were rarely mixed, and then only when I painted street scenes at home for relaxation – I never made work with a Caribbean theme at school. The work I did in school I liked for the pleasure of doing it. The work I made at home was my private world, a world I couldn't share with my teachers or anyone outside of the family. It was a world which constituted me, one too private for such exposure.

Mama bought hog-hair brushes of different sizes: flat, round, filberts and a few tubes of oil paint. I don't know how she put the correct brushes together with the oil colours, but she did. I read what I could find on the medium, searching words out in the *Oxford* dictionary.

Then one Friday afternoon Mr Goodwill brought in a pre-pared board and a small easel and started painting an oil of some of my fellow pupils at work. The large board interested to me because of its preparation, but so did the turpentine, linseed oil and the paraphernalia of oil painting. I watched quietly as he worked, familiarising myself with the process, the use of a rag to clean brushes, of turps to break the pigment down. The technique was utterly different from what I was used to, the results richer, the colours more translucent. That afternoon and on several subsequent Fridays I picked up the basic knowledge I needed for painting in oils. I loved the smell of pure turpentine, which became synonymous with oil painting. He used a palette, and an easel to hold the work, so I realised I would need yet more materials if I were to be able to work in this exciting new medium.

I should have sought Mr Goodwill's advice, let him know that I was keen to work in oils, but my relationship with staff was such that I couldn't find the confidence to do so, didn't dare ask him about his technique, the materials he used or the surface on which the painting was made.

Before long I was experimenting with pieces of cardboard, painting straight on to the untreated surface, but the results were not half so rich, the images not so alive, as Mr Goodwill's. I knocked together an easel out of lengths of timber, and it held the work precariously in position; a palette was made from a piece of scrap ply. My family encouraged me, if only by leaving me to get on with it, though Mama's commitment was more direct. A supportive ethos was created where no one at any point questioned what I was doing or suggested that I should take up a different interest. My parents and brothers accepted everyone as they were in respect of their interest and didn't make specific demands on them. As far as everyone was concerned I had ability and they would have been disappointed had I not become a professional person, but even there, had I chosen not to, I would not have been seriously challenged. My ambition to fulfil their ambitions for me was largely driven by me and my own mind-set: I simply didn't want to disappoint them. They didn't pretend to understand what it was about, but they saw this as a fulfilment of my preordained role within the family, that of someone who would one day do work that required significant mental engagement.

For my fourteenth birthday, George, mindful of my interest in painting, gave me a book on the life and work of the nineteenth-century French painter Camille Corot. It opened my eyes to new ways of using paint and representing flesh. Corot was of the classical school of French painting and painted women in natural surroundings, quite often nude. I was struck by the beauty of the reproductions. Corot's use of colour, the mood and sensuality of his women, introduced me to a whole new range of possibilities. I copied some of the figures and tried to replicate his technique. This practice led to drawings of figures from newspapers and even the television. A family friend came round one day and saw me copying a photograph of a scantily clad woman in a magazine. He upbraided my mother saying, 'Mrs Dash, how can you allow this boy to make drawings like this? This is shocking, shocking.' My mother calmly said I could draw what ever I wished, as far as she was concerned. One successful drawing made from television was of the Labour politician Hugh Gaitskell. I managed to create a pretty good likeness of him, and my success inspired me to make more drawings of that sort.

I began to take note of radio and television programmes which featured the life and work of artists, and thus got to hear of Impressionism, and of Picasso, da Vinci, Toulouse-Lautrec and many others. I was uplifted by the music used as soundtracks: symphonies, concertos and choral pieces. To my mind, classical music and painting were intertwined and cross-fertilising. I began to listen regularly and enjoyed the music of Mozart, Beethoven, Bach, Sibelius, Mahler and more. Their life stories became subjects of interest in their own right, as biography was later to do in respect of the lives of all artists. I had developed an interest in all forms of artistic creativity.

Staff and pupils at the school began to treat me differently. The boys complimented me on my work and often asked my advice on their own art, and staff, too, spoke of my paintings with enthusiasm. One day, while I was walking across the playground during mid-morning break, a member of staff stopped me and asked, 'Are you the artist Paul Nash?' I said, 'No sir.' By then I knew who Paul Nash was – his name had been mentioned on television or radio and I had seen a couple of reproductions of his work. The teacher was very embarrassed at his ignorance, but the significance of the moment didn't escape me: a teacher thought I was 'the artist Paul Nash'. The incident boosted my morale because it showed that people in authority were taking me seriously as an artist. An unfortunate spin-off from this, however, was that teachers had unrealistic expectations of all my visual work. The maths teacher scolded me for making a poor geometrical diagram in maths, because my work 'should be an example to everyone'.

My Barbadian grounding in cricket became apparent in the third and fourth years, in some decent performances on the pitch. I was terrible at football and useless at rugby, but I could play cricket well. The tricks and feints my classmates were capable of when playing football, I could parallel with a cricket bat. I could square-cut with the authority of Everton Weekes and late-cut with the finesse of Frank Worrel, throwing in a dummy for good measure. I had a good defence, and knew the rules of the game better than anyone else. I played for my house, Page House, at first, and then for the school. Later I was invited to play for Oxfordshire at schools county level. Walking on to the manicured turf of Magdalen College sports ground, for a game against Leicestershire, was a special moment in my school career. I took in every detail, the close-cropped grass, the redness of the clay soil, the precise whiteness and clarity of the whitewashed lines, the players in expensive whites as they awaited my arrival at the crease. The experience has stayed with me over the years as an extraordinary moment, especially in view of the backgrounds of the other players, who were almost all from grammar or private schools, and of the grounds where they played.

My passion for cricket resulted in a painful and almost calamitous experience. I was cycling to a ground where the school was due to play in a suburb of Oxford, with my whites and boots in a suitcase. I was going down a side road surfaced with loose gravel, when my knee caught the suitcase and I came off the bike. There was a loud bang as the suitcase exploded on the ground, and I skidded on my front for some metres. When I got to my feet, the gravel had taken all the skin off both hands – it was hanging in shreds. A kind lady saw what happened and came to my help, taking me into her home to bandage my hands.

The attitude of different members of staff changed towards me as news of my achievements got round. When I became an established cricketer for the school, Mr Shirley, who had come close to breaking my neck with that medicine-ball, revealed a different side to his character. Between overs, during a game in which when I was flailing the opposition's batting, and which he was umpiring, he noticed that my fly had not been properly done up – I was wearing a large box and one button had come undone. He informed me of the problem, but, instead of waiting for me to take my gloves off and deal with the matter, dropped to his knees and did the button up for me.

In 1961, after the Whitsun half-term break, I was at last moved to stream A and the top form of the school. Unfortunately this was done not in recognition of my abilities but for efficiency reasons, the two fourth-year forms merging because of the high number of early school-leavers. I was a little bitter about it, thinking if only things could have been better.

The two groups were thrown together under the tutelage of Mr Chance (we called him Charlie Chance), the form eight teacher and deputy headmaster. He was a small man, who smoked heavily. His colouring had a tobacco-like tinge, as if nicotine had seeped through his pores leaving a permanent stain. His greying hair was streaked with gamboges; even the whites of his eyes were a dull buff, his teeth and nails seemingly dipped in a fluid the turgid yellow of a pub ceiling.

Charlie Chance compensated for his diminutive size by a carefully massaged reputation for toughness. As deputy headmaster he regularly beat pupils; he was literally Clibborn's chief whip, and he ruled by sheer intimidation. I never saw the man smile. He eye-balled children by coming up close to them, literally in their face, and they didn't dare move or avert their eyes for fear of inviting a beating. He kept a cane on top of his desk, often picking it up and giving it a twirl as a reminder of the pain he could inflict. And he wasn't shy of bringing it into action, beating students for the slightest provocation or non-compliance with some insignificant rule. So what should have been an occasion for celebration turned out to be a period of tension and yet more fear of a beating. Yet all this flaunting of power was merely intended to create a space where he could prepare his fishing tackle, fishing being his hobby.

By now my work and prowess on the cricket field were highly spoken of everywhere. I received two prizes for art, one for the pupil making the greatest progress, and the other for the student who produced the most outstanding work. The prizes were paint-along books, one on watercolour, the other on oil painting, but I greatly valued their recognition of what I had achieved. Later that year, after my school-leaving exams, I was taken to one side by Mr Goodwill and informed that I had got one of the highest marks in Oxfordshire for art.

A few weeks before I left school I was interviewed by someone from the careers office in the presence of my father and Mr Clibborn. The interview was intended to provide me with advice me on my future prospects. On being asked what job I would like to do, I immediately said I would like to become a portrait painter. At that time I didn't know of any other means by which an artist could make a living, and portrait-painting did offer a profession as an artist, which was all I wanted to be.

The conversation then drifted to how I could turn this ambition into reality. I was too young to attend the local art college, whose minimum age for for acceptance was sixteen.

However, the careers adviser outlined two options. The first was to go out to work for a year and then apply to art college; the second was to go to the local college of further education for a year, sitting on a GCE programme until the following year, when I could apply to art college as a sixteen-year-old. She indicated that pupils who had been in the B stream of a secondary mod wouldn't normally be considered for GCE courses, but a temporary exception would be made in my case. I was delighted, because at last here was an opportunity to participate in meaningful learning, if only temporarily. This was a real opportunity to test my wits against the abilities of other students and begin to get the semblance of a decent education. There was no question of my doing anything but go to college for the year. Arrangements, I was told, would be set in train for me to go to Oxford College of Further Education. It was as if someone had thrown a switch within me.

I walked around the school on my last day and looked into a few rooms, feeling nothing but resentment, no loss except the loss of opportunity, no parting emotion except anger. For all that, the art room was a space where I had found a means to channel my frustrations, realize some of my potential. Art, I had discovered, was a subject which allowed one freedom to roam. That discovery was arguably the single most important thing I gained from the school. My talent had been recognised by Mr Goodwill, and through him I discovered what ability I had and it raised my self-esteem. The experience could, in that regard, be likened to that of someone with a disability who is thought to be without a mind, without the capacity to formulate simple views or make even the most basic communication with those around them. Then one day they gain access to a computer and their life is transformed: they find a voice, and the world discovers they have a mind.

The art room was my channel of communication, a lifeline I grasped with every ounce of my strength. Without it I would have drowned. I valued Mr Goodwill's celebration of my ability, and I shall always be thankful to him for creating the context that allowed my art to grow. When I left the school that final time, there was no goodbye either from or for Mrs Harris, but there was a shared moment of warmth of farewell with Mr Goodwill. I thanked him cordially for all he had done to support me; he shook my hand and wished me well for the future. With that I left school without a backward look.

My painting developed rapidly at home. The books provided useful information on the preparation of surfaces for oil painting and offered various other tips on the medium. I read of rabbit-skin glue and how it is used in preparing canvases. Not knowing where to get hold of it and lacking the money to buy it, I smothered pieces of hardboard with Gloy, a stationery glue, thinking it might do a similar job. My brother John still has a self-portrait from that period, painted on cardboard prepared with Gloy; apart from myself, John and Levi were my main sitters. At this time I was still largely self-taught and made many mistakes, mixed dull colours as I worked often at night, and so on. My favourite theme, however, was carnival. I had never seen one but carnival seemed to be in my blood.

Away from my art and last days at school, events elsewhere were concentrating the mind. The Cuban crisis exploded all over the contemporary world. Like everyone, I lived in fear for my life as President Kennedy issued his ultimatum to Khrushchev. Kennedy, it seemed was prepared to unleash a nuclear war on the world, ironically through fear of a nuclear attack from the Russians. There was real concern everywhere. Affected, like many people, by the media propaganda that assailed us daily, I went along with the notion that the Russians were bad and that Fidel Castro should be shot on sight. But I was afraid that nuclear bombs might explode in Oxford and the city be reduced to rubble. With local American bases and Brize Norton being not far away, the possibility of a pre-emptive strike by Khrushchev was a real one. I knew about radiation sickness and the near impossibility of escaping nuclear fallout so close to a target. The likelihood of escaping with your life was slim. It was a moment of fear and real concern, and the pressure showed on the faces of everyone around. When Khrushchev eventually acquiesced and removed his warheads from Cuba, the reduced tension was palpable. We were impressed by Russia, even if we were suspicious of her politics.

That autumn I enrolled at the college of further education. I was in Mrs Morgan's tutor group. She was a ginger-haired woman of fair complexion, who seemed to take a liking to me from the start. She had a gentleness of manner that was comforting and, though it was apparent from our conversations that she was aware of my peculiar status, she took me seriously as a learner. My timetable included history, maths, English language and literature, economics, geography, technical drawing and PE. At last I was carrying the bulging satchel I had always wanted. Chaucer's 'The Nun's Priest's Tale', Bernard Shaw's *Saint Joan* and Shakespeare's *Romeo and Juliet* were just some of the reading matter that I was required to familiarise myself with.

My ignorance of the great bard was made apparent when, within a few days of enrolling, I met a black student of about my age for the first time. He was a formally dressed character, who carried a briefcase and always wore a tie. Being black we gravitated towards each other, and he asked me about my course. I told him, saying I was studying Shakespeare. He asked which play or poems. I couldn't for the moment make the connection and merely said in response to his question, 'Shakespeare'. He asked again, 'Yes, but which play?' but got the same response. This was, indeed, a whole new world to me and I had a lot of catching up to do. I mingled with students from different institutions and backgrounds.

More importantly, for the first time I met girls regularly. It was strange sitting close to them every day. I quietly fell in love with every other girl in the class. Just commonplace conversations with some of these young women were a pleasure in themselves. The new pattern of work, the relatively patchy timetable, which allowed free time at odd times of the day, enabled me to find the courage to eat in public and be more outgoing.

My time at college was about keeping me off the streets until I was old enough to go to Headington (now Brook University) to take art. But I followed the lessons with all the earnestness I could muster. I didn't receive any special help or support from the tutors, who expected me to be removed within the year. The fact that my secondary-school education was dire and that I was now studying alongside students who had been better prepared, following courses which would lead to qualifications also being taken by students at Eton and Harrow, didn't make the slightest difference, but I was very aware of what was going on around me, very aware that I wouldn't be doing the same things as students at grammar and public school. While I had no intention of asking to be considered for GCE examinations, I wanted to make the very best I could, in those difficult circumstances, of my year at the college. It was a personal project.

Despite the more favourable environment for learning, there were difficulties with some subjects. My preparedness for the college was non-existent, because the work we had done at Cowley Saint John's was not a serious background for GCE study. Economics, English literature and maths were subjects I had to learn almost from the beginning. In English I heard for the first time of précis and subject clauses, the imperfect tense and puns; history exposed me to the world of Brunel, Trevithick and a host of other engineers, inventors and builders of the Industrial Revolution; maths was a new world of sines and co-sines, logarithms and algebra. Being timid, I lacked the courage to ask for detailed explanations of some of the more complex concepts, and struggled on as best I could. I knew I could do much, and could achieve some success. The college gym was a welcoming place. I played basketball, badminton and five-a-side football. Some days we did trampolining, a sport I knew next to nothing about and found quite terrifying. This was indeed a steep learning curve.

I had an individually designed timetable, which allowed time for self-direction. There were pockets of free time, which Mrs Morgan suggested I might fill by enrolling for classes at Oxford School of Art. I did as she advised, and over the coming weeks and months, when not attending GCE classes, I got on my bike and pedalled up the hill to the polytechnic.

The School of Art was a wonderful experience. In my first week I wandered around and took in the smells: the latex rubbers used for casting in the sculpture complex, the varnishes and turpentine solutions in the painting studios, the finely ground surfaces of lithographic stones worked in the traditional way by eager students in the printing rooms. In those rooms, with their bottles of nitric acid, containers of stopping-out varnish, and black greasy inks, I thought of Toulouse-Lautrec's Monmartre and Van Gogh's Antibes, could taste a world of picture-making.

Before long the staff began to take notice of me, partly because of my age – I was the youngest student there – and partly because my drawings were of reasonable quality. Many complemented my work, and gave me every encouragement. These were heady and wondrous times, a world of freedom and sheer joy in art.

I was black and surrounded by naked white women. It was the first time in my life I had seen naked women, and the embarrassment was heightened when I could see their genitalia, sometimes very exposed. I had a profound sense of being stared at, the hair stood up on my body, and it was difficult to focus or concentrate. But I got used to it and my drawings improved rapidly. Within weeks I came under the wing of Mr Hennis, the drawing teacher, who clearly liked my work. He encouraged me in his quiet way and made a lot of my drawings. Occasionally he illustrated a point of criticism with a beautifully worked sketch at the side of my paper. I sat enthralled as he worked at my donkey, his hand seeming to glide over the paper, creating the most elegant and sensuous lines. Under his tuition my art developed rapidly and my confidence grew. I painted a self-portrait in oils.

Art college was benefiting me and after a few weeks at the college of further education I elected to drop some of my subjects to devote more time to drawing and painting. I wasn't enjoying technical drawing, which I had known nothing about, the word 'drawing' being the reason why I had chosen to do it, and I wasn't enjoying geography. The removal of these subjects allowed more time for study at the School of Art.

I quickly made friends there. Lawrence Tainey, a Royal Academy-trained painter in the traditional mould, had a wonderful technique but worked in a very academic style. He was a bit of a recluse, who found it difficult to make close friends. Extraordinarily youthful in appearance and manner, though in his fifties, he lived with his mother; he had the top floor of their house, and had knocked walls down to create a good-sized studio. I respected his painting and drawing skill, honed from years of working in front of the nude model at the Academy. However, I found his style a stuffy throw-back to a pre-Impressionist world, one of chiaroscuro effects and concerns about form, long overshadowed by the scintillating colour world of Impressionism, Post Impressionism and other modern art theories, in which he took little interest. Harry Checkers was another with whom I got on very well. A very short, powerfully built man and an ardent pipe-smoker, he dominated a section of the studio, where he made his dull, uninspiring paintings.

Derrick G. became a close friend. He was in his late thirties to early forties and a great admirer of Fidel Castro, Mao Tse Tung and the Chinese revolution. About six feet in height, he was a large-boned, barrel-chested figure who sported a huge black beard, which stood out against his sallow complexion, suggesting a possible distant Latin connection. Derrick loved conversation, in which he excelled because of his skill with language. His broad knowledge, mellow voice and clear diction were compelling, and added to his articulation and intensity of communication. He read widely on commu-nism and maintained correspondence with contacts in China, from whom he received regular mail. He often showed me this material, beautifully designed publications printed on delicate paper, with idealistic images of red-cheeked, smiling Chinese women in Mao tunics. Despite his admiration for Mao and the Chinese, however, it could be argued that Derrick built his self-image around Fidel Castro, whom he regularly celebrated in conversation. The physical similarities were quite striking. He also admired Che Guevera, to whom he made reference in various contexts. Conversely, Derrick despised US capitalism, politics and culture, holding forth on the Americans' imperialist tendencies in strident and at times impassioned monologues. I wondered if this openly left-wing sympathiser might be kept under surveil-lance by the authorities, given his willingness to share his contempt for Western capitalism and love of revolutionary socialism. Though Derrick often came to my home to see my art, I kept his politics from my father, for fear that he might disapprove of our friendship, given his own admiration for American lifestyles and his adoption of many establishment principles.

Derrick's home was an Aladdin's cave of novels and political writings. He also had a magnificent collection of stamps and first-day covers, which he kept in shoeboxes, cupboards and stacked on chairs in the front room and elsewhere. I learnt about penny blacks, a damaged example of which he had in his collection, and other rare or fascinating stamps. I saw stamps produced by the Third Reich, and was gripped by their history. The cold, angular faces of German soldiers in metal helmets, swastikas and other trappings of the fascist movement were emblazoned on stamps which lay in my hands. I also held stamps produced by Mussolini's regime, his awful head a great boulder of granite on many of them. But there were more attractive images printed in Switzerland, the Netherlands, Poland, Hungary and elsewhere. The collection was an extraordinary encapsulation of key moments in modern history.

Derrick's mother was an elderly and gentle lady, who allowed her son to dominate their home. I met her on a few occasions, but our meetings were short: brief words of greeting were exchanged before we went in separate directions. Their house, behind its bushy, ill-kept hedges, was unreal, almost theatrical. Layers of dust and cobwebs covered stacked books, stamp boxes and bric-a-brac. Dust swirled and eddied in the front room, the back room, the corridors and elsewhere. I felt for the warm and kindly woman who lived in such conditions. Things weren't helped by the fact that Derrick didn't have a job. In all the years I knew him, he never worked, apparently regarding a job as compliance with the capitalist way of life he resented. How he made money to live on I don't know, but he was happy to get by on a very modest income. It was as if he saw himself as a professional revolutionary whose task it was to debate with the wider public on issues of politics and the revolution.

Nevertheless, he was an extraordinary lady's man and 'pulled the birds' by the hundred. He spent much of his time in an Italian café next to the clock tower in Carfax, and there he picked up many foreign students and hangers-on, beautiful young women beguiled by his smooth tongue, encyclopedic knowledge, strength of character and sheer charisma. In all my years I have never known anyone match his success with women. He could pick up three or four or possibly more women in a week, taking them back to his dusty lair.

Derrick taught me a great deal, and helped me cross the threshold from youth and childhood dependency to emerging adulthood (Fig. 11). Through him I learnt about Gauguin, whom Derrick idolised, admiring his willingness to give up family, security and home to live a bohemian life for his art.

Fig. 11 Emerging into adulthood: myself, aged about 15, at Fern Hill Road

I think he secretly saw himself in that role, taking up painting like the Frenchman when past the bloom of youth. He spoke of Tahiti and the Marquesas, Gauguin's art and life with young women of the South Pacific, his directness and uncompromising nature, his attempted suicide and death from syphilis. The colour and rawness of Gauguin's palette somehow brought that whole period together, creating a direction for my art that privileged colour and carnival in what were to be the most vital, optimistic and exciting years of my life in art.

I read about Van Gogh, and, like Derrick, was drawn to him. I became acquainted with Impressionism, particularly the work of Monet, Cézanne, Seurat and Pissarro. I was introduced, too, to the writing of Ernest Hemingway and to Thor Heyerdahl's *Kon Tiki*, about his epic voyage by raft from South America to Polynesia. Derrick gave me a copy of the book, which I devoured, living through every moment on the raft as it battled against the elements. There was Irving Stone's *The Agony and the Ecstasy*, a fictional life of Michelangelo, which gave me some sense of the life of a great artist, his frustrations and successes. I felt his drive to complete the Sistine Chapel ceiling, his pride in the powerful sculpted figure of Moses. It was the dawning of a whole new age for me, a time of real growth.

Mulling over cups of coffee in the Italian café while Derrick eyed women for possible pick-ups, I learnt, through scraps of conversation, of the Moulin Rouge cinema in Headington, about half a mile from the School of Art. Moulin Rouge screened the finest films by the most exciting directors, from Fellini to Goddard. I was advised to see *The Horse's Mouth*, which featured the work of John Bratby, an important contemporary British painter, and was about an artist who lived in difficult circumstances. I was impressed by the colour and vibrancy of Bratby's work, the strength of the story and the acting of Alec Guinness, who played him.

Then there was the Brazilian film *Black Orpheus*. The simple love story was in itself of little interest, but the power and colour of the Rio de Janeiro carnival, which acted as a back-drop to the film, was utterly gripping. The dynamic festival, its music and energy caught my imagination and inspired my art. Besides the energy, colour and rhythm of the movie, I was struck by the casting. This was the first film with an all-black cast I had ever seen, the first time I had seen black people had portrayed in normal roles. It opened my eyes to what was possible, and demonstrated that we could create our own compelling and magical cinema. *Black Orpheus*, along with the achievements and dazzling skills of Brazilian football, created a fantasy of Brazilian life that has stayed with me to this day.

In 1963 I painted a piece on an off-cut of glossy black bath-room hardboard. The material seemed utterly wrong for making a painting, but I was desperate and there was nothing else to use. I worked without sketches, constructing the image as I went along: people at a market stall in the Caribbean buying fruit and vegetables at twilight. The painting, which was made within a couple of weeks, represented one of those extraordinary spurts in my artistic development, an unexpected leap in intuition and skill. After months and years of painting similar scenes which showed promise but lacked resolution, this one was the fruition of all my hard labour, challenges and tribulations. The black background invested the piece with a charm unlike anything I had painted before, the colours soft and whispering, the tones translucent against the dark surface. Free of modernist theories, I just painted as my soul dictated, making statements about the Caribbean without artifice or pretence. It was a pure and direct response to a moment of sheer inspiration, a piece in which Corot's example held sway. It remains a work of which I have fond memories, one which suggests that my achievements today, given how far I had travelled at its completion, fall short of my potential.

Derrick saw the painting and liked it. He told an Italian friend called Pietro about my work, and Pietro came round to view it. Without any hesitation he offered to buy it from me for ten pounds, which I accepted. It was the first picture I ever sold. On reflection it was worth a great deal more, but I was happy to sell my first piece, just like a professional artist. That experience lifted my confidence enormously. I knew this was the type of work I wanted to make.

That was probably the happiest I have ever been as an artist. But it was a fool's paradise. A great deal was being made of my art, and I saw myself in the mould of a Gauguin or Toulouse-Lautrec, living a bohemian life, producing work not too distant in style from them and going on to become a successful artist. I hadn't heard of the modern movement, I knew nothing about Expressionism, Jackson Pollock or Max Ernst. My world as an artist was bounded by the influence of my two strong friends and the narrow life I had forged for myself in that artistic community in Oxford. My introduction to the wider world and the surprises it offered was to prove shocking and, from the point of view of my art, almost fatally disruptive in later years. There was no concern for my blackness and the very particular experience I had had as a black person. In making carnival paintings at home I was trying to come to terms with that in my own way: I had an agenda, but there was no support from the wider community. By fixing my art-making so firmly in Impressionism, I was sowing the seeds of difficulties that would erupt as distort my work in the future. The twin issues of style and content were therefore to raise their heads in subsequent years.

In 1963 the West Indies cricket team came to Britain to play England in a five-test series. They were captained by the great Barbadian batsman Frank Worrell, a member of the famous West Indies triumvirate of Weekes, Clyde Walcott and Worrell, the 'Three Ws'. He was in the twilight of his career – Weekes and Walcott had retired – but in those matches his brilliant captaincy shone through, burying for ever the myth that black people 'didn't have what it takes' for leadership. There had never been a black captain of the West Indies before, and we had always been made to feel that leadership was for white people.

During the series, people walked around with wireless sets held to their ears. Bus conductors and even the growing number of black bus drivers followed the games on transistors tucked in a pocket, or sitting on a dashboard. Factory workers listened as they worked, people in offices found creative ways of tuning in. Friends whom you might not have seen for a while, instead of sharing a word of greeting on meeting you, gestured a hello without breaking their concentration on the game. This was cricket and the West Indies were doing well against England. It was a sort of coming of age, not just for Worrell but of everything we believed in popular culture. It made us feel tall and good about ourselves.

The voice everyone wanted to hear was that of John Arlott. Some people seem born to occupy a particular position in life. I think of the blacksmith whose tunic, worn to shape by years of tending horses, is burnished and polished by wear. In other clothes, such as a three-piece suit, he looks awkward and clumsy, unlike the city type whose frame seems shaped for it. John Arlott, likewise, seemed born to cricket commentary. Through him we grew to appreciate the power of language, the poetry in stroke-play. Though few of us had read the great poets or were acquainted with the world of verse, Arlott's commentary touched the poet in us all. His descriptions gave form to play, by investing the arena with a magical and absorbing poetry. The timing of his comments, his ability to sum up a flurry of actions in a choice phrase, his eye for the unusual, brought to cricket commentary a dimension which made a temple of the stadium and gods of the players.

Cricket was a constant topic, not just on the playing field but in homes, church halls and elsewhere. I remember Darcy Brathwaite, a family friend, giving an extraordinarily colourful and humorous account of a Gary Sobers cover-drive. It was one of those impromptu situations where people seem to gather instinctively, and took place one Sunday afternoon in our home. We were in the back living-room. The occasion, as always with West Indians, was hot and impassioned, each person arguing their point with uncompromising forcefulness and with utter confidence in their own accuracy and knowledge. We were comparing the relative merits of Frankie Worrell, Everton Weekes and other West Indian cricketing immortals. Conversation settled on the quality of stroke-play. Some praised the relative strengths of their particular hero, the power of shot, timing or beauty of execution. Darcy argued the case for Gary Sobers's timing and footwork. When he described that cover-drive, he was speaking to an audience of my family and friends. The living-room was full – if not to bursting, certainly to a point where there was moment and conviviality of spirit. One after the other people spoke in favour of their own hero or praised a particular detail of play.

Darcy argued for Sobers's genius when batting: 'And believe me, Truman put one down like grease lightning and it reared up just short of a length outside de off stump and almost cut Gary throat.' By now Darcy had had a few slugs of Mount Gay rum; his eyes were bloodshot, his gaze intense, without even the shadow of a smile. 'Zip! De ball went straight through to de wicket-keeper. Gary watched it, man.' Darcy, his brow knitted, stared at Gerald's feet, where the imaginary ball had pitched. Someone tried to intervene, but was immediately silenced with a 'Wait, na man!' Darcy went on, 'And now he decide he gun teach Truman a lesson. Next ball Truman pitched it a bit fuller outside de off stump, and Gary walked down de wicket' – Darcy hitched up his baggy trousers and, with a mincing gait, his legs bent and tightly locked at the knees, proceeded to imitate the walk, using tiny shuffling steps. Coming to a rapid halt, 'Prax!' he shouted, while essaying a drive to the off side with a sharp flick of his left hand in recognition of Sobers's left-handedness. 'The ball went through de covers like a bullet; not a man move.' Pulling out of his crouched stance, Darcy was like a man possessed, his face expressing deadly earnestness as his gaze engaged everyone in the room. There was nothing in his manner to suggest that this description was anything but an awesome truth, rather than the fantasy it clearly was. While Darcy kept the intense expression of someone spoiling for a fight, rather than giving a description of cricketing genius, everyone fell about laughing. His demeanour, seriousness of expression, and most of all, impromptu 'dance' down the wicket, were a picture of inventiveness, humour and wit. Such moments brought us together as a community. They were beyond the reach of the English because they dug deep into our way of sharing experience. At times like that I lived as fully and richly as I did anywhere, because I could interpret every nuance of meaning in the fiction, appreciate the performance of impromptu Caribbean theatre.

This excitement about the West Indies team spilt over into local cricket. Many Caribbean men played; on coming to Britain, cricket fans often joined or tried to join local cricket clubs. In Oxford, several turned out for their works teams, playing for the Post Office, Pressed Steel, Morris's two local car factories, the Co-op and other firms. They punished English players not used to their fine technique. I remember Frank Francis, Ozzie Moore, Laker and many others as being especially good.

Each Saturday and Sunday afternoon, West Indians flocked to support 'the boys' as they went about the business of flaying the English bowling. The West Indian crowds brought their own bonhomie, cultural ethos and sense of fun. There were constant shouts to 'our man' to do this or that to the opposition, instructions on how to improve technique, and uninhibited celebrations of 'West Indian' performances. Most of all there was humour. Unlike the English, who focused on every delivery, the West Indian crowd brought a sense of moment to the game, recounting stories of past greats and giving an in-depth analysis of what each player was doing and how he could best improve his performance. Through cricket, connections were made and bonds were forged between local people and West Indian settlers.

President Kennedy's assassination on 22 November 1963 shocked the Oxford Caribbean community. We were all devastated. Not only was he much loved but he was regarded as a beacon of hope for black people in the United States and elsewhere. He captured the imagination by his oratorical skill, his apparent empathy with the plight of black people and obvious charisma. His charm communicated itself to black and white alike. My mother cried a lot. My father looked grim. My brothers and I were upset, confused and fearful. As the news filtered through that he had died we sat round our television, totally disbelieving. We watched the news with a keen hope for some semblance of sense in the madness, but none was forthcoming. When we saw the pictures of the procession and the figure of the president jolted by the bullets, we were alarmed and distressed. The image of Jacqueline Kennedy cradling the body of her dying husband was a painful moment; the grassy knoll became a place of infamy.

Gerald sought self-expression in sport, his interest in physical culture having started with our gymnastics on the streets of Bridgetown. At school in Barbados he grew interested in fast bowling and the high jump, becoming proficient at the straddle and the western roll; he also enjoyed sprinting. When we moved to Britain, to Annersley Road, he took up boxing and would shadow-box in the house, posing in front of the mirror, often punching a phantom opponent while making hissing sounds with each 'blow'. He looked the part in his boxing shorts and boots, and my father was keen to see him in the ring, being a great fan of the fight-game. He had good style and technique and looked every bit the boxer (Fig. 12).

My mother, though, became more and more concerned that he might take up boxing as a career, and possibly get hurt. When conversation turned to boxing, as it often did, she talked about the awful things that had happened to fighters.

We had heard of boxers being killed in the ring, and just about every fighter was scarred and marked by the trade.

Fig. 12 Gerald, every inch a boxer, photographed with my Box Brownie camera

There were gloves in the house, probably lent by the gym, usually badly worn and showing lengths of fibre at the seams. We played around with them, but I couldn't tolerate being hit, particularly in the face, so our games lacked real commitment. Gerald had a friend called Ruddy Vaughan, who became a heavyweight contender and boxed on television against one of the leading British fighters, but was knocked out. I remember thinking, when he came to our home some time after the fight, 'I saw him on television.' But Gerald lost interest in boxing on seeing close up what the game can do to a fighter's physical appearance. He cared a lot about his looks and couldn't bear the thought of having his nose flattened, his brows scarred.

Gerald continued to experiment with various sports in an attempt to find himself. Before long, he turned to long-distance cycling, racing groups of friends around the Oxfordshire countryside and as far afield as Reading, more than thirty miles away. Inner tubes, chrome wheels and puncture-repair kits had to be negotiated in various parts of the house. Most of us preferred the option and quietly delighted in his new interest.

By the time we moved to Fern Hill Road, he had started focusing on body-building. Each morning he went into the garden to train. The garden gym was his palette, each exercise a colour. Out there, he was transformed: no comic but a man in 'the zone' and focused on the one activity that represented who he was. Hendie, in particular, a friend from nearby, was a regular visitor. There was the hissing sound of intakes of air, and straining as they pressed, jerked and snatched, eyes staring, veins swollen on forehead and forearm. In between sets they walked around, arms held at odd angles to their bodies, like birds cooling themselves in midday heat, their wings lifted to allow air to circulate round them.

Gerald eventually became very large indeed. He trained with Wally Hammond, an Oxford-based England weight-lifting trainer who ran an optician's shop next to the College of Further Education – and who supplied my first pair of glasses. I learnt about pectorals and biceps, triceps and the solar plexus.

Meanwhile, my studies at the College of Further Education were going well, too. I was working alongside boys and girls from Oxford and the surrounding districts who had in some cases left grammar school to take their GCEs there. The vast majority, however, were able former secondary-modern students who had gone there to gain qualifications. One day while we were in the gym a youth came in and sat at the back of the hall on a box. Word soon got around that he was an Etonian. He was the first person of about my age with whom I had a measure of contact who had purportedly benefited from all that Eton had to offer. Given my ambition and drive to succeed academically, I was mesmerised by him, couldn't help thinking of all the privileges he had enjoyed. He was, by his educational background, a rare bird, a member of a select group that had mysteriously flown in among us.

Other people used the gym, too, people with a greater call on our admiration, though that didn't occur to me at the time. Oxford United football team trained there that winter. I remember Ron Atkinson and his brother Graham, who both played in the first team. The club had access to the gym for a few hours in the week, and my fellow students and I peered in through the gym doors to watch them play five-a-side and go through their fitness routine. We were all impressed by them because they were famous in the city and soon to enter the football league. I saw the occasional game at the Manor Ground. Two games stood out in particular, one against Preston North End in the cup and the other against Leicester City. It was quite impressive being that close to famous people who were talked about, had their photographs in the newspapers and were seen on television.

Gerald bought a cheap electric guitar and an amplifier, and we started playing together. My parents allowed us to use the front room, because it was the only free space in the house, and because the radiogram was there and we needed it for playing the records we copied. Most evenings the house rang with music. Gerald and I listened to blues, pieces by Howlin' Wolf, Muddy Waters, Sonny Boy Williamson and others. We got a firm feel for the music, and could appreciate its texture and mood, the rawness of Muddy Waters and the rasping tones of Howlin' Wolf. From our experience of black people in the Caribbean, we could identify with Williamson's timbre and mood, the way he stretched, smeared or grunted his words, the feeling he conveyed through his voice. This might have been a different culture, and indeed a different music, but the fundamentals sprang from a common source: we knew where they were coming from.

We also listened to R&B artists such as Chubby Checker, Bo Diddley and Chuck Berry. However, the first piece we played reasonably successfully was Fats Domino's slow and easy-to-follow 'Blueberry Hill'. I shall never forget the excitement at turning a few chords in harmony. We fought to stop ourselves breaking into idiotic grins as we tapped out a 4/4 rhythm with our feet and hummed the melody. We played 45rpm records of the music on the gramophone, going over sections over and over again until we understood how they were pieced together, how the chord sequences worked. Then we tried to reproduce the sound as faithfully as we could. My father occasionally joined in, humming and giving advice, though he wasn't really into blues as a genre. But we respected his understanding of musical notation if not of the beat and rhythmic patterns of contemporary popular songs. We were fortunate in having parents who showed the flexibility of mind to create a context that allowed our interest to flourish.

Our success with 'Blueberry Hill' and other straightforward tunes encouraged me to study a wider range of piano chords. I practised in my spare moments and before long could play a number of majors, minors and sevenths and diminished sevenths. I longed to develop the skill to play more demanding but subtle chords, but knew that was beyond the requirements of the music I was playing. Over the next few months we became more competent. Then Bob Reid, a friend of Gerald's, became involved. He was interested in playing bass and bought himself an electric bass guitar. That was lucky, as we needed someone to hold the bass line. It took a while for Bob to settle into the rhythm of our music: he had to learn his new instrument. Within a few weeks the sound was becoming fuller with the introduction of the bass. As Bob gained in confidence and skill, the three of us began to form something of a unit. But we realised that the small confines of a front room didn't allow the music to breathe.

The idea of forming a proper group arose. We needed a drummer and a vocalist to complete the unit. Before we found a singer we acquired George Applewhite, who played the saxophone. George could sightread. Though lacking in experience as a musician, he was worldly wise and could turn a tune reasonably well. The Carib Six was being formed and we were even beginning to think of putting our wares in a shop window.

Within a few months we had our first gigs; sessions in pubs, at a party at the Cowley Shopping Centre and a few in youth clubs. We were well received by the Caribbean crowds, who didn't have another band to support which played the kind of music we did. I didn't have a portable piano and was dependent on an in-house instrument for these gigs – some of them were poorly maintained, not to mention out of tune.

We didn't have the right microphones for amplification and so my contribution was wasted. To make myself heard, I thumped the keys with such force that my fingers and thumbs were very sore indeed.

It was clear that, if we were to create a viable rhythm section with a keyboard component, I would have to acquire a portable piano. Daddy generously bought me an electric piano and an amplifier. This was a huge step in the right direction. For the first time my music could be heard and I could contribute meaningfully to the band.

In 1964 I applied, as planned, to Oxford School of Art for a place on the full-time art course. I was called to interview and met the principal and other members of staff whom I had seen in the buildings. I was informed that, since my last application a year earlier, the whole nature of art and design, education had changed from a National Diploma in Design (or NDD) to the Diploma in Art and Design or DipAD, which had degree status. Therefore, I was told, I needed a minimum of five GCEs or the equivalent to be considered for acceptance. I was disappointed at not being able to start the course but was generally philosophical about the whole thing, realising that I was broadening my educational background after a particularly fallow period in my education. Though I had worked hard from the outset, the situation now was such that I would have to work even harder to get started on the art course I wanted. But the prospect of studying for a degree was a huge motivator; the fact that I wasn't told that it was beyond me to obtain the qualifications. I never seriously thought that one day I would be considered for a degree, the ultimate academic recognition, which seemed destined for others from different backgrounds and educational environments. A degree was something too fabulous and special for me. I needed a mentor, someone who could say, 'Yes, you can do it,' but there was no one, no one to provide the clarity I needed. I cannot remember discussing it with Derrick or Lawrence. So caught up in their own lives were they that conversations about personal issues like this simply did not arise. My family had no way of measuring what was required for a degree, couldn't clearly indicate how far I was along the road to acceptance or compliance in respect of qualifications. As a pioneer within the family, I had to make these discoveries for myself, find out what a degree qualification was about and even what was required to succeed on GCE courses.

That year, at the age of 18, I took my GCEs and gained the qualifications I needed to enter the school of art. My father picked me up in town in his car and told me the results; he had opened my letter to read how I had done. I was enraged but remained silent. There was no way of challenging his action; he was beyond reproach. To this day, though, I still fiercely resent the arrogance of that deed, the insensitivity and sheer bloody-mindedness. That letter was arguably the most important one I had ever received in my life, taking into account its implications for my future, but my father was in there reading it first.

I had organized myself at college to do GCEs, had made arrangements to study at the school of art with the helpful advice of Mrs Morgan, was beginning to learn how to operate moderately effectively in a whole new world, one which my family were not party to, least of all my father, but when important letters came to my home from that world, he pulled rank and read my mail. I felt humiliated and deeply angry. I knew it was time to move on.

In September I returned to the college of further education, to discuss a few matters with Mrs Morgan. During our conversation she indicated that I had got more from the college than any other student. I appreciated what she said, but smiled quietly to myself, thinking that she didn't know the full story. The educational system had created me in a mould designed for black pupils, and they were astonished to find that I didn't fit the stereotype. I couldn't help thinking that we construct fictions about each other which can do permanent damage to the chances of many. Fortunately, I survived the negative experience and kept my focus. Once again I applied to the School of Art to do a foundation year, which I hoped would lead to a Diploma in Art and Design. I was interviewed by Mr Grimshaw and other staff, and offered a place. I felt as though I was walking on air. It was quite an honour being the first member of my family to take a degree, something I had once thought would never happen. I would take the opportunity with both hands and give it my very best shot.

That autumn I duly enrolled at the school, and started work in earnest under the guidance and supervision of Len McComb, without doubt the finest teacher I have ever known – of any subject. I had applied for a grant and got a full one. For the first time in my life I had real money in my pockets. Being selfish, and being used to taking from my parents, I didn't think to offer them anything for my upkeep, I had never had to do that before, and they didn't ask me to. It was a stupid and mean of me.

I worked from the model, made prints, sculpted, poured liquid bronze into clay moulds and stitched designs into textiles. I prepared lithographic stones to an unblemished perfection and glass-like smoothness, polishing the rock for hours under running water. Then I tried my hand at lithographic work, thinking of Toulouse-Lautrec's delicate creations for the Parisian theatre. By such exposure to traditional crafts, I developed a taste for texture and line that shouldn't be compromised by working with inferior materials. I made etchings on steel, zinc and copper plates, and engaged in other crafts and art and design skills. It was a rich and broad-based experience, which created a strong and informative foundation for my studies in later years. It was without doubt the most enriching and purposeful year in my career at art college.

Toward the end of the year Len McComb asked me to take care of a life-sized clay figure he was making in his home. I went round to his house and he stripped the piece of its moist coverings and the plastic sheets that shrouded it. I cannot forget the shock I experienced on seeing the nude form of a woman I recognised from college. Len showed me how the clay was to be kept moist by the application of damp cloths, which were then to be covered by the plastic sheets. I was greatly uplifted by the trust Len placed in me. He could have asked any student and they would have gladly looked after the piece for him, but he asked me. The sculpture, of Nicolette, which was later cast in bronze, led to others of similar strength, sharp observation and delicate sensitivity. In that piece, his uncompromising attitude and focus on the truth embodied in his subject echoed the talks he gave in college. Len's acclaimed *Gold Man*, which followed, is based on a man who worked at the college. It stands proudly today in

Tate Gallery Britain, recognised by many as one of the finest British sculptures of the twentieth century. In later life, Len won first prize in the summer show at the Royal Academy. He became a leading academician and was ultimately appointed Keeper of the Royal Academy. His watercolours, oils and prints are sought after throughout the art world, and his sculptures sit in many important museums and private collections.

Len has the ability to peel away superficialities and delve deeply into a subject to understand it better. He spoke lovingly of Cézanne, the way he used colour, his distortions of the picture plane, his compositional sense. Len's words caressed the piece and brought clarity to it; they sparkled. I remember him talking, during a drawing lesson, about the underlying structure of a goat's skull. He was trying to get us to explore structure and form, to move away from mere superficial, external representation. He held the skull and pointed to details in its structure with a pencil, tracing over the surface lines of tension which depicted its nature, lines which retained the energy of the skull. That word 'energy' was central to his vocabulary. Initially I couldn't quite grasp his meaning, but over time it became clear. This probing and stripping away, this uncompromising search for truth, was the hallmark of his style and the lasting gift he bequeathed to all his students. In his hands a skull or a shell became an object of intense beauty, something one had to scrutinise in a wholly new manner.

Len regularly read from Van Gogh's letters, about his relationship with Theo, the dreadful incident near the Yellow House when he cut off a piece of his ear, his incarceration in a mental asylum. But more often the everyday letters in which Van Gogh described the process of making work and his uplifting experiences when painting a landscapes, a still life, a prostitute or any other subject. I shall always remember Len, this tall, gentle man, seemingly locked into an other-worldly zone of concentration and intensity of understanding, his round glasses sitting on the bridge of his nose as he walked back and forth in the studio, the students quietly listening to his every word as he read.

He was like a preacher reading a sermon from a pulpit, bringing us into the light, sharing the artist's words, so totally caught up in the quest for truth that his words burnt with a fierce intensity. One felt welcome into a shrine, a special and privileged place to be as an artist. Each word he uttered seemed to burrow under the layers of Van Gogh's vision. Through Len's respect for his profession, for the world, for the commonplace and everyday, the possibilities he saw in every object, one appreciated the special gift of the artist and the barriers we have to break through to make work of any real quality, for what he spoke about was enormously challenging. That peeling away and constant reflection required a total and intense commitment. There could be no compromise.

When I entered the School of Art I was confident and totally self-believing as an artist. I had a good reputation at the college, and it seemed the world would open out for me as a painter. But my education in art was narrow, focusing on movements in Western art from the Renaissance to the Impressionists. I had little appreciation of what was going on in the contemporary art and design world. Hockney and Picasso, for example, didn't exist for me. Instead, at home I continued to make work based on my memories of the Caribbean, pieces intended to speak of my broader experience.

Nothing could have been better than making work at home in my shared bedroom. This was a magical world, cut off from the rest of the art environments to which I had grown accustomed. I created paintings which spoke for me without worrying about modernism or breaking new ground. I merely painted for the love of painting, so as to experience again a life long since lost to me. It was the time when I was happiest making art work. The skills I acquired at art college further enhanced this. It was wonderfully fulfilling and totally absorbing.

Meanwhile, the band which we had named The Carib Six was going from strength to strength. Encouraged by the reception we met with at most venues, we practised regularly and developed a reasonable if not particularly original sound. We bought ourselves suits – just about every respectable band, from the Platters to the Beatles, wore suits on stage. Ours were made from an attractive grey fabric with a stagy black stripe down the outside of each trouser-leg. We improved the quality of our amplification by investing in

Marshall equipment, and bought extension speakers. By now there were six of us: Gerald, rhythm guitar; myself, electric piano; Bob Reid, bass; George Applewhite, lead saxophone; Kenrick Davies, second saxophone; and Roger Constant on drums (Fig 11).

Fig. 11 The Carib Six; I'm at the extreme right, playing the piano

We also picked up a crooner, who was the inheritor of an awful ego and massive self-belief but very limited ability. He had a girl friend who was bewitched by him and seemed prepared to follow him into the jaws of hell. They spent a lot of time in bed together, and we sometimes had to go round to his place and drag him out of bed for rehearsals. To my mind he was the male organ personified, with his skinny frame, leaning demeanour and highly charged libido. His partner, a pale, thin woman with long, dank brown hair, was difficult to communicate with. She blanked out the rest of the band and communicated only with her partner. I can't remember hearing her speak once. When he was on stage she sat alone and feasted her eyes on him.

The fellow warbled all over the place. 'Harbour Lights' was his favourite piece but he mangled it badly, making the band cringe and the audience melt away. He couldn't hit the top notes and was always way off key. The band couldn't move forward with him and he had to go.

He did leave the band and disappeared off the scene altogether. We then started working with a guy called Wally, an irritable and moody man, and a weightlifter. He had a reasonable voice but spent much of his time looking angry or at best annoyed with the band, in rehearsals and at times on stage. However, he brought a greater force to the group by his better singing and firm presence. We began to have a real impact in Oxford and elsewhere.

My father was appointed manager of the group, as we needed someone to deal with bookings and that side of our business. Before long we were playing in Slough, High Wycombe, Wolverhampton and elsewhere. We did gigs in Oxford town hall and even in London, at the 100 Club and other venues.

We also played at the university. The experience should have been special but it wasn't, because of their lack of coordination and withitness. When dancing, most of them hardly knew where to put their feet and looked generally oafish and out of touch. Far from inspiring us to great heights, we felt demoralised by the lack of interaction and emotional response to our music. The group was deflated after gigs at the university by the obvious lack of appreciation of our rhythms and skills: we were just the band supplying the party music.

Much of the time the students kept themselves at some distance from us; few if any came up to ask about the music. Instead they talked among themselves, and one or two danced in their stiff, clumsy way from time to time. There was never a rush to the floor when we played our best numbers, though they often drove people to heights of excitement in other places. This was a different world indeed, one in which we felt like intruders. The behaviour of the undergraduates, their closed world and remoteness from us, the lack of eye contact or conversation with the band, highlighted that gap. Their behaviour and sense of fun were very different from ours. Whereas in Cowley there was informality, in the university there was formality. There was an obvious disinclination on the part of most students to relax and 'chill out'. It was hard work playing for that lot.

West Indian gigs at the town hall were extraordinary occasions. People of all types attended: women in lacy trimmings, others in hot-pants, some in trouser-suits; lads from the Cowley boozers with pub-crawling white women who sought their fun in the company of black men, and who were often as excluded from white society as the black men who courted them. Youths in dark shades and sharp suits, eager for a bit of fun on a Saturday night roamed the hall, many looking the part of city slickers but in reality bored in a comparatively docile city which couldn't provide the challenge they needed to test their mettle. Curried goat was freely available, and the bar sold Mount Gay Barbados rum, Scotch, bottled beer and Coke. During the interval the audience danced to a Jamaican sound system with its attendant giant speakers and overpowering sound; the music was by Prince Buster and Fats Domino, Jimmy Cliff and Brook Benton. Such dances, as everywhere where young people congregate, were pick-up points for dates. There were lots of young men standing around in dark glasses and holding cans of beer, hoping for a sensual liaison.

The personnel of the band changed very little, but new members joined us from time to time. Our reputation spread as people from a wide area heard us and spread the word about us. Three women joined us as a vocal group and one of them – Jascinta Limerick – and Gerald later married. V, a talented Jamaican musician, smoked weed before going on stage and would proceed to play with fire and passion but not in time with the rest of the band. We admired his solo work, but were exasperated by his lack of timing. I wondered what it was in a spliff that elevated the spirit in the way that was apparent in his playing. His playing was truly impassioned – his face beaming with intensity, his brow lathered with sweat, his eyes bloodshot with ganja. He was truly a character.

Bob drove us to gigs in a Ford Transit. I remember the cold nights travelling in the back of the van, the steamed-up windows and occasional smutty jokes. I feared accidents but fortunately we never had one. Bob was a good driver, and one felt safe with him. But there was the danger of coming off the road in winter when driving on black ice or frosty surfaces. Comfort was minimal: there was seating at the front only, and we took it in turns to ride next to Bob. Those in the back sat on amplifiers or were squashed up between drum kits, my electric piano, the large speakers and other kit. It was the lot of the small band on the road.

We had some extraordinary experiences. At the American airbase at Upper Heyford we ate massive steaks and paid for our food with American currency. It was strange playing R&B to the very people who had invented it. Initially we were tentative but the audiences were generous in their praise and treated us with the utmost respect and courtesy. Those gigs were strangely proper and decent, with no rudeness or improper behaviour on the part of the audiences, the band or its hangers-on. Inevitably other people came along as helpers and roadies to gigs which were a magnet for many Oxford West Indians.

One particularly notable gig was at a large club in Wolverhampton. We played to a packed audience, without doubt one of the most packed I have ever played to, and the atmosphere was electric. There must have been at least five hundred people in a space which could only comfortably hold about three hundred, and there were still more queuing to get in. We were inspired and developed a good rapport with the crowd. But the majority of them were smoking ganja. The air was thick with its acrid smell; you could cut it with the proverbial knife. Then, late in the evening, the police arrived in force. The band was playing and we could see everything from our high perch on the stage, which allowed us an uninterrupted, if hazy, view to the main entrance at the back of the hall. When the police arrived, I thumped my piano with my eyes popping out of my head, wondering what the hell would happen next. But the police gathered at the back of the hall, took one look at the scene, turned on their heels and walked out. I couldn't believe it. I expected the police to take action each time there was clear evidence of criminal activity, but that night the sheer numbers must have made it impossible to do anything. Astonishingly, the people in the hall hadn't seemed to care about the police's arrival, and carried on smoking weed as if nothing had happened.

Another memorable but almost fatal event took place at a club on the Cowley Road. One Saturday night while we were on stage, a row broke out between two guys on the club's main staircase, and in the ensuing mêlée one slashed the other, from shoulder to shoulder, across the chest. As always, the band kept playing, but during the interval we peeped into the hallway to see what the trouble was about and were met with a sight of apparent carnage. There was blood everywhere: on the walls, the staircase and the landing. Never in my life had I seen so much human blood. The injured man, Na Teet – so named because his front teeth were missing – was taken away swiftly by ambulance; happily, after lengthy rehabilitation he recovered.

At a gig at a dance hall in Reading I saw a woman sexually manhandled. While two men danced with her, one in front, the other behind her, and both pressing tightly against her, another character got down on his knees behind the man dancing behind the woman, thrust his hands between the man's legs and up the woman's mini-skirt, presumably fondling or even penetrating her genitals. I was so shocked by the incident that I made a painting of it, called *Dance at Reading* (Plate 3).

Most evenings I spent painting in my shared bedroom. I placed prepared boards on a chair beneath the window and worked. I had by then acquired an old mains radio on which I listened to the Third Programme. Working in front of a board, brushes and palette in hand, I was transported into a different world, one where I couldn't be touched by anybody, but sadly one in which my family played only a tiny part, with the exception of my mother, who kept a distant and discreet vigil over my right to practise my art. There were endless cups of tea and buttered teacakes and sometimes, in momentary pauses to take in the development in a work, a few scraps of conversation. Mama had a special insight and sensitivity to our needs from which we all benefited. I only wish we had found the capacity to reciprocate.

I was confident and felt capable of achieving almost anything in art and design. My life was on a very different trajectory from those of my brothers and other relatives. I was reading texts that no one else in the family had even heard of, and, more importantly, my art had taken me into areas unknown to them. My work on the foundation course was progressing well, and people made a great deal of me. Lawrence's and

Derrick's influence was also significant. They pointed me in the direction of literature and of exhibitions which greatly enhanced my understanding of art practice.

My first visits to the Ashmolean Museum, for example, came about as a result of city-centre café conversations with them. I saw Uccello's work and drawings by Raphael of staggering quality. Canvases by lesser-known artists also attracted my interest because they were far superior to anything I had seen before. My appreciation of how light could be rendered with paint, in the sky, say, or on the shimmering surface of a pool, or how the softness of skin could be conveyed in portraiture, was increased by that exposure.

In my bedroom studio I created a world that was empowering, a world in which I was very happy. I made carnival paintings on hardboard. One was so large that it had to be made in two separate pieces. When working on it I often played steel-band music from Trinidad, which helped create the ethos of the work. My drawing was good and my use of colour heavily influenced by the Impressionists; the work was vivid and full of energy. I never made preparatory drawings but allowed the visual narrative to emerge as the work developed. This process was not dissimilar to improvised riffs in jazz or blues. On the hardboard I created a world which referenced places I had never seen but which were clearly Caribbean. My observations of dancers at gigs provided a wealth of material and ideas. I merely placed them in different contexts. I observed the way people moved, the arching of the back and twisting of the body as they danced, and fed this research into my paintings. Almost all my carnival paintings are constructed from above, allowing a clear view of the revellers and the patterns created by people at Mas' (Masquerade).

The time was rapidly approaching when I would have to leave home. I was doing well on the foundation course but the Oxford School of Art hadn't yet been granted a licence to award degrees in fine art, so I would have to study elsewhere. I found it difficult to accept the fact of my departure from my mother, and those elements of home life that I held dear. But I had to go, and she, like other members of the family, would have it no other way.

In spring 1965 I applied to Chelsea School of Art, with Kingston as my second choice. I opted for them because, with the Carib Six uppermost in my mind, I wanted to be as close as possible to Oxford, and they were the closest to offer the Diploma in Art and Design (which had degree status and was the precursor of today's fine art BA). The piano was central to the rhythm section and there wasn't anyone else available to play it. Gerald greatly enjoyed playing and I was close to the other guys in the group. The last thing I wanted was to do something which would lead to the collapse of the band.

Round about this time Derrick's mother died. She was a quiet, self-effacing lady who did her utmost not to cause offence. Whenever I went to their home she welcomed me cordially, but soon found a reason to leave me with her son: they lived in the same house but led wholly separate lives. She had seen service in India with her husband, and there was an echo of the past in the fine objects with which she surrounded herself: exquisite china, silver photograph frames, books in fine bindings, Victorian vases and so on. Despite the dust, the feel was one of character and refined quality.

Theirs was a strange relationship, but it was clear that Derrick was deeply affected by her death. I saw him in tears for the first time. Because of the way he and his mother had lived, there was no one but Derrick and me at the funeral (Lawrence, who didn't know Mrs G. well, also appeared but kept a discreet distance from the ceremony): Derrick, myself, his mother's coffin and of course a priest, in a church in Cowley. It was a distressingly brief service. The priest was a gaunt man with tobacco-stained teeth. He rattled through the reading as if each word was a hot potato that couldn't be allowed to settle in the mouth. There was no compassion, and no eye-contact with Derrick or me. It was as if the woman being buried was a pauper, a nobody whom the state wanted to be rid of with as little ceremony as possible. Throughout this fiasco, Derrick stared at the man, his expression betraying a cold loathing.

Derrick was appreciative of my presence, and not only said so but gave me a bronze statuette as a way of showing his thanks. It remains one of my most prized possessions.

If television and the movies failed to represent black people in an acceptable manner, in the arena of sport we were confident and assertive. Within our family, we knew little about the finer rules of football, but could appreciate the brilliance of Pele, enjoying his skills whenever he played for Brazil. He was a great black icon. Gerald became very animated when the Brazilians played, even though he wasn't a football fan, whooping with delight each time a black Brazilian, especially Pele, touched the ball. Garincha's bandy legs and Pele's bulging eyes led to outrageous comments in celebration of our favourites, the fantastic, largely black, world-beating Brazilians. Those in the team who were not obviously black were regarded as having the 'blood' of colour, Gerald swearing blind that every Brazilian was partly African, meaning they had African ancestry. Despite this adulation, cricket, a game we were all brought up on and understood, gave us a greater sense of what we could achieve as a people. We were nurtured on the game, lived inside its aesthetic, felt the pulse of its rhythm on the field, on the wireless, and more recently on television.

Boxing, like cricket, was a sport in which we invested a great deal of pride and self-esteem. We were weaned on accounts of Joe Louis's greatness. My father told us of his bouts with Max Schmelling, lacing the accounts with references to Germany's racism and the requirement by every black person that Louis should 'do the business' and knock the man out. Heavyweight boxing for us was the domain of black gods: brilliant, fearless athletes who dominated by their superior ring-craft, strength and determination.

During my time in Oxford, we often woke in the early hours on many occasions for the broadcast of a big fight in the USA. There would be a cup of tea or cocoa with crackers and cheese as we huddled round a paraffin heater. We listened to the pre-fight comments with keen interest. When a BBC commentator predicted what for us would be an unsatisfactory result, there would be a storm of abuse, my mother showing her annoyance in every gesture, screwing up her face, sucking her teeth, pouting and generally looking miserable. The rest of us argued with no one except our hero's hated foe, encapsulated in a squat radio smelling of warm valves and ancient wiring. We were psyching ourselves up for the bout, finding ways of giving vent to our excitement.

When the fighters came into the ring and were introduced by the MC, the tension was almost unbearable, some of us fidgeting and showing our nervousness by frequent trips to the loo and irritation with each other. When 'our man' was hit and rocked, you measured the degree to which he was hurt by the reaction of the crowd and the words of the commentator. When the person we supported scored a knock-down or rocked his opponent in turn, we cheered and celebrated without inhibition, some leaping to their feet, grinning from ear to ear and whipping their fingers, characteristic of the 'licks' gesture popular among Caribbean people. And if our boxer won, as he usually did, we cheered and leapt about, smiles breaking out all over our faces with joy.

It was in this mode that we listened to the fight between Cassius Clay (as Muhammad Ali was then called) and Henry Cooper in May 1966. I had travelled to Oxford that weekend from Chelsea. We followed the build-up with enormous interest, as Cooper was British and white and Clay a brilliant young black American boxer. We had much respect for Cooper's left hook: he had often used it to devastating effect and we were fearful that Clay might be caught napping. But the odds seemed stacked against the Englishman, who was easily cut and had lost many fights to that trick of nature. Apart from that, Clay's guile and brilliance was unlike anything we had seen in the heavyweight division, and there seemed little hope of Cooper winning, so long as Clay kept out of his reach.

When the fight got under way Clay was his usual dazzling self and we heard the constant refrain, one two three four jabs by Clay. It looked as if we were going to have a delicious and trouble-free evening, though there was the danger of that left hook and of Ali's tendency to drop his arms to do the shuffle in the middle of a fight. Then towards the end of round five it happened. Cassius Clay was caught with a beauty of a left hook and he went down like a sack of potatoes. It was one of the most awful moments we had ever known. Clay our absolute hero, was losing the fight. We could tell by the excitement of the British crowd and the hysteria of the commentator. The bell went, and the great man dragged himself to his feet and staggered to his corner. Our hearts almost stopped; we were lost for words. Surely Clay wouldn't let Cooper beat him! How could we survive that? We respected Cooper's ability, but this was Clay we were talking about.

Gerald had visions of workmates giving him stick, my mother was faint with worry, my father scratched his head with disbelief, my tongue was cold with shock. Our disappointment was so intense we couldn't look each other in the eye. The ringing of the bell was a miracle which surely saved the great man from a humiliating defeat. We didn't know how we could face an Englishman in the street the next day should Ali be beaten, given the eagerness of the British to see the outspoken and super-confident black man whipped. More was at stake than Clay facing possible defeat: black pride itself was on the ropes.

When the bell went for round six, our hearts were beating like the complex rhythms of a drum workshop. We didn't know what state Clay would be in or if he could defend himself properly. We waited with baited breath for description of his appearance, how steady he was on his feet, to gauge just how much he had to offer.

Almost immediately he began to perform as we had hoped. There was the usual flurry of punches and a wonderful exhibition of his supreme ring-craft. He threw the full range of shots at Cooper, concentrating on the Englishman's vulnerable face. By then we were cheering wildly, relieved that the great man had clearly got the sting of the knockdown out of his head and was boxing with the seriousness and focus we had hoped for. Cooper was cut badly above his eye, and there was a lot of blood. It was quite clear that he wasn't going to survive, and eventually the fight ended in a technical knock-out. We leapt around in joyful relief. Clay had survived when he seemed destined for ignominious defeat. Equally importantly, we could face the street in the morning, cheered by the fact that our man had won.

When a recording of the fight was televised we all watched with great intensity. My father loved boxing, and identified totally with his heroes. During the screening of the Clay–Cooper fight every hook, cut, jab reverberated through his body. When Clay ducked to avoid a blow, my father gestured a feint; when Clay threw a snapping punch, my father's clenched fist fired a short jab which travelled no more than an inch from his body, his face contorted with concentration, eyes staring, lips puckering, temples dappled with perspiration. When, on the other hand, Cooper threw a punch, he rolled with his hero, snorting anger and determination, sometimes uttering a stifled gasp as he worked his body in imaginary struggle. Each time the bell went, there was a sudden release of tension as he sat back and scratched his head or nervously drew the back of his hand across his nose, sometimes asking my mother for a cup of tea or saying, 'Got some cream crackers? I hungry.' Though she was as addicted to the fight game as any of us, my adoring mother always obliged, Daddy's pleasure being of paramount satisfaction to her.

I had first seen Clay in the 1958 Olympics when he won a gold medal. I remember saying to my mother that he would be world champion one day, so mesmerised was I by his dazzling skill in the ring. When he turned professional we watched those fights, too. Then of course his sheer cheek, or as some would have it his arrogance, and his ability to predict the round in which many of his opponents would be knocked out or stopped became legendary, adding to his mystique and charisma. Clay was a dream come true to many black people, a handsome heavyweight boxer of extraordinary skill and speed, assertive, brilliant, beautiful and black. We invested our hopes and aspirations in him. By this yardstick, he seemed to carry the weight of black communities everywhere on his shoulders.

We followed Clay through the great fights, enjoying his skill and brash confidence. Sonny Liston was a frightening man, who had a reputation for toughness and sheer brutality. It was said that he had connections in the criminal under-world and was used to back-street brawling. His steady gaze, muscular build and unsmiling demeanour added to this rep-utation; that of an executioner ready to dispense merciless justice. The build-up to their first fight in 1964 was marked by a tension so delicious that few in our family could speak without revealing the concern in our voice. But Clay outfoxed the 'bear', knocking him out in the second round. On seeing the big fellow go down we felt extraordinary relief mixed with unbridled elation. Our hero had knocked out the most feared man in boxing in less than two rounds. On reflection, it was clear that Clay had seen through Liston's veneer of invincibility, refusing to be cowed by an adversary who probably psyched his opponents into defeat more than beat them by superior ring-craft or power. After the knock-down

Ali presented an extraordinary picture, arms held aloft, white gum-shield flashing triumphantly as he did the Ali shuffle. It was a wonderful moment.

When he fought Floyd Patterson our hearts were there with him because we didn't want him to lose to a white man's stooge. Patterson had shown himself to be a spineless fellow, milking the role of white man's favourite, as we saw it, against Clay, the people's warrior. This Uncle Tom therefore represented much that we despised. We threw every blow delivered by Clay, and dodged every punch returned by Patterson. It culminated in a defeat for Patterson after several gruelling rounds during which he was beaten into submission by Clay. The great man showed off his full array of skills, from the Ali shuffle to his mesmerizing speed of punch, and Patterson got the hiding the vast majority of the black community hoped for. Clay united the black community in a manner rare in the history of sport. The beauty of his movement, his anticipation and speed were electric, his aural defiance of our white oppressors a rapier. He was the living embodiment of black rebellion and dignity. In him we had a true champion who did battle with the object of our fear and hatred.

Cassius Clay's conversion to Islam, and adoption of the name of Muhammad Ali, was his own affair, but it took us by surprise. Having been brought up in a notional Christian household, with all its attendant values and prejudices against other religions, it was difficult to accept Islam. We saw Ali's conversion as a flaw in the great man's make-up, an aberration which we hoped he would overcome. But his embrace of Islam, and his 'in your face' avowal of it, made us question the logic of the religion in which we were immersed. I began then to question how the Christian Church worked. One began to think privately of the lack of representation, the dearth of black icons in the Church, the lack of presence. In my confused mind I tried to conceive of the Christian deity: what colour was 'he'? How come the angels in heaven were always white? Could it be that Islam was a space for a more significant black presence? After all, most of those who followed Islam had dark faces like my own.

Islam was practised largely by people of different shades of black and brown, while Christianity, as I knew it, was a white faith. White missionaries and evangelists had spread the tentacles of the religion to colonies and it embraced the peoples of other nations and 'races', but the icons of the Church, the central players, in it were all white. Other religions and belief systems seemed to follow a similar ethnic or race-specific pattern and were as much cultural as indicators of an absolute and neutral cross-cutting force. Islam in America, in my imagining, was difficult to accept, because it had been transported from the Middle East to the lap of another culture. But on reflection I realised that this has always been the way of great religions, Christianity included.

The Beatles were by now the world's most famous pop group and their music affected everyone with an interest in popular music. Some of us had very little time for the Beatles, certainly in the early days, preferring Fats Domino, Little Richard, Chubby Checker and other black artists. We were bitter at the limited success of black musicians who failed to attract the same level of interest as the Beatles, the Rolling Stones and other white artists. The Rolling Stones were looked on with some suspicion because they borrowed heavily from black blues musicians like Muddy Waters, Howlin' Wolf and Sonny Boy Williamson who remained relatively unsung by the wider public.

Young white consumers, with their growing financial power and youthful energy, drove the music and determined who would be successful. The vast majority of the successful musicians were young white men with a particular sensuality, while the black originators of much of the music they played were middle-aged men and women, in some cases the living embodiments of characters white children were taught to mock. These black musicians, however, played music of real power, originality and energy, which couldn't be matched by their more popular white imitators.

There was frustration in the Oxford Caribbean community at black people's inability to break through the white structures that held them back. At that time there wasn't a significant black press in Britain, and television and radio didn't offer black artists the opportunities they needed to reach a wider public, so we were unable to speak out in favour of black representation. But while people were going wild over Elvis, the Beatles, the Rolling Stones and others, we quietly admired the work of James Brown, Wilson Pickett, Aretha Franklin and many more.

The exception in our family was Levi, who loved the Beatles and other white bands. He had no time as a teenager for traditional black music. Ska, Rock Steady and, later, Blue Beat and Reggae had no resonance for him; he preferred heavy rock bands, the likes of which we had never heard. This preference placed him outside the popular musical taste of most of us. A new way of living, a new culture, was emerging, and it made some of us uneasy because we had no way of dealing with it. We weren't prepared for a relationship like this with the white world, and it seemed a rejection of our roots; we simply couldn't understand how that could be.

Levi, a member of a generation brought up from an early age in this country or born here, had no real appreciation of Caribbean values. There were few black children of his age, even some years into our sojourn in Britain. He was well integrated into white British culture. At times one felt somewhat discomfited by that, though the process of integration is perfectly healthy and understandable. I guess we were becoming so used to the notional cultural polarity of different peoples, were so steered by what sense we could make of events in the wider world, that we couldn't easily adjust to what was going on in his world, a world quite separate from our own. I didn't have the vision to equate his experience with my own in respect of classical music, though apparently, unlike Levi, I enjoyed traditional black popular music as much as anyone.

When I applied to Chelsea School of Art I knew nothing whatever about the college. I hadn't spoken to Len McComb about it, not to Lawrence and Derrick, for their way of making and thinking about art was light years away from the avant-garde approaches on which Chelsea had built its reputation. As far as I was concerned, the college was comparatively near Oxford, and it was an art college, and that was it. But Mr Hennis, my former art tutor in the drawing studios, had continued to follow my career closely, and was alarmed at my first choice. One day, when walking down a street in Headington, I heard a distant voice calling my name. On turning round I saw a white-haired figure running towards me. It was Mr Hennis. I was surprised to see him run, because he must have been about sixty and was quite solidly built; clearly, he urgently wanted to speak to me.

'I hear you have applied to Chelsea, Dash' he said, addressing me by my surname, as in the past.

'Yes I have, and Kingston is my second choice'.

'But why did you apply there?' he asked. 'You do know that it is a hard-edge school and you will find it difficult to fit in?'

I was a bit alarmed by this but didn't fully grasp the significance of what he was saying. so merely shrugged and mumbled something about hearing it had a good reputation. My mind was set and I simply wasn't prepared to listen to his advice.

I was called to interview at Chelsea soon after Easter in 1965. Psychologically I was wholly unprepared: my work was sloppily thrown together; I hadn't made the best plans for getting to London. I remember arriving at Paddington Station from Oxford with a bulging portfolio. I took a 49 bus, and stood on the lower deck for the duration of the journey, greatly inconveniencing a few pensioners as they boarded and alighted from the bus. Going round corners was very uncomfortable.

In the courtyard at the front of the art school was a sculpture by Henry Moore, a governor of the college. I couldn't believe that I was applying to a college which was associated with the great man.

Applicants were required to show proficiency in a foreign language. I did the test in Spanish as best I could. It was evident that my attempt at self-education was offering benefits beyond my wildest dreams, though in all honesty I don't think the outcome of the test had any bearing on the school's decision.

During the lunch break I took myself off to the Kings Road, found a workers' café in a side street and bought myself pie and mash, followed by apple crumble with custard. It was the first time I had ever done something like that. The experience of applying to Chelsea was already changing my life in a small way.

Norbert Lynton and Lawrence Gowing were members of the large panel of interviewers, some ten to twelve. I later discovered they had high reputations in the art world as educators and critics. Gowing, principal of the art school, had a severe speech impediment and dribbled when he spoke; there were strands of saliva beading from his very thick lips to his chest, staining his shirt, jacket and tie. Several of the interviewers stood to either side of a long table at which Gowing, Lynton, Myles Murphy, Norman Blamey and a few others sat. I was asked about artists whom I liked, and responded by giving details of various Impressionists. They asked me about the Ashmolean Museum, presumably to establish whether I visited the place of my own volition, and to ascertain my level of commitment to art. I explained that I went there frequently. Gowing then asked me what I thought of *Hunt in the Forest* by Uccello in the Ashmolean. I said I didn't like it much because the figures were too stiff. I remember this had an effect on the panellists, many of whom stifled a laugh, perhaps out of embarrassment for me. I thought I had blown it.

I hadn't taken with me many pieces from home. Even here I regarded my home art as something private and preferred not to expose it to the scrutiny of outsiders. I never recorded my work, and the market scene I had sold to Pietro was not preserved in any form. A large carnival painting then in progress was also left behind, and *Dance at Reading* was too big to carry on the train.

I had taken a small – about ten inches by eight – gouache of a nude figure. It caught the interest of Norman Blamey, who expressed a lot of enthusiasm for it. This piece also resonated with other members of staff. A few other figure paintings, my sketchbooks and some large drawings also drew positive comments. By the end of the interview it was quite clear that the panel were favourable towards me. Nothing was said directly, but it was apparent from their mood that, barring some unforeseen circumstances, I would most probably be offered a place at Chelsea School of Art.

A few days later I got a letter confirming it. My parents and brothers were pleased for me, but everyone kept their cool. No one in my family or the local Caribbean community had won a place to study for a degree or the equivalent before, and they were not prepared for the implications because I was breaking entirely new ground. But for the moment life continued as usual. I continued my art course and my other usual activities, including practising and playing in the band and making work at home.

At the end of the college year Len McComb was very warm to me and wished me well. He is a dear friend, with whom I am still in contact, and he has been one of the shining lights in my life. My parents said little. They didn't quite know how to handle it all.

That summer Gerald, Bob Reid and I went to Basle in Switzerland to stay with Pia Senn and her cousin Marianne Weber, friends we had met in Oxford while playing in the band. They had become good friends of our whole family as well as of Gerald and me, had won the trust of our parents and had been accepted in our home. They actually ate our meals and wandered in and out of the back living-room and elsewhere in the house without any qualms whatever. It was peculiar to think that in my years in this country I had never got close to English girls, Leila not withstanding. My time at the College of Further Education brought me into contact with young women for the first time but I didn't get close to any of them. Pia and Marianne were trusted and admired by my parents as well as the rest of us.

To get to Basle, we took the ferry and drove through France. I remember how impressed I was by the French roads, their straightness and simple layout. We didn't stay in a hotel or camp out, but drove directly to Switzerland. Bob, a motor mechanic, was an excellent driver and drove fast, safely and beautifully 'on the wrong side of the road', as Gerald and I saw it. After what seemed an interminable journey, we reached Geneva. I didn't know what to expect, but Switzerland had a reputation for cleanliness and sophistication. We were therefore shocked, when we we went for a pee in a public toilet, to find to discover some of the most disgusting public urinals we had ever seen: covered in a thick lime and urine deposit, and with a broken flushing system which no one had bothered to repair. The urinals had gone a nasty mouldy green and gamboges colour. The stench was almost unbearable, and hit you with the force of smelling salts. I winced at the smell and filth.

We stayed with Pia's family in Basle. They were generous and afforded us the heartiest welcome. I cannot forget, though, how confused I was at seeing a bidet. I had never seen one before, didn't know what they were for. It had an opening not unlike that of a loo with a small neck. Happily we all had the wit to use the right bowl.

After this very successful trip we visited the Senn family. We toured around Zurich with them and went on a brief trip into the foothills of the mountains. On the way, we passed lots of the chalets for which the Swiss are famous: pretty timber buildings with neat window-boxes. In the fields the haystacks were perfect and the hay lush and immaculately tended. When we stopped in the mountains, I was surprised to see scenes of poverty, which I hadn't expected in Switzerland. Some of the people were unshod, as many were in my days in Barbados, and the chalet was semi-derelict, with lots of gaps in the unpainted, timbers and so on. We stayed there for a couple of days, and slept for the first time under a duvet.

The mountains, with their great height and beauty, were like nothing I had ever seen – and were clearly why our friends had wanted us to take us there. The scale and physical beauty were overpowering. Gerald, Bob and I stood on a ridge one evening, overlooking an apparently bottomless valley with a massive mountain range on the other side. The way the mountains rolled into the distance, taking on subtle shades of grey and blue, was breathtaking, and left me numb with emotion. We stood and drank in the beauty and power of nature, and said nothing. Back in Oxford I made paintings which were inspired by my experiences on the trip. I am particularly fond of one of Lake Geneva with sailing-boats, the huge fountain playing in the foreground.

In later years we lost contact with Pia and Marianne, but they embody a very happy and special moment in my youth. They somehow managed to penetrate the Dash family citadel and opened up our insularity, breached our wall of inhibition. Largely as a result of their influence, 'continentals' remain, for me and my family, people with a zest for life and an openness of view which is truly refreshing. Recently, friends have spoken of European women asking for the Dash family in the Cowley and Blackbird Leys areas of Oxford. I have no doubt who they were.

For the rest of the summer vacation, I worked as usual, though I was to get a full grant. I didn't know how to take myself off to London and find myself a place to live, and I didn't think to make enquiries through the College. I was in mild shock over the whole extraordinary experience. The boy from Oxford who had never been allowed to make basic decisions for himself, had never cooked a meal or done his own washing, was taking this momentous route out of the city and into the big wide world, away from his parents and brothers.

That summer was strange, almost unreal. I was at the point of leaving home but the reality of this was not faced up to. I just carried on as if life would remain the same. I painted and played cricket as usual. I saw my friends in town and we socialised with others. A teacher on the foundation course who lived in Forest Hill, south London, asked me to ring him because he would help me find accommodation, but nothing came of it. I still had nowhere to live and did absolutely nothing to find a place. Within myself, I had settled for commuting. Then, the penultimate weekend of the vacation, I received a phone call from a fellow foundation student called Georgina, offering me a place at a friend's home in the Oval. Without seeing the place I accepted the offer. The following weekend I left Oxford for London.

The journey on the A40, on what was a bright and sunny afternoon, was long and tedious. I thought of the trip from Victoria to Oxford all those years earlier, and the high expectations then. At that moment, as I was travelling the other way, the full implications of what was happening struck home; I felt a bit like a condemned man walking to the gallows. I was leaving home. Apart from George, who still lived in Oxford, I was the first to leave home, and I would be miles away from the family. The prospect was daunting.

It was a fine afternoon and the journey was trouble-free. My father and his friend George Brown sat in the front of the Austin Cambridge and chatted. Knowing my father as I do, I am sure he realized the turmoil I was going through, could see the tears in my eyes. I knew I was leaving home for good. That is not to say that I wouldn't be back – my intention was always to come back home regularly – but *that* life was over, at least in the form I knew it. My father kept up an endless conversation with George, who presumably wasn't aware of the tensions in the car or perhaps didn't want to draw attention to my distress.

When we arrived in London, though, it became more stressful, partly because of the circumstances of the journey but also for the practical reason that my father never travelled to London with an *A to Z*. He has the unfortunate habit of attracting attention by making a sibilant sound between his teeth, like the catcall some men make when they spot a pretty woman. 'Huish! Huish!' was constantly being sounded as he sought advice from people on the other side of the road, often in heavy traffic. As his hearing wasn't good, they had to repeat things at the top of their voice. Things became a little fraught.

Eventually, however, we were guided by various helpful people to the Oval and we found our destination. I met my fellow lodgers, my possessions were unpacked, and Daddy and George, concerned about the return journey, soon took their leave. The people with whom I stayed were mostly students and professionals. They were an educated and cultured group who filled the house with classical music.

That evening I made rice with corned beef – Mama had packed some corned beef for me. One of my housemates was an American, and as he was around at the time I stupidly invited him to dine with me in the communal dining-room. The meal was a disaster. My mother made cooking look easy but I soon discovered my limitations. The rice was overcooked and became a nasty, sticky swill, the corned beef was lumpy and tasteless. I had fried it with onions and butter, and somehow it just didn't work. The poor man bolted the meal and beat a hasty retreat; we didn't have much to say to each other after that.

For some weeks after the move I went home at weekends with my dirty washing. By then my mother had a washing-machine but she still did much of the family laundry in the bath, being mistrustful of new technology. I sadly added to her burden of work until I became more worldly-wise and independent. I think she was glad to maintain the connection with me, but I don't offer that as an excuse.

Over time I settled into a rhythm of playing music and making work during the week at Chelsea, and going home to play with the Carib Six at the weekend. The band was doing well, occasionally playing gigs in the Midlands and London. In my second year we were contracted to do a residential spot at a club in Milan for a month. The group saw it as their big break, an offer they couldn't refuse. They arranged to have leave from work, but of course I couldn't go – and that was how I came to leave the band.

Chelsea was a huge disappointment. The lecturers took little direct interest in me, or my work. The world I had created as a young man in Oxford disintegrated, but there was nothing to take its place, and no Derrick or Lawrence to talk to. Students didn't work from the life model; figurative work was frowned on. Constructivism and minimalism were the flavour of the moment. This was light years away from that I wanted to do.

While in Oxford, I hadn't engaged in any theoretical debates about art-making: where we are today and should be tomorrow. I just lived the style of 'the artist', and produced work I enjoyed, work which spoke for me at that time. The concept of breaking new ground didn't occupy my mind in any way. In that respect, going to Chelsea was a traumatic experience, because the students and certainly the staff favoured avant-garde work. The tension between those two diametrically opposed positions almost destroyed me, the only thing that kept me going was my own passion for making work. And of course I couldn't work at home as I used to: the special, insular world I had created in Oxford was gone for ever. From now on I would be much more exposed. The whole culture of art college in the big city was turning out to be a bigger challenge than I had anticipated. The experience deeply undermined my self-confidence, though not my determination to continue. I tried different approaches to win the respect of the staff, but the harder I tried the more distant they became, and my work suffered.

In my third year at Chelsea I met John La Rose, one of the chief architects of the Caribbean Artists' Movement (CAM). He recruited me into the movement and I met Andrew Salkey, Wilson Harris, Ronald Moody, Eddie Brathwaite, Beryl McBernie, Ann Walmsley, Errol Lloyd and others. I was greatly uplifted by the experience of being with people from middle-class West Indian backgrounds who had been steeped in literature and reading, and had been taught to analyse text and extract meanings from a wide range of sources. These very able people lived in a different world from mine. A reading from *Islands**, at the now defunct West Indian Students' Centre, by Eddie (now Kamau) Brathwaite will long stay with me. He captivated his audience by the quality of his work and wonderful presentation.

One passage he read was of particular interest to me as a Barbadian and cricket fan. Part of it (from p.45) is reproduced here:

Boy, dis is *cricket.*
Then Laker come down wid he third
One. He wrap up de ball in de palm
O' he han' like a package
AN' MAKE CLYDE WALCOTT LOOK FOOLISH
Mister man, could'a hear
All de flies that was buzzin' out there
Round de bread carts; could'a hear
If de empire fart.
An' then blue murder start:
'Kill one o'dem, Clyde,' some wise-
wun was shoutin', 'knock he skull off.'

I respected and admired Brathwaite and the others, but couldn't relate to their lifestyles; nor could they to mine. They had read the classics of English and Caribbean literature, and I had not. But through them I heard of important black writers such as Martiniquan poet and politician Aimé Césaire, William (known as WEB) Du Bois, Ralph Ellison and others. As a result of John La Rose's introduction, I met Ellen Wright, wife of the late American novelist Richard Wright, at her home in the rue Jacob in Paris. Ronald Moody, the outstanding Jamaican-born sculptor, was a man of immense dignity and presence. The brief meeting that I had with him in 1969 was uplifting and humbling. The Jamaican novelist Andrew Salkey held CAM meetings in his home. I loved him. I bought a copy of his *Havana Journal* which I took home and read immediately. John was always the calming influence, the linchpin who held the whole machine of CAM together,

* *Islands*, by K. (formerly Eddie) Brathwaite (Oxford University Press, 1969)

at least for me. He was the person I looked to for guidance and reassurance in this high-powered group who were achieving success in many spheres. Being a member of CAM was liberating. It was almost as if I had been imprisoned for many years, and then suddenly set free.

I left Chelsea in 1968. Two years later, in 1970, I began playing with a group which later evolved into Curved Air. I was living in Saint George's Drive in Victoria at the time. Oliver Hunt, a composer, lived nearby. While walking to and from Victoria Station, where I caught a bus to Chelsea, I used to see him composing at the piano in his front room. Some evenings there were other musicians playing the double bass, violin and other instruments. One day I couldn't resist introducing myself. I expressed an interest in his music, and explaining that I played blues piano. Oliver was warm to me and we became friends. He introduced me to Francis Monkman, who was looking for someone to play blues piano in a band he was forming. I joined the group and we started practising in the home of one of its members. Most of the musicians were upper-class people with a public-school background. The house we practised in was huge, with extensive lawns, statues and a fountain. We rehearsed in the front room, which was the size of a small hall. It was a whole new world.

Francis Monkman was a brilliant pianist, far more skilled than I was. However, he had a passion for the guitar and played Jimmy Hendrix, whose style he copied and married to his classical approach (that was to be the defining feature of the Curved Air sound). Unfortunately, after a lot of infighting – I wasn't involved in the rows – the band broke up. Afterwards I was invited by Francis to rejoin the band, which was to become Curved Air. By then I had decided to devote more time to my art and turned down his invitation. Within a year Curved Air were in the charts with 'Air Conditioning'. Francis in later years went on to play with Sky, a very successful band of which the well-known classical guitarist John Williams was a member.

Through Oliver I met other young musicians and composers from the Royal Academy. There was Phillip Pilkington, of the Pilkington Glass family. He was wealthy and owned an old Bentley and had a girlfriend called Gloria, who was colourful and expansive where he was reserved. Phillip had got a good degree at the Royal Academy of Music, but had since gone on to study philosophy at university. Later he returned to the piano and played some concerts, at least one of which was positively reviewed in the broadsheets.

My abiding memory of him is at soirée at Oliver's: he was leaning against the upright piano, his bottom against the closed keyboard lid. People there were mostly musicians and, as always, were talking music, and as ever in that company they were far more knowledgeable than me. Phillip was making a point about a piece of music, and elected to illustrate his point by playing the passage concerned. He stood up and, facing his audience and with his back to the piano, proceeded to play it accurately with both hands, fingering the keys the wrong way round, so to speak. I was stunned by his dexterity and technical excellence. I could never have conceived of doing such a thing.

At some of these evenings I saw the organist Nicholas Jackson. I heard a recording of his on Radio Three late one evening. I also met composers at Oliver's. Brian Fernihough was one; I heard part of a symphony by him on the radio and was suitably impressed. Another was John Tavener. I had never heard of him, but Oliver singled him out as being a special talent. I shall never forget the lanky blond young man with the mop of hair that fell over his brow, sitting on the floor and sipping wine. He had charisma, and everyone was respectful of him. Since then he has, of course, risen to worldwide fame.

I have many precious memories of that period and those people, but something I shall always cherish is Oliver's belly-laugh, which seemed to rise not from his belly but from his feet and rocked his whole body. It was quite the most contagious and warming laughter I have ever known. One of the things we did to set him off was act out farcical moments. One of these was the collapse of a squashed tomato, which I did in front of some of his friends. Oliver almost dissolved into a pool of sweat with the intensity of his laughter. It was a very special and delightful moment.

In 1971 I played with another band, Protoplasm, which took over a jazz-rock slot from Osibisa, at Ronnie Scott's. Osibisa had gone on to bigger and better things after getting into the charts with a single. Protoplasm turned out to be arguably the most enjoyable of the three bands to work with, because of the type of sound they produced and the venues where they played. Besides Ronnie Scott's, we played at Speakeasy, the 100 Club and other top venues.

Music and literature were not the only things about which I was learning more. All round the world, profound social changes were in the air.

Martin Luther King's growing reputation in the United States was beginning to have some impact in Britain. His extraordinary ability as an orator filled me with pride as a black person, although I had misgivings about his non-violent stance: the idea of black people standing up to rabid white racists, shielded only by their faith and a strategy of turning the other cheek, worried me. Yet there was the shining example of Mahatma Gandhi, who had used this form of resistance to great effect against the British in India. I knew of and respected Gandhi, but I wondered if similar tactics could work in the domain of the Ku Klux Klan.

I sometimes saw photographs of Klansmen in their white robes, and tried to understand what went through their heads as they hunted black men down. I remember images of cold-faced white men, women and children in the Deep South, bawling black people out of their properties, their eyes filled with hate. I quaked at the thought of the violence that could be visited on the Black Power Movement if there were to be a crackdown. We read of lynchings and burnings of property and even people. The words 'Ku Klux Klan' had a special obscene cachet, even though few of us had been to the United States. We were familiar with the black resistance in Little Rock and Alabama, were aware of the merciless brutality of American racists. Pictures of slavering Alsatians snarling at the heels of black protestors assailed us from our television sets and newspapers, people tossed aside like confetti by powerful jets from water cannon.

I tried to make sense of such hatred, wondered what people of that ilk saw in a black skin. It is an extraordinary thing when you see a people who have embraced a philosophy of racial hatred. In many areas we have similar values in respect of the simple and the everyday, but when they see me I become an object of hate. Despite this I couldn't help but try to make sense of madness.

This continued to form a challenge to which I had no firm answer then. As the product of a skewed and unrepresentative education, I had no means of engaging meaningfully with evidence which seemed to confirm white scientific and mathematical superiority. As a black person I sought answers but knew of no one to whom I could turn for insights, for acceptable explanations. Nothing I was familiar with even began to provide answers to these issues.

Enoch Powell's infamous 'River of Blood' speech in 1968 had a similar effect. As I listened, I was both fearful and perplexed: fearful for the future, because as a black person one felt very exposed and vulnerable in British society at that time; perplexed that a capable white man should have such difficulty seeing us as people just like himself. Powell removed the veneer of common human respect that we all live by. It was like the gardener lifting a stone and finding a delicate creature there, exposed and vulnerable, almost entirely at your mercy. He was merciless in his onslaught. And there was no one out there speaking for us, not with the same passion and purpose, or even the same charisma, as Powell.

Nelson Mandela was mentioned as a figure of protest in South Africa. I knew little of him, and the anti-apartheid movement in that country was not publicised to the same extent as the resistance movements in the United States. Apartheid as a concept was known to us, but we were more focused on the USA because of the relationship Caribbean people have always had with America. New Zealand and Australia, too, were seen as tough environments for blacks. I heard of the difficulties many black people had gaining access to Australia, and my dislike of the country became intense. I was slowly becoming bitter at the powerlessness of black people worldwide in the teeth of white oppression. I wondered how we had managed to survive in the Western world since the sixteenth century, how we could prosper in the future, given our systematic brutalisation.

Reading *The Autobiography of Malcolm X* was a turning-point in my life. Many of the questions to which I was seeking answers were dealt with in a forthright and compelling manner. Malcolm X articulated many of the myths and complexes that traditionally had been left unsaid. In the process, he explained how we were trained to hate ourselves by the white hegemonic structure for its own purposes. For the first time there I had access to a someone who spoke of our shared blackness in a way which truly celebrated our physical differences from the white physiognomy. Through him and the whole Black Power movement, I felt a growing confidence in myself and what I could achieve.

Our views were greatly influenced by the British media, and Malcolm X's confrontational stance scared me. It was difficult to reject the published word of the British media, which was critical of much that he stood for. His autobiography did much to clarify matters, and put the record straight.

In 1967 my father sold the house in Fern Hill Road. A house was bought in Barbados and Mama went to live there with Levi and John. I went to Oxford after the house had been sold but before the new owners had moved in. Daddy had swept the family bric-a-brac into a heap in the middle of the floor. In the midst of this mess was my personal property, items so precious that I hadn't trusted myself to look after them in London. My stamp collection, started after meeting Derrick, was scattered around the floor like trash: twisted, torn, dust-covered, water-splattered. Lewin Bassenthwaite, a lecturer at Chelsea who suffered from multiple sclerosis, had given me an exquisite gouache, which had once featured in a well-known glossy magazine, as thanks for the support I had given him in preparing for a show at the Piccadilly Gallery. The painting was lost. It remains one of the great disappointments of my life. This throwing out of much of the paraphernalia of my youth and early adult years was a full stop, a metaphorical drawing of a line under my life at home and my emotional dependency on my parents and family.

Mama eventually returned to England. She and my father moved into a council house on the Blackbird Leys estate and within a couple of years they bought it. My mother died there of a heart attack in 1987.

In 1974 I went with my partner, Jean, to Barbados. It was the first time time I had been back, and I found the visit very uplifting.

Seeing Aunt Elise and Uncle Samuel – he was as quiet as ever – my cousin Pearl and the rest of the family was especially moving. There was a warmth and dignity to them all which I treasured. The yard seemed much smaller but it was still recognisably the place where I had spent such happy times. It still held a rabbit hutch my cousin Sam Sam and I had built together, and it still housed rabbits; but Rose the dairy cow was long gone. The house had taken on many of the trappings of the modern Barbadian chattel home with its modest fitted kitchen and canopied porch.

Across the way, Grazettes plantation was no longer growing as much cane, and houses and factories dotted the landscape. The cricket pitch was still there, though, and the centre of a thriving cricket club.